MW00717474

THE STORY OF
THE MIDDLE AGES

Second Edition
by
Suzanne Strauss Art

Copyright © 2014 by Wayside Publishing

All rights reserved. No part of this publication may be reproduced, stored in a retrieval system, or transmitted in any form or by any means, electronic, mechanical, photocopying, recording, or otherwise, without the prior written permission of the publisher.

Printed in USA

3 4 5 6 7 8 9 10 KP 17

Print date: 255

Softcover ISBN 978-1-938026-65-2

CONTENTS

To Dorothy and Herbert Art

Once again, I gratefully acknowledge the tremendous commitment of time and effort that my friend and colleague, Dick Upjohn of the Fay School history department, has put into reading my manuscript. As he has done in the case of each of my previous books, Dick has tirelessly reviewed my early draft, making thoughtful criticisms and insightful remarks as well as pointing out any inaccuracies. I feel fortunate indeed to have the continued aid and support of such a learned scholar. And I am grateful to the Parents Association of Fay School whose Endowment for Faculty Enrichment provided me with a grant to visit the Cathedrals and monasteries of northern France.

PROLOGUE

Try to imagine an old, white-haired scientist, sitting in his wooden rocking chair and looking back over his life. He smiles as he fondly recalls his happy, carefree childhood when he first became intrigued with the mysteries of the natural world. Then his thoughts quickly shift to the proud moment when he won the Nobel Prize for his brilliant discoveries at the age of seventy-five. Between these two highpoints of his life stretch the many years he spent experimenting in his scientific laboratory. Should he dismiss that long period of trial and error as unimportant? Of course not, for it is when he explored all sorts of data, rejecting some and pursuing others until he arrived at some unexpected conclusions. This was a lively and exciting period of his life.

And yet, historians writing in the sixteenth century dismissed all the events and discoveries that occurred during the one thousand years separating the grandeur of the Roman Empire and what they considered the glory of their own times, lumping them into a vast and vague period known as the Middle Ages. They were convinced that little of value was accomplished by the people who lived in Europe between the fifth and the fifteenth centuries. In their minds, western culture had fallen into a deep slumber, a slumber from which it did not awaken until scholars rediscovered the ideas of the ancient past and began improving upon them. In fact, the term given to the new age that dawned in the late fifteenth century is the Renaissance, which in French means "Rebirth."

Fortunately, this view of history has been cast aside, although the term Middle Ages (or medieval) is still used. Historians now appreciate the richness of the multi-faceted culture that slowly evolved during those thousand years. The Romans had considered northern Europe a wasteland of dense forests inhabited by uncivilized barbarians, but after the fall of the Roman Empire it was this northern region that gradually became the political and cultural center of the western world. Despite many backward steps, great strides were made in the areas of art, architecture, literature, music, philosophy, and politics, and these led to the creative outpouring of the Renaissance.

The aim of this book is to bring to life the story of a wide diversity of people who helped to mold a new civilization on the smoldering embers of an old one. The cast of characters includes bloodthirsty warriors, pious monks, brilliant military leaders, unscrupulous religious leaders, skillful craftsmen, greedy opportunists, thoughtful scholars, hard-working peasants, and many more. The episodes occur in a variety of settings – humble thatch-roofed huts, huge fortified stone castles, crowded buildings in bustling towns, towering cathedrals, colorful country fairs, and among the hills and woodlands of the countryside. This was a time of tremendous contrasts: Gallant knights followed a code of chivalrous behavior among their peers and yet committed acts of unbelievable cruelty; royal courts engaged in brilliant pageantry while famine and disease struck great numbers of the population; a thirst for knowledge flourished amid a world of superstition and blind religious faith. In the end, compromise and the merging of many opposing attitudes created something new, something better.

But it all started with the dying civilization of the Romans, so it's there that our story begins.

PART I
IN THE ASHES OF ROME

CHAPTER 1

THE BARBARIAN INVASIONS

For nearly five hundred years the Romans ruled a huge empire covering about two million square miles. It stretched across the sands of northern Africa, the rugged terrain of western Asia, and the woodlands of southern Europe, completely encircling the Mediterranean Sea. Its border was nearly 10,000 miles long! The empire was divided into many provinces that were linked by a vast network of roads, governed by an efficient bureaucracy, and protected by a mighty army.

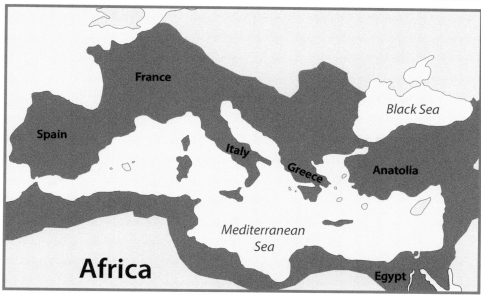

The Roman Empire

GERMANIA

North of the Roman Empire was a vast region of dense forests. It was inhabited by nomadic Germanic tribesmen whom the Romans referred to as barbarians. Today we think of a barbarian as someone who is uncivilized or uncouth, but the Romans applied the term to anyone who did not live within their borders. We know something about the primitive cultures of northern Europe through the writings of early historians. In the first century CE a Roman writer named Tacitus composed a large volume entitled Germania. It describes in great detail the life style of the people who lived just north of the Roman borders at that time. Others writing a few centuries later have left lengthy accounts of what conditions were like when the tribesmen began to pose a serious threat to the survival of Rome. Further clues come from the artifacts, ruins, and human remains that date back to those early times.

The Germanic tribesmen were tall and robust people with fair skin, blue eyes, and reddish blond hair. They looked very different than the shorter, dark complexioned Romans. The men wore their hair long and sported shaggy beards. They dressed in knee-length shirts made from coarsely woven wool, cloaks buckled at the right shoulder, and long leather trousers. The Romans, who wore short tunics and togas (long pieces of cloth that they wrapped around their bodies), considered trousers the sign of an uncivilized and inferior warrior. The women's ankle-length dresses were dyed "earth colors" using crushed minerals and plants. The tribesmen bathed very little, according to the remark of a fifth century Roman: "Happy the nose that cannot smell a barbarian!"

A timber hut

The tribesmen dwelled in villages of rude, timber huts with thatched roofs and earthen floors, a family often sharing the living space with the livestock. They grew a variety of crops (barley, rye, wheat, peas and beans) and tended herds of sheep, cattle, and goats. Most of the farming was done by the women, children, and the slaves who had been captured in battle. The men were warriors. They spent much of their time hunting and protecting their land from enemy intruders.

Because all of the Germanic tribes sprang from common ancestors who lived in Scandinavia around 1000 BC, they spoke similar languages and shared many customs. Their religion was based upon the worship of the forces of nature. Like most primitive peoples, they believed that particular gods and goddesses were responsible for

such natural occurrences as a rain storm, the birth of a lamb, or a bountiful harvest. A set of myths evolved around a family of gods who lived in a place called Asgard. We'll learn more about these Nordic deities in Chapter 4.

The tribesmen had no cities, no roads, and little trade. Their basic social unit was the family clan, which usually consisted of about twenty-five relatives. A group of clans made up a tribe. The strongest and bravest warrior in the tribe became the chief. The people depended upon their kinsmen and their chief for protection and support. When a boy was old and strong enough to become a warrior, a ceremony was held in his honor in a sacred grove under the light of a full moon. On this occasion he was given the weapons he would wield for the rest of his life— a spear, and perhaps a sword or an axe. Barbarian warriors were aggressive, skillful with their weapons, and absolutely fearless. To lose a weapon or shield was considered a loss of honor.

A battle ax

Unlike the Romans who lined up in orderly rows on the battlefield, the barbarians used a triangular battle formation, with the bravest and best armed men placed near the point at the front. As the army of warriors advanced forward, they murmured a war cry that increased in amplitude until it became a terrifying roar. Then

Barbarian warrior

they charged! Each man followed the orders of his chief unquestioningly, and he was willing to die with him. If the chief was killed, his warriors were quick to avenge his death. Barbarian women urged their men into battle and had great contempt for cowards.

The tribesmen often gathered in assemblies to discuss issues that arose within the community, such as land disputes and causes for going to war. When it was time to make a decision, they would murmur among themselves to demonstrate their disapproval or clash their weapons on their shields to show their support. Blood feuds were common. If a kinsman was murdered, his clan would seek revenge. The Frisians, who lived on the coast of the North Sea, would hang the corpse of a murdered man from the rafters of his home; his relatives could not bury the body until they had killed one of the enemy clan. In later years, a concept known as wergeld came into use. Wergeld (which literally means "man money") was the amount of gold, or oxen, or grain, that a murderer had to pay the family of his victim in order to avoid being killed by them. This was intended to curtail the blood feuds, but it was not always effective. We will learn more about it later in this chapter.

For hundreds of years the Romans successfully protected their frontiers from the barbarians, but toward the end of the third century the empire's economy began to weaken. This meant that there was less money to pay its soldiers, so the army was diminished. When it was no longer possible for the Romans to patrol the thousands of miles of border, waves of tribesmen began to push

Rocky shores of the Danube River, which flows from modern Germany eastward to the Black Sea

into the territory near the Rhine and Danube Rivers. (These rivers formed the borders of the northeastern part of the empire.) Many of these barbarians were attracted to the well cultivated farmland and moderate climate of the Roman land. Others were simply looking for a good fight.

THE GOTHS AND THE VANDALS

The Goths were the first major group of barbarian tribesmen to settle within the Roman borders. The Ostrogoths ("eastern Goths") had lived in small communities above the Black Sea, while the Visigoths ("western Goths") inhabited the banks of the Danube River. When the Visigoths first began staging raids into the Roman territory, the Emperor Aurelian tried to bargain with them. In 271 he gave them the Roman province of Dacia (modern Romania) in return for their promise not to cross the Danube. His strategy worked, for a while anyway, and the tribesmen coexisted peacefully with the Roman citizens, farming the rich soil of Dacia and trading their produce as well as slaves they had captured for luxury items. They adopted many elements of the Roman culture, and some even became Christians.

But the peace was broken when the Goths were threatened by the Huns, savage horsemen who swept in from the steppes of central Asia. The Huns terrified everyone. Their faces were deliberately scarred in early childhood, and they carried powerful bows that shot arrows with enough force to pierce a Roman armor at one hundred yards. In 375 the Huns conquered the Ostrogoths and then invaded Dacia, where they defeated the army of the Visigoth king. Frantic, the king sent a message to the Roman Emperor

defend the border against other invaders. He was thinking, of course, of the Huns.

Unfortunately, the Roman soldiers were scornful of the new settlers and treated them poorly. At the same time, the local officials pocketed the funds sent by the Emperor to support the Visigoths until they could raise their first crops, leaving them with no source of food. So they rebelled and tried to form their own kingdom within the Roman territory. Fighting broke out, and in 378 the tribesmen defeated the Roman army at the battle of Adrianople. Valens was slain in the battle.

Countryside in modern Romania (Roman province of Dacia)

Valens begging for permission to lead his people across the Danube to safety within the Roman territory. Valens agreed and so thousands of Visigoths poured across the river with their wives, children, and animal herds. Valens' one stipulation was that the newcomers help to

Theodosius, the next Emperor, made peace with the Visigoths and allowed them to remain where they had settled as allied troops under their own leaders. Like Valens, he hoped that the Goths would serve as a buffer against other barbarian tribes. All was well until he died and the Roman Empire was split in two parts to be ruled by his sons: Honorius in the west and Arcadius in the east. It is Honorius that concerns us here. He was a weak ruler (some have claimed that he was mentally retarded). When a new Visigoth king named Alaric led his armies into Greece and then Italy in search of new land, Honorius and his court fled from Rome to Ravenna, a city in northern Italy surrounded by impregnable marshes. Thousands of slaves escaped from their Roman masters and joined Alaric's army as it ravaged the Italian countryside. They regarded him as a great liberator. After surrounding the city of Rome in 408, Alaric demanded that all the silver, gold, and movable property be sent out to him. "What will be left?" the Romans asked. "Your lives," he replied. The tribute he exacted was enormous: 5,000 pounds of gold, 30,000 pounds of silver, 4,000 silk tunics, 3,000 scarlet dyed skins, and 3,000 pounds of pepper. And even then Alaric was not satisfied! As his forces multiplied, he besieged Rome twice more. In 410 he actually burst through the gates and plundered the city for three days. This entire episode was a great catastrophe for the Romans. Their capital had not been invaded in eight centuries. Now it was at the mercy of hordes of barvarian warriors. The mighty empire was on its knees.

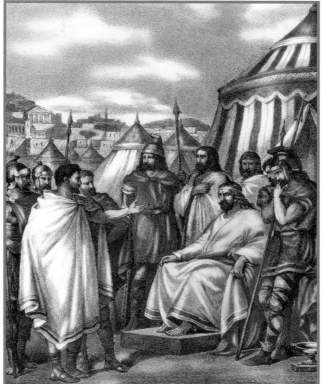

Alaric meets with the Romans

Soon after leaving Rome, Alaric died. He was buried in the Busento River in southern Italy. His followers diverted the water from its course into a temporary channel in order to dig his grave in the river bed. After burying the king's body with a rich treasure, they turned back the water to its original course. Then, in hopes of guarding the secrecy of the grave's location, they put to death the grave diggers. Alaric's successor led the Visigoths to Aquitaine in the southwestern part of the Roman province of Gaul (modern France). Some of them remained in that fertile land, but most moved on to settle in Spain.

The Vandals were another tribe who felt threatened by the Huns. In the winter of 405 the Rhine River froze. One moonlit night 15,000 warriors accompanied by their families and animals walked across the ice into Roman territory. Their arrival was unopposed, and they soon spread out and headed south, pillaging and ravaging the countryside along the way.

When they got to Spain they finally settled down. But, as we have just learned, the Visigoths were also in that region, and conflict between the two groups was inevitable. So in 429 a Vandal king named Gaiseric ferried his entire people across the strait of Gibraltar to Africa. He then marched along the coast, and within a decade of hard fighting he had gained control of northern Africa. His conquest of the city of Carthage in 439 cut off

The Rhine River

much of the Roman grain supply; this led to a food shortage that further weakened Rome's ability to fight off the invading barbarians. Gaiseric built a huge fleet of pirate ships, which enabled his people to gain control of the western Mediterranean. In the process they became very rich.

ATTILA THE HUN

In the early fifth century the Huns were led by a particularly bloodthirsty king named Attila. (Oddly enough, his name means "little Daddy.") He negotiated a treaty in 434 with Theodosius II, the Emperor of the eastern half of the empire, agreeing to keep out of that Roman territory in exchange for an annual tribute of seven hundred pounds of gold. But after six years of peace, Attila suddenly disregarded the treaty and crossed the border, plundering several cities and defeating a Roman army. Once again he was temporarily bought off by the Roman negotiators, but in 445 he launched a new campaign. This time he announced his intentions to conquer the known world. He led his army westward, ravaging everything in sight. Attila once boasted that grass was never green again where the hooves of his horse had trod, and the terrified Roman Christians referred to him as the "Scourge of God."

In 450 Attila crossed the Rhine. According to one legend, he demanded the sister of the Roman Emperor as his bride, plus one half of the Roman Empire as a wedding present; when it was refused, he invaded Gaul. The general in charge of the Roman legions in that province (a man named Aetius) quickly enlisted the support of the barbarian tribesmen living there. United by a common fear of the Huns, an army of Roman soldiers, Goths, and Burgundians (who lived near the Rhone River) defeated Attila's warriors at Chalons in 451.

Rebuffed but not discouraged, Attila turned south into Italy. When he reached Rome, Leo I (the Bishop of Rome) confronted him and somehow convinced him not to enter the city. (It was reported at the time that Attila was frightened off by an apparition of Saint Peter in the sky above Leo's head.) Soon after the withdrawal, an epidemic broke out among the Huns and Attila died. Deprived of their leader, the fearsome horsemen of the east were no longer a threat.

Not long after Attila's death, Rome was sacked again. This time the invading army was made up of Vandals, who attacked from the sea in 455. The Vandals' assault upon Rome was so vicious that ever since the term "vandal" has referred to someone who causes senseless damage and destruction.

THEODORIC THE GREAT

In 476 the last Roman Emperor, Romulus Augustulus, was overthrown by a Germanic chieftain named Odoacer. The Emperor was, in fact, only a boy (Augustulus means "little Augustus" in Latin), and he was sent off to live in a quiet villa. The barbarians now controlled the western half of the Roman Empire.

In 493 Theodoric, king of the Ostrogoths, entered Rome and assassinated Odoacer. He made Ravenna his capital and ruled Italy wisely, preserving many of the old Roman forms of

Ruins of the Palace of Theodoric, Ravenna

government. Theodoric was anxious to maintain peace between the Romans and his own people. In fact, he was the first king in Europe to recognize different nationalities as equals.

For thirty-three years Theodoric maintained order. Roads and aqueducts were repaired, new buildings were constructed, and prosperity returned to the Italian peninsula. Although illiterate, Theodoric was very interested in education, and he invited a number of Greek

Attila and Leo I

scholars to his court. They translated many ancient writings into Latin. Theodoric was tolerant of different religious beliefs, and although he supported the Church (Christianity was the official religion of the Romans), he did not compel his subjects to do so. He once remarked that no man could be compelled to believe against his will.

When the king died in 526, he was succeeded by his daughter. But her reign was short-lived: She was murdered by her husband and co-ruler, Theodahad. This caused her allies from the east to seek revenge and attack Italy. By the middle of the sixth century the Ostrogoths had lost power. Would all of Theodoric's reforms be forgotten? Meanwhile, another group of tribesmen, the Lombards, had settled in the valley of the Po River in the northern region of the Italian peninsula.

THE CELTS

Long before the Germanic invasions took place, another group of tribesmen inhabited central Europe. These were the Celts, an Indo-European people who had settled there as early as the second millennium BCE. Most Celts were farmers, but they were also fierce warriors when fighting was called for. Their appearance was rather startling. They shaved their beards and grew long mustaches that covered their mouths. Just before battle, a warrior poured lime on his hair and brushed it back like a horse's mane. The Celts collected the heads of their enemies (which they considered sacred) and displayed them in their huts. They were the first warriors the Romans encountered who wore trousers rather than tunics. (In fact, "breeches" is a Celtic word.) They were a creative people, and they excelled in metalworking.

As the Roman Empire expanded most of the Celts were slowly absorbed into its civilization. The Romans named the province where they lived Gaul, which is Latin for Celt. Not all Celts had remained on the Continent, however. In the eighth and seventh centuries BCE large numbers had crossed the North Sea and settled in the British Isles, where they created their own unique culture, worshipping the sun and believing in giants, dragons and other monsters. Their priests, who were called Druids, often performed ceremonies involving human sacrifices.

A Druid ceremony

BRITAIN

Britain (Britannia) became a Roman province in 43 CE and remained one for almost four hundred years. The Romans referred to the Celts living there as Britons because they wore blue paint when they went to battle. (Briton comes from the Latin word for "paint".) But in 407 the Emperor withdrew his troops from the island and sent them to reinforce his northern European borders where the Visigoths were raising havoc. This left the Britons at the mercy of the savage Picts and Scots who lived in Scotland and Ireland.

About this time, groups of Angles, Saxons and Jutes (all Germanic) began crossing the narrow

Map of modern Britain

had to defend their land against the new invaders (their former allies). In the fighting that ensued, Horsa was killed, but Hengest later founded a new kingdom (Kent). Among the Briton leaders was a chieftain named Ambrosius Aurelianus. It is very likely that he was the source of the legends of King Arthur, about whom we'll learn more in a later chapter.

Around 500 the Britons won a great victory against the Angles at Mount Badon. They drove the invaders from the British midlands and held them in check for half a century. They were finally defeated by the Angles and Saxons in 577 at the Battle of Deorham. Afterwards, groups of Britons retreated to the mountain districts of Cornwall and Wales. (The Saxons called them Welsh which, in their language, means "foreigners.") Some Britons fled to Gaul and established villages there. This region in modern France is still called Brittany.

channel that separates Britain from the European continent in long rowing boats. Most of these people had lived near the mouths of rivers along the North and Baltic Seas. They were attracted to Britain's fertile soil and mild climate, which contrasted so dramatically with the bleak and windswept lands of northern Europe.

According to legend, the Briton king Vortigern asked two Saxon chieftains, Hengest and Horsa, to help him defend his people from their fierce enemies to the north. The Saxons easily subdued the poorly organized Picts and Scots in 442. But then, much to the Britons' despair, they began helping themselves to large portions of choice farmland. So now the Britons

The Sword in the Stone from the legend of King Arthur

By 600 the Angles, Saxons, and Jutes (whose merging culture could now be referred to as Anglo-Saxon) controlled most of present England and southern Scotland. They built huts of wattle and daub (a framework of woven branches smeared with mud plaster), clustering them around their fields. Because they disliked cities, they left those built by the Romans to crumble. In fact, they believed that the deserted towns and villas were haunted by the people who had lived and been slain there (they referred to them as the cold harbors). They also neglected the roads, since they feared that well maintained highways would enable their enemies to cross their land and attack them. Besides, they had no interest in trade.

The Anglo-Saxon communities held assemblies to deal with local issues. These were called folk moots. Over the years, as groups of tribes were united to form kingdoms, the folk moot developed into the Witan (an assembly of advisors to the king). Society was now divided into three groups: the thanes (who owned large

A hut made of wattle and daub, with a thatched roof

portions of land), the churls (who owned small amounts of land), and thralls (slaves).

Anglo-Saxon justice was derived from the Germanic system we have already learned about. As you will remember, if a tribesman was killed, his kin sought revenge or claimed wergeld. (It shouldn't surprise you that a thane's value was six times that of a churl!) In most cases an accused person would pay the fine in order to avoid bloodshed. But a large fine could force a small farmer to deed his land to someone wealthier. He would continue to work the land, but he would have to share his produce with the new landowner. His descendants would never know the liberty he had once enjoyed.

Paris was founded on the island in the Seine River where Notre Dame now stands

There was also a fixed value for any part of the body that was injured by another person, an eye or a leg being the greatest. Cutting off a man's right hand cost more than cutting off his left one, and fingers which held the bowstrings were worth more than other fingers. Some people convicted of murder or assault refused to pay the wergeld and fled to the forests. However, the life of an outlaw was difficult indeed. He was called a "wolf's head" because he could be slain on sight as freely as a farmer would kill a wolf.

Some crimes were punishable by death. Runaway slaves could be killed on the spot, as could people who helped outlaws. In such cases death occurred by hanging, beheading, stoning, burning or drowning. Certain lesser crimes were punished by branding, scalping, scorching, or blinding. Someone found guilty of spreading nasty rumors could have his ears cut off or his tongue cut out!

By the seventh century the Anglo-Saxons had established seven small kingdoms, known as the Heptarchy. These were: Northumbria (literally, the land to the north of the Humber River), Mercia (the middle region), East Anglia (the land of east Angles), Kent (which had become the land of Jutes), Wessex (the land of the west Saxons), Essex (the land of the east Saxons), and Sussez 9the land of the south Saxons). In time, all the land was controlled by the three most powerful kingdoms: Northumbria, Mercia, and Wessex. The entire region came to be known as Angleland (England), and the language of its Germanic inhabitants would evolve in modern English. (Even today, the French refer to England as Angleterre, meaning "the land of the Angles.")

THE FRANKS

Now let's return to the European continent and see what was happening there. The Franks were a loose confederation of tribes who crossed the Rhine River in the fourth century and settled in the Roman province of Gaul. Their name is derived from the franciscas (short-handled axes) that they hurled at their enemies at close range. Unlike the Goths, who wandered from place to place in search of the best land, and the Vandals, whose main interest was plunder, the Franks settled in Gaul and became allies with the Romans and Celts living there. Of all the tribes we have learned about so far, the Franks were to have the most long lasting effect upon the development of medieval culture.

At first each Frankish tribe had its own king. Clovis (his name was an early form of Louis) inherited a kingdom of 5000 warriors in 481 when he was only fifteen years old. He managed to unite the people of northern Gaul under his rule, and then he conquered the other Germanic tribes that had settled in other regions of the province (the Burgundians and Alamanni). Clovis eliminated those Frankish chiefs who challenged his authority and became the first generally recognized king of the Franks. He established a dynasty, the Merovingians. The name is derived from Clovis' grandfather Meroven, a Frankish chieftain. His new kingdom came to be known as Francia ("Land of the Franks"). Francia was the first significant political organization of the early Middle Ages. Its modern name, of course, is France.

Clovis established a capital in Paris. This bustling town was named for the Parisii, a Celtic tribe that lived there before the Romans invaded Gaul. Clovis rewarded his military leaders with large tracts of land. Because the Franks had no experience in ruling a large empire, Clovis adopted the Roman machinery of government, which was still in place at the time of his conquest. He appointed officials called counts and sent them throughout the land to help govern as his personal representatives. They administered districts of land known as counties. Clovis had many tribal laws written down, as well as the fines that had to be paid if someone was killed, injured, or insulted (wergeld).

When Clovis died in 511, his kingdom was divided between his four sons. Unfortunately, they did not have the leadership qualities of their father. When they later divided up their kingdoms among their own sons, the kingdom Clovis had fought so hard to establish was broken up into many small parts. Most of the people lived near the old Roman villas, which continued to thrive. Farmers worked for the wealthy landlords, who protected them in times of war.

The later Merovingian kings were known as the "do nothing" kings because they devoted most of their time to amusing themselves. One allegedly spent hours each day arranging his golden locks with a jeweled comb! By the seventh century the Merovingian monarchs were merely puppets. And who was running the government? Officials known as the Mayors of the Palace.

THE EASTERN EMPIRE

Although the western half of the Roman Empire crumbled in the late fifth century, many aspects of that rich civilization survived and became an important part of medieval culture. We'll learn what these were in the following chapters. Gradually the cultures of the Germans and the Romans would merge to form a new type of society.

But it is important to remember that while the western half of the Roman Empire was

Dagobert, King of the Franks, seventh century

being devastated by the barbarian raids, the eastern part continued to prosper. It had a strong government and a well trained professional army that successfully protected its borders. It also had a highly educated class of administrators and enterprising merchants who brought great wealth to the major cities. Because its capital (Constantinople) was built on the site of the Greek city of Byzantium, the civilization that flourished in the eastern empire after the fall of Rome is known as Byzantine.

QUESTIONS

1. What was the original meaning of the word "barbarian?"
2. What were typical weapons of barbarian warriors?
3. What was wergeld?
4. Why did Valens allow the Goths to enter Roman territory?

5. What catastrophe did Alaric cause (catastrophic from the Roman point of view)?

6. Who was called the Scourge of God and why?

7. What did Theodoric do to preserve peace?

8. How did the Welsh get their name?

9. What did the word England mean originally?

10. What did Clovis accomplish?

FURTHER THOUGHTS

1. The barbarians were the first people to produce felt, a fabric made from a matted sheet of tangled wool, hair, or fur. After heat, pressure, and moisture caused the tangling and shrinking of the fibers, the material was clipped. Felt was used in early times for hats, padding, even mattresses.

2. After the Roman army withdrew from Britain in the fifth century, many wealthy inhabitants buried hoards of coins and other valuables for safekeeping. In 1979, many gold and silver objects from this period were found buried in Thetford, Norfolk.

3. Sutton Hoo, in Suffolk, East Anglia, was the site of the greatest archaeological find in England. It consisted of a royal graveyard with several large mounds. In 1939 the largest mound was excavated and archaeologists discovered an eighty-nine-foot long boat. This was probably the coffin for King Raedwald of the Angles who died in 624. Although the wood had rotted away, its design was indicated by the dark marks the wood had left in the soil (and the nails were still in their approximate position). In the center of the former boat were the remains of a burial chamber. It contained jewelry, coins, a helmet, a lyre, weapons, a scepter, a splendid shield, a

purse, buckles, cauldrons, shoes, combs, drinking horns, bottles, and ornamental iron chain work. But there was no evidence of the body. What do you think happened to the remains of the king?

4. In the seventh or eighth century an Anglo-Saxon poet wrote an epic poem *Beowulf* in an early form of our English language. The story had been recounted orally for centuries before it was written down, and it is the earliest existing poem of the Middle Ages composed in a modern European language. More than 3,000 lines long, *Beowulf* is one of the longest poems ever written.

Although it was written in England, *Beowulf* takes place in fifth century Denmark. The villain is a monster named Grendel who carries off and eats one of the Danish king's courtiers each night. Beowulf, the young hero who comes from southern Sweden, kills the monster; then he kills Grendel's mother and becomes the new king. He rules for fifty years. In his old age Beowulf fights a dragon, and although he manages to kill the beast, he dies of the wounds received in the fight.

Beowulf reflects the heroic code which we will study in a later chapter. The young hero embodies loyalty and bravery, ever striving for lof (the fame that will survive his death). All but one of the written copies of the epic have vanished. The single, surviving manuscript written in about 1000 was readable until the eighteenth century. Fortunately, copies of it were made at the time (the original is now illegible).

5. The word "book" comes from the Anglo-Saxons. In their language, *boc* meant beech tree (the early settlers wrote on its bark).

6. The several centuries following the fall of Rome used to be called the Dark Ages because we knew so little about them. Now we know more, so the term is seldom used. Some Renaissance scholars referred to the period in that way

because they believed it was a time when nothing happened. We'll soon see how wrong they were!

7.   The dates we are dealing with originate with the year 1, Anno Domini ("the Year of Our Lord"). This is when Jesus was born, and it serves as a convenient point for marking time. Since everything between 1 and 100 makes up the first century AD, three digit dates that begin with 1 (142, 198, and so on) make up the second century AD. Remember this when you're thinking about dates. The hundreds' or thousands' digit of a date will always be 100 years less (accounting for those first 100 years!) than the number of the century. So 877 is the ninth century, and 1994 is the twentieth.

PROJECTS

1.   Draw a map of Europe, western Asia and northern Africa (see fig. 1). Then make a key, attributing different colors to the major tribes of barbarians. On the map draw arrows in the appropriate colors to indicate the movement and settlement of each tribe.

2.   Many of our towns, cities, and regions have names that are derived from the Anglo-Saxons. For example, the word endings -ton and -ham mean "village" (Burlington and Framingham). The ending -ing means "homestead of a tribe or clan" (Reading). The ending -ley means "clearing" (Henley), -burh or -burgh means "fortified place" (Pittsburgh), -Chester means "a place with an old Roman fortification or army base" (Winchester), and -ford means "river crossing" (Westford). Make a list of towns and cities that you know about in the United States or Great Britain whose names are derived from the Anglo-Saxons.

3.   Find a modern version of *Beowulf* and read several chapters. Then make a report to your class.

4.   Justinian (482-565) was a remarkable Byzantine Emperor who managed to "turn back the clock" and recapture, for a while at least, the "good old days" of a Roman Empire that (nearly) encircled the Mediterranean. He also did a lot for Roman law. Find out more about Justinian and write a report.

Mosaic of Justinian

CHAPTER 2

THE EARLY CHRISTIAN CHURCH

Christianity arose in the eastern provinces of the empire when Rome was at the height of its power. The early emperors resisted the new religion, persecuting thousands of people who practiced it, but they could not extinguish the fervent belief in a single, all-loving God that was rapidly spreading throughout the civilized world. Early in the fourth century the Emperor Constantine converted to Christianity. About fifty years later his successor, Theodosius, made the new faith the official religion of the Roman Empire.

Statue of Constantine

HOW THE CHURCH WAS ORGANIZED

As the Christian Church grew, its leadership adopted the very efficient bureaucracy of the Roman government as a model for its own organization. So when the western empire fell in the fifth century, a well-established network of church officials was already in place to take over as the guardian of law and order. Medieval society would be guided by the spirit of the Christian faith rather than the ardent patriotism of earlier times.

Let's take a look at the structure of Roman government that so influenced the Church. Late in the third century the Emperor Diocletian had split the empire in two. He further divided the vast territory into twelve military districts called dioceses, each to be ruled by a vicar. So, following his example, the Church divided the regions where Christianity had spread into ecclesiastical (church) dioceses. Several dioceses made up one province. Each diocese was governed by a bishop (a word meaning "overseer"). His duties were to maintain order, preserve justice (local law-breakers were tried in his court), and provide leadership for the officials of the local communities. He also performed religious ceremonies, such as the "holy orders" in which priests were confirmed. Those bishops whose dioceses included major cities were called archbishops. An archbishop not only had authority in his own diocese but also outranked all the other bishops in his province. Those archbishops whose territories included Rome, Milan, Constantinople, Antioch, and Jerusalem became very powerful.

On the local level, a diocese was divided into several parishes. Each parish was ruled by a priest, usually a man of humble origin. It was his job to conduct services and to cater to the religious needs of the local people. The parishioners had to pay a tithe (one tenth of their animals and crops) each year. Most of this went to the bishop, but the priest kept about a quarter of it to help the sick and the poor as well as meeting his own basic needs. He was paid an additional fee each time he performed a special ceremony, such as a baptism, wedding, or funeral.

In the sixth century the Bishop of Rome claimed supremacy over the Christian Church in Europe. He became known as the Pope (from the Latin word papa meaning "father"). The power of a Papacy (the office of the Pope) was derived from St. Peter, the first Bishop of Rome. Peter was one of the twelve Apostles of Jesus according to the New Testament. During the Middle Ages the Pope would become one of the most powerful men in Europe.

Statue of Saint Peter in Rome

THE CHURCH TEACHINGS

The Christian people believed in the existence of heaven (a blissful place of eternal peace and happiness) and hell (a fiery inferno where the devil saw to it that his victims suffered endless pain and despair). Purgatory was a misty, intermediary place where the soul of a person who died in a state of grace (having God's favor) atoned for any small sins he had committed before entering heaven; afterwards the soul would spend eternity with God and the spirits of the saints (holy people). The living were expected to offer prayers on behalf of those waiting in purgatory. The souls of the damned (super sinners) went directly to hell!

Life was difficult during those early times, and the potential of war, famine, and disease made death a common fear. But the people were sustained by the hope that if they did all the right things in this life, their souls would make it to heaven. But the Church said that everyone sinned. (The seven deadly sins were pride (this was the worst), anger, avarice, envy, gluttony, lust, and sloth.) So how could a person gain God's favor? One way was to participate in the holy sacraments (religious rituals): these were baptism, confirmation, penance, holy orders, matrimony, and anointing of those who were about to die. People also prayed to the saints to "plead their cases" before God.

The supreme act of worship was to attend a service called the Eucharist (Mass). Part of the service was called Holy Communion. This was a special ceremony in which a participant consumed a wheat wafer and sipped a small container of wine. The wafer and wine represented the body and blood of Christ. The purpose of Communion was to remind the worshippers that Christ had died for their sins; by consuming the wafer and wine they "communed" with the spirit of Christ. This inspired them to demonstrate their gratitude for His sacrifice by leading moral lives.

But even conscientious Christians worried about ending up in hell after they died. So the Church offered other aids. For example, an indulgence was an official edict that reduced or even erased the amount of time a person's soul would spend in purgatory (or even in hell) in exchange for a particular deed or a sum of money. (Can you see how some wealthy people might be tempted to "buy their way" into heaven?)

The Pope could dole out some fearsome punishments to those who did not follow the teachings of the Church. Perhaps the worst was excommunication, which forbade a person to participate in the holy sacraments, to attend mass, or to be buried in sacred ground. In other words, it closed the door to any future in heaven. An interdict was a general excommunication that affected an entire region. No Christian services of any kind could be held there until the interdict was revoked.

During the early centuries a number of scholars wrote books that would greatly influence the thinking of the Church. These men were called the Church Fathers. Among them was St. Jerome, who translated the Old and New Testaments of the Bible into Latin. His work, known as The Vulgate, would become the official Bible of the Church. Why was he called St. Jerome? Many of the clergy we will be studying were canonized (made saints) by the Church after they died. The abbreviation for saint is "St."

St. Augustine wrote a long work entitled The City of God to defend Christianity against accusations that Rome had been sacked by the Visigoths in 410 as punishment for having abandoned the pagan religion of the ancient Romans. According to Augustine, Rome would

have fallen under any circumstances because of the wickedness and greed of its people. In contrast to a city in which people immersed themselves in early pleasures (A City of Men), he proposed that the Christian city devoted to the worship of God (A City of God) offered the only hope for a better society.

Statue of Saint Augustine

THE MONASTERY

One of the strongholds of Christianity during the Middle Ages was the monastery. Monasticism is a term that refers to a solitary and secluded way of life. (It is derived from the Greek word monos meaning "one.") Among the earliest Christians were hermits who lived alone in the desert and in caves. St. Anthony was an Egyptian who retired to the wilderness to escape the wickedness of society and to spend his hours in prayer. Word of his sanctity soon spread and drew visits from other pious Christians. This eventually inspired St. Anthony to organize a community of hermits.

Before long, similar groups were springing up in Asia and Europe. These communities were the first monasteries, and the men living in them were known as monks. Although each monk spent much of his time in private prayer, he was also responsible for performing particular tasks for the group, and he was bound by certain rules of behavior. The monks gave up all worldly possessions when they devoted their lives to prayer, fasting, and meditation. In an increasingly corrupt and violent society, the monasteries would become havens of tranquility and security.

Some monks sustained great physical hardships because they believed that suffering made them better Christians. They slept on beds made of thorns, wore hairshirts, and frequently whipped themselves. (A hairshirt was made of hair from the manes and tails of horses. It was incredibly scratchy and uncomfortable to wear.) In the fifth century a Syrian named Simeon Stylites lived for thirty years on the top of a sixty-foot pillar. That was a record for seclusion and self denial!

FOUNDING MONKS IN BRITAIN

St. Patrick was a Briton who was born in Wales in 385, the grandson of a Christian priest. He was kidnapped by pirates while still a young boy and spent his youth as a slave in Ireland. Eventually he escaped to a French monastery where he was trained as a priest. In 432 Patrick returned to Ireland, firmly determined to spread Christianity throughout the island. He was made a bishop, and he devoted his life to preaching,

baptizing people, and ordaining priests. He must have been enormously convincing, because within thirty years most of the Irish had been converted to Christianity. According to legend, St. Patrick taught the people the Christian concept of the Holy Trinity (Father, Son, and Holy Ghost) by showing them a shamrock, a three-leafed plant. This is why the shamrock is always associated with Ireland.

St. Patrick encouraged the building of monasteries, which were to become great centers of learning. He introduced the Roman alphabet to the Irish monks so that they could write down and thus preserve much of the Celtic literature that had been passed down orally from generation to generation. He died on March 17, 461. Ever since, that date has been celebrated as Saint Patrick's Day. He is also the patron saint of Ireland.

During the years when Britain was being invaded by the Angles, Saxons, and Jutes, Ireland was protected by the sea, and so it remained a stronghold of the Christian Church as well as a preserver of Celtic culture. Because of its great

Statue of Saint Patrick holding a shamrock

distance from Rome, the Irish Church had little to do with the Pope, and it evolved somewhat differently than the churches on the Continent.

In 563 an Irish monk named Columba (later St. Columba) sailed with twelve companions to the small island of Iona off the southwestern coast of Scotland and built a monastery there. He believed in extreme piety and self-denial.

For example, he felt that no monk should go to bed until he was already asleep on his feet. As a result, much of the time the monks of Iona were propped up against the walls, in slumber or in a daze! But despite his austere philosophy, Columba loved animals and flowers, and he was often seen with a squirrel on his shoulder. He later left the island and traveled in Scotland, converting many of the Picts to Christianity. Then he continued his preaching in Northumbria. Iona would become the center of spiritual life for Ireland, Scotland, and Northumbria.

In 635 Aidan, an Irish monk from Iona, built a monastery on the island of Lindisfarne off the coast of Northumberland. It was later known as the Holy Island. English boys were trained there to become missionaries. We will learn about the manuscripts produced on Lindisfarne later in this chapter.

THE BENEDICTINE MONKS

Benedict of Nursia (St. Benedict) was born to a wealthy Italian family in 480. He was educated

Iona Abbey, founded by Columba in 563

Stained glass Image of Saint Columba

upon the ruins of the palace of the Emperor Nero. There he lived as a hermit, wearing a hairshirt and existing on the bread that was brought to him by a faithful friend. His ascetic life style enabled Benedict to feel at peace with himself and close to God.

As had been the case with St. Anthony, St. Benedict's reputation for holiness attracted many followers who wanted to share his way of life. The concept of a community of pious men living together appealed to Benedict, so he left his cave, and in 525 he founded a monastery (Monte Cassino) between Rome and Naples. It would become a major center of monastic life.

Even monks needed to follow rules if they were to live together harmoniously, so St. Benedict devised a comprehensive set of regulations (known as St. Benedict's Rule), which became the model used by later monasteries. He had come to scorn the extreme hardships endured by some religious men, preferring a life of balance and moderation. He divided the day

in Rome in preparation for a life of government service. But he was appalled by the ruins of the once glorious capital of the Empire that had been sacked by the barbarians, and he was disgusted by the rowdy behavior of the young Romans who lived there, just as St. Augustine had been. So he gave up his studies and went east into the hills. He found a lonely cave that looked down

Ruins of the Abbey of Lindisfarne

Medieval painting of St. Benedict

poverty, chastity, and obedience. He had no personal belongings (he gave everything he owned to the monastery), he was rarely allowed to speak, he was forbidden to quarrel, and he was expected to walk with his eyes fixed on the ground, thinking about all the sins he had committed. He would remain in the monastery for life, unless he was sent on a special mission.

St Benedict's monastery at Monte Cassino

into three equal parts, allotting eight hours each to work, prayer, and sleep. This does not mean that a monk would sleep for eight hours, then pray for eight hours, and finally work for eight hours. Rather, his working and sleeping time was interrupted at regular intervals (eight times a day, or about every three hours) so that he could pray. Work time was spent laboring in the fields, preparing meals, cleaning the monastery, studying the writings of the Church, educating young boys, or making copies of books. St. Benedict once said that idleness was the enemy of the soul, so his monks were never idle. Monte Cassino was self-supporting; it prospered without any sort of outside aid. In his lifetime St. Benedict founded fourteen monasteries, all regulated by his Rule. He later became the patron saint of Europe.

St Benedict's monastery at Monte Cassino was destroyed by Allied bombing in 1944. It was later rebuilt and greatly expanded, as is shown here.

Each Benedictine monastery (also called an abbey) was governed by an abbot, who was elected for life by his fellow monks. He was responsible to no one except the Pope. The abbot was assisted in his duties by the prior. When a monk joined a monastery he took a vow of

Anyone wishing to become a monk had to wait at the monastery gate for four or five days in order to prove his patience. Once admitted within the walls, he became a novice and spent the next year carefully studying every principle described in Benedict's Rule. Once he had accomplished this task, he could become a monk. In a simple ceremony he promised to live according to the Rule and then put on his habit—a heavy, black hooded robe made of coarsely woven wool (this is why the Benedictines were called the Black Monks). The top of his head was shaved, leaving a round, bald spot called a tonsure. From then on the monastery community was his family: The abbot was his father and the other monks were his brothers.

The buildings of a monastery were usually constructed of stone. Over the centuries, the design of a monastery became standard. The most important structure was, of course, the church. On the south side of the church was the cloister: It consisted of four long sheltered walks (colonnades) forming a square around a central garth (a lawn or small garden). This is where the monks spent many hours, walking along the colonnade or sitting on the stone benches placed at intervals beside the pillars. It was the perfect spot for prayer and meditation. The other buildings were grouped around the cloister. These included the refectory, where the monks ate their meals; the chapter house, where they conducted business; the dormitories, where they slept (in French dormir means "to sleep"); special cells for study and meditation; a kitchen, a bakery, perhaps a brewery, workshops, storehouses, and an infirmary.

Some monks had special responsibilities: The precentor was in charge of the conduct of services; the sacristan looked after the church and its furnishings—the altars and the hangings, the candles and the lamps, and any treasures—and saw to the ringing of the bells; the cantor directed the music; the cellarer was in charge of the food; the chamberlain took care of the clothing (repairs and washing); the infirmarer took care of the sick; the almoner distributed gifts, generally food, to the poor in the local community; the guest master received the guests and provided hospitality; and the porter guarded the gate.

A Benedictine monk's robe

Cloister of a medieval abbey

As we have learned, every day a monk attended a series of religious services. Each service was called a recitation of the Hour. Here is the schedule of a typical twenty-four-hour period. Just before midnight a bell rang and the monks arose from their beds (they slept in their habits on straw mats covered by wool blankets). Yawning and shivering, they passed in silence to the choir of the church (the area near the altar where they prayed). Once assembled there, they were led in Matins and Lauds, the first services of the day. These consisted of an hour of hymns and psalms and other readings, all spoken or chanted in Latin. During the services one monk went around with a lantern and shone it in the eyes of the sleepy worshippers; if someone was found dozing, he had to take over lantern duty. Anyone who arrived late was expected to lie face-down on the floor in the middle of the choir to indicate his contrition; he remained there until the man leading the service knocked on the wood of his choir stall, signaling permission for him to get up. After the services the monks returned to bed.

At sunrise they were again awakened by the bell and immediately proceeded back to the choir for Prime (more prayers and hymns). Afterwards they went to the lavatorium to wash in the basin

Bells in the bell tower summoned the monks to prayer

that day. Afterwards, punishments were doled out for such infractions as speaking or making a noise in the cloister, doing work poorly, or falling asleep during prayers. Typical punishments included living on bread and water for a few days, eating meals alone, and being whipped. If a monk committed a serious crime, he might be placed in solitary confinement for a while or even expelled from the monastery. One abbey listed the ten chief sins of monks; at the top of the list were 1) thinking too much about comfort and 2) being tempted by rich food! The chapter meeting was conducted by the abbot or prior. All the brothers listened in silence. If someone had something to say, he would stand up and patiently wait until he was given the signal to speak.

After the meeting, the monks went off to do their jobs. One group went to the fields to tend the crops. Monks were great innovators in farming techniques. They drained swamps and diverted excess water into canals. Monks later developed many new ways of cultivating crops and experimented with animal breeding, producing new lines of cattle, sheep, and horses. They also became famous for the crabapples, gooseberries, plums, and cherries they grew in their orchards. Carthusian monks developed the breed of the Andalusian horse in Spain

After the next service (called Sext), the brothers finally sat down to dinner in the refectory. This usually consisted of soup, bread, and vegetables (peas, beans, and cabbage). Sometimes the meal included cheese, eggs, and fruit. No red meat was consumed, although fish was often served on Friday. The monks drank ale or wine with their meal (water was often impure). Before dining, grace was sung by all the brothers. Then they sat in silence on benches at long narrow tables while the food was served. The abbot and prior sat in the front at the high table (so-called because it was placed on a low

(monks were much cleaner than the average person of the times). Unless it was a Holy Day or Lent, the young novices and the elderly brothers then had breakfast (a quarter of a pound of bread and a third of a pint of ale or wine) which they consumed while standing up. Most of the brothers abstained; they had only one meal a day. The few who did eat were thus breaking the period of fast (and this is the origin of our word breakfast!).

The third service of the day was called Tierce (held at nine o'clock AM). It was followed by a High Mass, which was often attended by the people of the local community. After Mass, a morning meeting was held in the chapter house. At the beginning of the meeting a chapter was read from St. Benedict's Rule (this, of course, is why it was called the chapter house). Then announcements were made and the monks were told what particular duties they would perform

An Andalusian horse

measured the daylight hours (and were totally useless on a cloudy or rainy day). So they used a water clock. It was a simple device: A clay jar with a hole at the bottom was filled with water. The water leaked through the hole at a certain rate and slowly filled a second jar. All the monks had to do was to look at the lines painted on the inside of the second jar to find out how much time had passed. The only problem with this primitive clock was that the water often froze in winter! In 1280 the monks at Dunstable Abbey created Europe's first mechanical clock. (The Chinese had been using them for centuries.) In the late fourteenth century the first alarm clock was devised for use by the brothers of a monastery in Wurzburg, Germany.

platform). During the meal one monk stood at a pulpit and read aloud from the Bible.

After a short rest period, it was time for another service (called Nones). Those brothers working in the fields put their tools aside when they heard the church bell and had a private service there. Then back to work for awhile until, once again, the bell chimed. It was time for Vespers. By now it was late afternoon. The young and the elderly were allowed to eat a bit of bread and cheese (another breakfast!), while the other brothers enjoyed their leisure time. This was the one time during the day that they were allowed to speak. Some even played board games. At seven o'clock it was time for another service. This one was called Compline, which means "completed" in Latin (it marked the end of the day). Before going to bed they attended Nocturnes, then they slept until they were awakened for Matins the next morning. Later on, this arduous schedule was revised, and two services were often combined to open up longer stretches of time for work projects.

The monks needed a way to determine when it was time for the next service. Sundials only

Medieval clock on an early church

It's important to mention here that although the monks had a twenty-four-hour day, not all hours were of equal length. Wishing to take advantage of the longer periods of daylight in the summer, they stretched the hours of the day at that time of year so that each hour was more than sixty minutes long. In the winter they did the opposite: They compensated for the shorter period of light by shrinking each hour of the daytime. Nighttime hours, therefore, were shorter in summer and longer in winter. Perhaps the modern concept of Daylight Savings Time has its roots in the medieval monastery.

Beginning in the late sixth century hundreds of Benedictine monasteries sprang up throughout Europe, all of them modeled on Monte Cassino. In fact, from the sixth to the eleventh centuries, the greatest medieval builders were the monastic orders. We will learn more about their beautiful stone churches in a later chapter. Benedict's sister, Scholastica, established a convent for women, and before long nunneries also appeared in many places. Some women joined a convent because they could not find husbands - in those days, an unmarried woman was considered an old maid at the age of twenty-one!

Early painting of St Benedict and Ste Scholastica

THE MONKS RETURN TO BRITAIN

When Monte Cassino was pillaged by the Lombards in 577, the monks living there quickly scattered. Some who took refuge in Rome came in contact with a man who would later become a powerful force in the Church as Pope Gregory I (the Great). Like St. Benedict, Gregory came from a wealthy family and received a good education. At the age of thirty he was named prefect of Rome (a high government position). But he became disheartened with city politics and decided he would rather lead a life of piety and contemplation as a monk. His father died soon after he made this decision, and Gregory used the large fortune he inherited to set up six Benedictine monasteries in Sicily. His own house in Rome became the seventh. In 584 he was elected abbot of one of the abbeys.

Gregory became Pope in 590. He was the first monk to attain this high office. He was an able leader who tried to be a patient listener while maintaining an image of strict authority. He increased papal power by asserting his right to intervene in the secular (non-church) matters of the Christian community. Gregory wrote many books, including a biography of St. Benedict.

Before becoming Pope, Gregory had noticed a group of blond-haired blue-eyed boys who had been brought to Rome to be sold at the slave market. He asked who they were (blond hair was unusual in Italy), and when he was told that they were Angles from Northumbria, he responded that they were Angels, not Angles (the pun works in Latin as well as in English). When he became Pope, Gregory remembered the blond-haired boys and, in 597, he sent a band of forty Benedictine monks led by a man named Augustine (later St. Augustine) to convert the pagan Anglo-Saxons.

Painting of Pope Gregory

(This was not St. Augustine, the Church Father.) Christianity had been established in Britain back in the days when the Roman soldiers occupied the island, but the churches were abandoned when the army withdrew to the Continent.

Augustine's expedition landed in Kent. They marched ashore carrying a silver cross, a picture of Christ, and a letter from Gregory addressed to the King of the Angles. (This was when the Europeans first started referring to Britain as Angleland.) But King Ethelbert of Kent was suspicious of the black-clad monks. He insisted upon meeting with them only in the open air, where (he hoped) their "magic" would have no effect on him. Ethelbert's wife Bertha was a Christian Frank, so he was somewhat familiar with the religion. With Bertha's help, Augustine managed to convince the king of the advantages of Christianity, and on Christmas Day in 597

Ethelbert was baptized, along with ten thousand of his subjects. Soon afterwards the religion spread to Essex.

Gregory had cautioned Augustine not to destroy the pagan temples, so they were converted to Christian churches. Similarly, many of the old heathen festivals were transformed into Christian ones. For example, the Germanic winter feast of Yule became associated with Christmas, and the Saxon spring goddess Eostre lent her name to Easter. Augustine established the see (center) of his new diocese at Canterbury, and that city would become the headquarters of the English Church. Augustine himself served as the first Archbishop of Canterbury. Ever since, the man occupying that position has been regarded as the most powerful churchman in England.

Paulinus, one of the monks who accompanied Augustine, traveled on to Northumbria, where he converted the king (Edwin) and his subjects to Christianity. Paulinus became the first Archbishop of York, the major town in Northumbria. From the sees of Canterbury and York, a network of churches gradually spread throughout England until, by the end of the seventh century, most Anglo-Saxons were Christians.

Eventually a conflict arose between the Celtic Church (founded by St. Patrick in Ireland) and the Roman Church (founded by St. Augustine in England). Remember how Columba built his monastery on Iona and then proceeded to convert the natives of northern Britain? By the seventh century there were large numbers of English Christians following the practices of both churches (Celtic in the north and Roman in the south). Although their religious beliefs were similar, a difference in cultural backgrounds had led to slight differences in church services, the concept of monasticism, the date upon which Easter was celebrated, and, most significantly, the recognition of the authority of the Pope. (As we have learned, the Irish-Celts did not consider the Pope to be the supreme head of the Church.)

In 664 King Oswy of Northumbria called a synod (a religious conference) at Whitby to discuss how the two churches could be brought together. After much discussion, the king supported the traditions and policies of the Roman Church, and the authority of the Pope was thus assured in Britain. Gradually the Celtic Church accepted the basic doctrines and procedures of the Roman Church. In 669 a Greek monk named Theodore was sent by the Pope to become the Archbishop of Canterbury. He organized the English Church into a system of dioceses and parishes. So, although England was still made up of several kingdoms, the people were united by the Church.

THE NORTHUMBRIAN RENAISSANCE

Not long after the decision was made at the synod of Whitby, Northumbria became the focus of a great cultural awakening that would affect all of western Europe. This is known as the Northumbrian Renaissance, and it was sparked by the merging of the Celtic and Germanic/Roman traditions of scholarship and art that had been thriving in the monasteries for years.

Perhaps the greatest achievement of the period was the production of beautiful manuscripts. We learned earlier that the copying of books was one of the major tasks performed in the monasteries. There were no printing presses or bookstores in those early times, so the monks produced their own manuscripts by making copies of the few books available in the abbey. (The word "manuscript" is derived from the Latin words for hand (manus) and written (scriptum).)

The most important books were the Bible, the Psalter (a book of psalms), and the writings of the Church Fathers. (This should come as no surprise!)

A monk worked on his manuscript in a special room called the scriptorium. He sat in a high backed armchair or on a stool with his materials spread out before him on a writing desk. He wrote on parchment (sheepskin) or vellum (calfskin), dipping his goose quill into an inkhorn (made from a cow's horn). If he made a mistake, he simply scraped the surface of the material with a knife and then smoothed away the roughness with the tooth of a goat or boar.

He spent long hours copying page after page. It was a tedious job that produced aching muscles, numb fingers, and a bent back. But he was inspired to press on by the belief that for every stroke of his pen a sin would be forgiven. Sometimes he relieved the boredom of his task by drawing little pictures in the margins to illustrate the text. The illustrations were called miniatures (not because they were small, but from the Latin word miniare meaning "to paint or write"). The pictures were often entwined in curving lines that spiraled and intercepted one another, producing

A modern monk at work on a manuscript

an intricate pattern. This design, known as curvilinear, dates back to Celts living in Gaul during the sixth century BC. It was passed on to the Irish monks by the descendants of Celts who had settled in the British Isles, and from them the technique went to the English. The copyists of Northumbria employed the Celtic pattern to decorate not only the miniatures but many of the letters themselves.

Celtic illuminated letters

Over the years, the monks found that a division of labor in the production of a manuscript worked well, each man performing the task that he did best. One monk (called the antiquaric), who was skillful at calligraphy, copied all the letters except those starting a new paragraph, for which he left large spaces. The rudicatore then drew elaborate letters in the spaces, decorating them with interlacing spirals, whorls, and ribbons as well as animal figures, all of which he painted in many bright colors. After the miniatore filled the margins with pictures and more spirals, the page was complete.

The monks made their own quill pens for writing as well as illustrating. This is how a pen was made. A goose feather was soaked in water and then dipped in hot sand to make it hard and springy. Once the feathery parts were stripped from the quill, the nib was shaped and split with

Quill pen, parchment, and ink

a special sharp knife. The monks also made their own paints from plants, parts of small animals, and minerals. The various colors came from a wide variety of sources: crimson was produced from the gum of a tree, scarlet from a tiny red insect, bright red from an Indian shrub, indigo blue from an Indian plant, purple from a sea snail that lives in the eastern Mediterranean, green from copper mixed with the juice of a rotten apple, bluish green from malachite, and yellow from saffron (this was incredibly expensive) or from arsenic salts. Gold coins were pounded to make thin sheets of gold leaf, which was glued to a page to provide a shimmering background. The brilliant colors and the gold so brightened

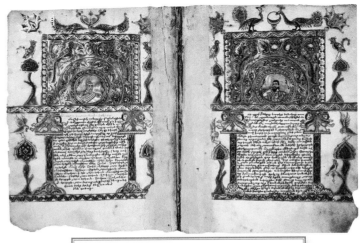

Pages of an illuminated manuscript

the texts that they came to be called illuminated manuscripts. Elaborate book covers were often made from velvet and decorated with gold, silver, or precious stones. Simpler covers were made from leather, to which were attached straps to buckle the books shut.

In the late seventh century (about 698) the monks of Lindisfarne completed a book of Gospels that is considered a masterpiece of Christian Celtic art. (A Gospel is a scene from the life of Christ, especially as described in the first four books of the New Testament.) The Book of Kells, produced at the monastery at Kells, Ireland, is a magnificent manuscript of the New Testament. It was stolen in 1007, and when it was later found buried in the ground, it had been stripped of its gold paint. Nonetheless it remains one of the finest examples of an illuminated manuscript. The Lindisfarne Gospels can be seen in the British Museum (London), and the Book of Kells is displayed in the Trinity College Library (Dublin).

The illuminated manuscripts of this period would later inspire the creation of beautifully handwritten prayer books for laymen. A prime example is the Book of Hours, which included materials for private devotions at each of the Hours of prayer, as well as passages from the Bible and a calendar of the saints' days. Only the wealthiest people could afford these lavishly decorated volumes. Many of them have survived to our times, and their illustrations tell us much about the medieval world. The Book of Hours made for the Duc de Berry, exhibited in Chantilly, France, is considered one of the finest examples.

The Northumbrian Renaissance was not limited to illuminated texts. Beautiful stone crosses were carved in England and Ireland. The Ruthwell Cross has survived relatively intact to this day. It is eighteen feet high, and nearly every inch of its surface is carved with scenes from the Bible. The earliest surviving example of Anglo-Saxon poetry was written during this period by a monk named Caedmon.

The greatest intellect of the times was Bede, an English monk. At the age of seven he had been sent to a Benedictine monastery to be educated; he later transferred to a different abbey at Jarrow. The abbot there had once visited Rome and brought back many books. Bede ravenously read them all. He also delighted in hearing the stories and poems that had been passed on by word of mouth for generations. The vast knowledge he accumulated from his reading and his listening later inspired Bede to write The Ecclesiastic History of England, which he completed in 731. It is the earliest written history of the English people. It was Bede who introduced to English speakers the Christian practice of dating events from the year of Christ's birth - BC for before the birth and AD (Anno Domini) for after the birth. (Today most historians use BCE (Before the Common Era) and CE (the Common Era) for dating.) Because of his brilliant accomplishments,

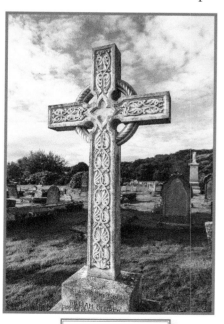

A Celtic Cross

Bede was given the title Venerable, meaning worthy of respect. He has been known as Venerable Bede ever since.

The flourishing of creative and intellectual activity that took place in Northumbria ended all too suddenly when England was invaded by the Vikings at the end of the eighth century. We will learn about these invasions in Chapter IV.

CHRISTIANITY SPREADS EAST

Irish monks were the first missionaries, and Columban (543-615) is credited with bringing Christianity to eastern Europe. He later settled in Burgundy (in modern France) and founded the monastery of Luxeuil, which became a famous center of learning.

Winfrith was a monk who was born the same year as Bede (673). He was reared and educated in a monastery in Wessex. As a young man he traveled to Rome to obtain the approval of Pope Gregory II to carry the Christian faith into eastern Francia. The Pope gave Winfrith not only his permission but also a new name, by which he has been known ever since: Boniface ("Doer of Good"). In 716 Boniface led a troop of Benedictine monks across the Rhine River (in modern Germany). Almost single-handedly he founded new Benedictine monasteries throughout the region and spearheaded a movement to Christianize the local people, converting thousands to his faith. Boniface was killed in Frisia in 754 by a mob of pagans who were offended by his missionary zeal. But in great part because of his efforts, western Europe was predominantly Christian by the dawn of the ninth century.

Engraving of Pope Gregory blessing Boniface

THE MUSLIMS

During the period of the Northumbrian Renaissance (the seventh and eighth centuries) a new army of invaders conquered half of the known civilized world and ended the long-lived Christian domination of the Mediterranean Sea. These were the Arab Muslims, and although they did not successfully penetrate Europe beyond the Pyrenees Mountains that separate modern Spain from France, their culture would have a significant effect upon western civilization.

Who were the Muslims? They were followers of a religious prophet named Mohammed, who was born in Arabia in about 570. Mohammed was a camel driver until he was forty, when he claimed that an angel appeared to him and said that he had been chosen to spread the word about a single god (called Allah). Further revelations came to him over the remaining years of his life. These were later written down by his followers in the Koran, the Bible of the Muslims. And the message? That there was only one god

(Allah) and that Mohammed had been chosen to warn the people of the coming Day of Judgment (when Allah would confront the powers of evil) and to remind them of Allah's goodness. The new religion was called Islam (which means "obedience to the will of Allah").

Mohammed inspired his Arab followers to fight a holy war (called a jihad) to spread his teachings. Their enthusiastic support was bolstered by the belief that anyone who was killed in a jihad would automatically go to heaven, and upon Mohammed's death in 632 all of the Arabian peninsula was within the sphere of Islam. His followers then set out to conquer Asia as far east as the Indus River and as far north as Syria.

The new leaders were called caliphs ("successors" to Mohammed). They treated the people they conquered fairly, allowing Christians and Jews to keep their religions. (After all, they regarded Moses and Jesus as prophets as well as Mohammed.)

In 661 Damascus (Syria) became the capital of the Muslim Empire. Nearly one hundred years later the caliph of Damascus was overthrown and a new government and capital were established in Baghdad (modern Iraq). This city became an important intellectual center where Arab scholars worked with their Jewish and Christian counterparts to translate many of the great works of Egypt, Greece, Rome, Persia, and India into their own language. Arab culture became one of the most advanced in the Mediterranean world. Learned Muslims used the ideas translated from ancient texts to create new concepts. For example, the Arabs invented algebra (from the Arabic al-jabr which means "the joining of broken parts"), and they borrowed the zero and numerals (with base ten) from the Hindu mathematicians of India and later passed on the "new math" to the Europeans.

The Muslims also gained control of the northern coast of Africa. In 711 an army crossed the Strait of Gibraltar from Africa to Spain, where they crushed the Visigothic kingdom established there. The Muslims who settled in Spain were called Moors. For the next four hundred years their rich culture flourished in that country. They built many beautiful churches (called mosques). The Alhambra, a Moorish palace later constructed in Granada, is considered the finest example of Islamic architecture in Europe.

The Muslims founded academies for the instruction of medicine and philosophy in Baghdad, Cairo, and Cordova. They also created the first school of pharmacy (and history's first drugstore). Arab doctors were the first to discover that blood circulated from the heart. Ibn Sina wrote an encyclopedia of medicine (The Canon of Medicine) that was used for five hundred years.

Part of the Alhambra Palace

Baghdad was also a great trading center, and Arab merchants traveled from there to all parts of the known world to bring back products as well as ideas. These were then passed on to the West. This is how new technologies like papermaking, the spinning wheel, the windmill, and the magnetic compass entered Europe.

Medieval magnetic compass

CHRISTIANITY IN FRANCIA

In the last chapter we learned how Clovis conquered and united most of Gaul. In 493 the Frankish king wed Clotilde, a Burgundian who was a devout Christian. She constantly tried to convince him to convert to her religion, but he wasn't interested. One day, however, while he was engaged in a difficult battle against the Alemanni, Clovis called upon Christ for help, promising to be baptized if his army was victorious. As it turned out, he soundly defeated his enemies, and soon afterwards he and three thousand of his warriors were baptized at the Cathedral at Rheims. His motives for converting were more political than religious, however. He knew that it would be easier for him to rule the people who had been living in Gaul for centuries if he and his warriors shared their religious faith. In any event, the bishops of Gaul enthusiastically hailed him as a protector of the Church, and within a single generation most of the Franks were Christians.

Early in the eighth century the Moors crossed the Pyrenees and attacked several French coastal towns, burning churches at Bordeaux and

Poitiers. The inhabitants of Aries were so worried about the raids that they turned a Roman amphitheater into a fortress and lived within its walls. Do you remember how Clovis' successors were known as the "do nothing kings" whose government was controlled by officials known as the Mayors of the Palace?

An old engraving of the baptizing of Clovis

When the Moors invaded Francia the Mayor was Charles Martel. He was called "Charles the Hammer" because of his skill with that lethal iron weapon. When he heard about the invasion he quickly mobilized his forces. In 732 Martel and his armed horsemen intercepted and defeated a large Muslim army near Tours. (Some scholars believe that he was called "The Hammer" because he attacked the Muslims over and over again.) This victory not only made him a great hero, but it also determined the religious fate of Europe: had things turned out differently, most Europeans might have become Muslims.

Charles' son, Pepin "the Short," succeeded him as Mayor of the Palace. In 741 Pepin invited Boniface (remember him?) to reform the Frankish Church, which had become rather corrupt. This act placed him on friendly terms with the Pope.

Pepin later took advantage of his good relationship with Pope Zacharias by convincing him to support his campaign to win the French crown. At the time, only a Merovingian could technically rule in Francia, but Pepin wanted to be king in name as well as in power. Zacharias agreed that it was better to give the title of king to a man of political talent than to a hereditary monarch of questionable ability. So, supported by the papal endorsement, Pepin had himself "elected" king of the Franks. Childeric III, the last of the Merovingians, had his long, kingly locks shorn and was sent to a monastery. He died three years later. Pepin established a new dynasty of Frankish rulers, the Carolingians (named after his father, Charles Martel).

Pepin the Short

When the Lombards later invaded central Italy and threatened Rome, Pepin marched south and defeated them. He gave a large piece of land in northern Italy which included Ravenna and twenty-one other cities to the Pope. This gift, known as the Donation of Pepin, would be the basis of the Pope's claim to power over the Papal States of Italy for centuries. The Pope was so grateful that he anointed Pepin with Holy Water (in the manner of Old Testament kings), proclaiming that he was king "by the grace of God." He then issued an edict forbidding the Franks to select a king from any family but the Carolingians and declaring that any revolt against a Frankish king would be considered a sin in the eyes of the Church!

QUESTIONS

1. How was the organization of the Church modeled on that of the Roman government?

2. From whom did the Pope derive his claim to power?

3. What is an excommunication?

4. How did St. Columba spread Christianity to Britain?

5. What was the purpose of St. Benedict's Rule?

6. What incident caused Pope Gregory to send Augustine to Britain?

7. What was (and is) the highest church position in England?

8. Why are the manuscripts referred to as "illuminated?"

9. Describe the Celtic designs used to decorate the manuscripts.

10. Who brought Christianity to many parts of eastern Europe?

11. What is a jihad?

12. What part of Europe was conquered by the Muslims?

13. Who was the first Frankish king to become a Christian?

14. Who were the Mayors of the Palace?

15. What dynasty was established by Charles Martel?

FURTHER THOUGHTS

1.   In the early Christian Church, the secular clergy consisted of the priests, bishops, and popes. In Latin in saecula means "in the world" or "among the people." The regular clergy were the monks and nuns, who lived according to a strict rule (regula). Anyone who was not a member of the clergy was considered a layman. The term can be confusing, however; sometimes society is divided into two parts, clerical (church) and secular (non-church). The meaning of the word secular, then, depends upon the context in which it is used.

2.   Parchment was made from sheep (and sometimes goat) skins. Vellum, which was softer and had a smoother surface, was made from the skins of lambs (and sometimes kids). The hides were cured with tannin from oak trees to prevent them from rotting; then they were soaked in tubs of water and urine to bleach and soften them.

Afterwards they were dried and stretched on a frame. The last step in preparing a piece of parchment or vellum was to polish the hide with a pumice stone.

3.   Bede wrote that St. Columba saved one of his monks from a "savage water beast" at Loch Ness by frightening it off with the sign of the cross. This is the first record of the Loch Ness Monster!

4.   The word clerk is a mispronunciation of cleric (clergyman). As we know, the men of the Church were the only literate people in most medieval communities. Similarly, a modern clerk spends much of his time reading and writing.

5.   The fleur de lis (a lily-like flower blossom) became the symbol of French royalty. According to legend, Clovis was awarded an iris by an angel when he converted to Christianity. It was called the fleur (flower) de (of) Louis (Clovis, you will recall, was an early form of the name Louis). In no time the name had evolved to the fleur de lis.

The fleur de lis

PROJECTS

1.   Find a book containing illustrations of the texts of medieval illuminated manuscripts. Study the artwork closely. Then take a large piece of blank paper. Think of a sentence about the Middle Ages. Leave a large blank space for the first letter, and then carefully write the words of your sentence in the middle part of the paper. Then draw the capital letter. Decorate it, as well as the margins of your page, with Celtic designs. Remember, a medieval monk might have spent a year on one letter! You need not spend that much time, but allow several hours for your project.

2.   Make a timetable of a monk's day. Illustrate it with pictures of the monk performing his many activities.

3.   Do you know the musical round that begins "Frere Jacques, Frere Jacques, dormez-vous? dormez-vous?" Tie in the story of the sleepy monk with what you now know about the schedule in a Benedictine monastery. Explain why he was so sleepy.

4.   What are the five pillars of Islam? Find out, and write a short report.

5.   Mohammed forbade the worship of idols. He said that Allah had created living creatures, and so it would be a sin to make drawings or statues of them. This is why Muslim art does not depict animals or human beings. Instead, it consists of geometric designs of intertwined flowering vines. Find a book about art, and examine an illustration of Muslim art. Then compare the twisting vines with the swirls of Celtic art (you'll need a book about Celtic art for this). Write a paragraph or two about the differences and similarities between Celtic and Muslim art.

6.   Read *A String in the Harp* by Nancy Bond. It's a fantasy about sixth century Wales, first published in the 1970's (winner of a Newbury Book Award) and still popular.

CHAPTER 3

CHARLEMAGNE

Charlemagne was the son of Pepin the Short (and Bigfooted Bertha!). His name means "Charles the Great"—a title he well deserved, as we shall soon see. He inherited the Frankish throne in 768 and ruled for forty-six years. Fortunately for us, much was written about Charles during his lifetime. Certainly the most useful work is The Life of Charlemagne by Einhard, the king's personal secretary and trusted advisor. This scholarly monk lived in the royal household and was constantly making notes about his observations. He was somewhat of a hero-worshipper, however, so some of his descriptions are undoubtedly exaggerated.

Charlemagne was crowned according to traditional Frankish ritual: He was raised by his nobles on a leather-covered wooden shield (the shield represented his willingness to fight for his people). According to Einhard's account, Charlemagne was very tall (he was 6'4" when the average man was less than 5'6"). He had an athletic build, a long nose, a thick neck, and a pot belly. His long, flowing hair and beard plus his piercing blue eyes enhanced his regal appearance. Oddly enough, he had a very high-pitched voice. He was an extremely active man, who arose at the crack of dawn and exercised daily to keep fit. He particularly loved hunting and swimming.

For state occasions, the king wore a gold, bejeweled crown, gilded boots, and a golden cloak. The rest of the time, however, he dressed rather simply. His standard attire was a linen shirt, a woolen tunic, and breeches (trousers that end at the knee, like knickers). He wrapped linen strips around his feet and calves (stockings had not yet been invented) before putting on his high leather boots. In the winter he kept warm with a thick coat of ermine or otter skins. Charlemagne's ordinary attire contrasted with that of his nobles, who preferred to flaunt their wealth by wearing fancy embroidered clothing and gold jewelry most of the time.

Charlemagne in his formal attire

CHARLEMAGNE'S ARMY

Charlemagne gathered around him an elite group of armed horsemen (whom he called paladins). He conducted sixty major campaigns and participated personally in over half of them. His army was more highly disciplined than the forces he opposed, and his foot soldiers were uniformly well equipped. Charlemagne's striking force was his paladins. They were well armored and they carried lances, swords, and sometimes bows and arrows. Their role was to charge through the enemy line, making a gap through which the Frankish foot soldiers could follow in order to engage in hand-to-hand combat. This was the model medieval army, the standard which later rulers would try to emulate.

Charlemagne had a genius for organizing and inspiring his men. Before launching a campaign he made careful plans, studying the terrain, the local culture, and the fighting strategies of the army he would be confronting. (By contrast, most battles in those days were fought in a relatively haphazard manner.) His favorite tactic was to divide his army in two sections in order to score a one-two punch: Just when the enemy thought they might recover from the initial attack, they were bombarded again. The speed with which he moved his men became legendary; it enabled him to catch his enemy off guard and unprepared to retaliate against his assault.

THE MAJOR CAMPAIGNS

In 773 the Lombards tried to regain the lands Pepin had seized and given to the Pope. (Remember the Donation of Pepin?). The current Pope, who was named Adrian, sent an urgent message to Charlemagne, asking him to rid Italy of the "perfidious, stinking Lombards." Without giving the matter a second thought, Charlemagne marched his army across the Alps and defeated the intruders. To prevent further trouble he seized the Lombard crown for himself. So he was now king of Francia and Lombardy.

The Saxons were Germanic tribesmen who lived across the Rhine (in modern Germany). The name "Saxon" is derived from the sax—a single-edged knife that each warrior carried as a tool and weapon. We learned earlier how large numbers of Saxons migrated to Britain, but there was still a large population on the Continent. Charlemagne's most difficult campaigns were

against these fearless warriors. In addition to the sax, each Saxon carried a spear. He had a small circular shield made of light wood, often covered with a tanned hide, with an iron boss at the center which he used to deflect blows.

Modern replicas of Saxon shields

The Saxons were continually raiding towns and monasteries in the Frankish territory, and Charlemagne spent over thirty years fighting them. The conflict really heated up in 772, when Saxon warriors burned a Christian church. Charlemagne was so furious that he launched a massive attack, forcing the Saxons to surrender. But that wasn't enough for him. He ordered his men to destroy the Irminsul, a huge tree trunk that was central to the Saxon religion. (The Saxons believed that it held up the roof of the world.) The trunk had been laden with rich sacrificial offerings, all of which were plundered by the Franks.

In 777 Charlemagne ordered the pagan Saxons to convert to Christianity, threatening to execute anyone who was not baptized. But it is difficult to force a religious belief upon anyone (as Theodoric had once so wisely pointed out),

The Irminsul looked a lot like this

frontier), most of his successes were small and at very great cost. So he retreated to Francia. In a minor incident of this campaign, the rearguard of his army was wiped out at the mountain pass at Roncesvalles by a band of Christian Basques. This event later inspired poets of the eleventh century to compose one of the great medieval epics, *La Chanson de Roland.* We'll learn more about it in a later chapter.

In 787 the Franks marched into Bavaria and conquered that region, but then another threat lurked on the southeastern border of Francia. The Avars were nomadic horsemen from the steppes of Asia who were allies of the Bavarians. They were a colorful sight as they charged across a field of battle on their stocky little horses, their long hair bound and tied with flowing ribbons. In 795 Charlemagne's army seized the camp of the Avars' leader (Khagan) and discovered, much to their delight, a tremendous treasure. Charlemagne had to summon fifteen four-oxen wagons to transport his hoard of gold, silver, and silk back to his home base. It would help him significantly in his later building projects. In 805 Khagan converted

so these conversions were at best half-hearted. And as soon as the Frankish army withdrew, the Saxons rebelled and resumed their raids. This scenario was repeated again and again: Charlemagne would defeat the Saxons in battle, negotiate treaties with them, and then, as soon as he left, they would conveniently forget their promises and resume their attacks. Their last raid, led by their hero Wittekind, was quelled by the Franks in 782. Charlemagne had had enough. He ordered 4500 captured warriors to be bound and then beheaded in a single day. After that, there was little fighting, and by 804 all Saxon resistance had ended.

In 778 Charlemagne launched a campaign against the Muslims in Spain. But although he managed to win the region around Barcelona and to obtain a long stretch of border land on the Spanish side of the Pyrenees Mountains (known as the Spanish March, or

The Pyrenees Mountains separate France and Spain

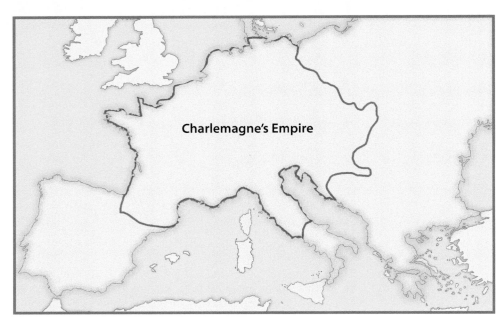

Charlemagne's Empire

to Christianity and placed himself in the hands of the Franks.

By now Charlemagne's conquests had doubled the size of the Frankish kingdom. It included modern Belgium and Switzerland; most of France, Germany and the Netherlands; and parts of Italy, Austria, and former Yugoslavia. It stretched from the Pyrenees Mountains eastward to the Danube River, and from the Elbe River South to the Adriatic Sea. Charlemagne was now the most powerful ruler in western Europe since the days of the Romans.

EMPEROR OF THE ROMANS

Pope Adrian was succeeded by Leo III, an arrogant man who had many enemies. In 799 Leo was ambushed by a mob of Roman aristocratic rivals, who tried to gouge out his eyes and cut off his tongue. Fortunately, he was rescued by some of his followers and fled to Francia. Charlemagne offered his protection and saw to it that Leo was quickly restored to power. The Pope showed his gratitude on Christmas Day 800. While Charlemagne was worshipping at St. Peter's

Cathedral in Rome, Leo descended from the altar and placed a jeweled crown on Charlemagne's head. The people who witnessed this act immediately hailed the Frankish king as Charles Augustus, Emperor of the Romans.

Charlemagne later claimed that he would not have attended church if he had known what Leo was planning to do. Not that he disliked being Emperor of the Romans, but he was annoyed that Leo's gesture implied his power was a gift from the Pope. He would have preferred to receive his title according to his own set of conditions and circumstances. So, although he accepted the crown, Charlemagne was careful not to acknowledge any submission to the Pope. He also made certain to retain the title of King of Franks and the Lombards along with his new title. (Some scholars have interpreted his reaction differently, but most agree that Charlemagne wanted to obtain power on his own terms.)

This coronation marked the beginning of a very long period of conflict between the leader of the Church and the rulers of the emerging nations of Europe. It also symbolized the dramatic shift in European political power from the south (the heart of the old Roman

Stained glass window depicting Charlemagne

Empire) to the north. The rulers of the Byzantine Empire resented Charlemagne's new title. They considered themselves the true heirs of the Roman Empire. In their eyes, the Franks were the heirs of the savage barbarians who had destroyed the Western Roman Empire.

After the crowning at St. Peter's, Charlemagne spent some time in Rome's libraries, studying the histories of the ancient emperors. He began to consider it his mission to revive the old Roman ideal of a Christian empire. This made him more determined than ever to stamp out paganism in his domain and to unite all the Germanic peoples in a Christian commonwealth as was envisioned by St. Augustine in *The City Of God*.

GOVERNING THE EMPIRE

Charlemagne had always depended upon the support of his top warriors, and, like his predecessors, he rewarded them with the plunder gathered in military campaigns as well as large tracts of land. He also sent representatives to each of the villages in his realm so that, in their presence, all of his subjects could swear an oath of loyalty to him. He appointed two officials to help him run his empire: the archchaplain advised him on religious matters and the chancellor dealt with non-religious business. He divided his empire into three hundred counties, each under the rule of a count. (As you will recall, Clovis had previously divided his empire in a similar manner.) The districts on the frontiers (the marches) were ruled by margraves. The role of the counts and margraves was to collect taxes, raise troops for the army, and serve as Charlemagne's representatives in local courts. Superimposed on his framework of government was the Church network of dioceses and provinces which were, of course, controlled by bishops and archbishops. Charlemagne personally appointed the men for every position, whether government or church.

Traveling supervisors called *missi dominici* ("envoys of the lord") worked as two-man teams (a priest and a layman) who served a one-year term. They visited the various districts to hear complaints of local people against the local count or bishop and to make sure that Charlemagne's orders were obeyed and that his revenues (taxes) were not being pocketed by unscrupulous administrators. Once a year the king summoned his counts and margraves to a national assembly. This gathering enabled him to maintain his authority over them and to keep up-to-date on the state of his vast empire. He also spent a great deal of time personally traveling throughout the counties and making recommendations for the running of his royal estates.

The roads that had been built centuries earlier by the Romans were in poor condition. Wishing to encourage trade throughout his empire, Charlemagne saw to it that they were repaired, and he ordered the construction of new roads and bridges. One particularly impressive bridge was built across the Rhine at Mainz. He even made plans to build a canal connecting the Rhine and Danube Rivers, but this project was later abandoned.

Charlemagne standardized the systems of weights, measurements, and coinage throughout his empire. His currency was divided into pounds, shillings, and pence. Since the Latin words for these coins were libra (pound), solidus (shilling) and denarius (pence), the terms were abbreviated as L (pound), s (shillings) and d (pence). This system (with the abbreviations just mentioned) was used in Britain until the 1970's. Charlemagne also fixed the maximum price that landowners could charge for grain or that bakers could charge for bread.

AACHEN

At first the Frankish court moved about from one estate to another, but in the 780's Aachen (Aix-la-Chapelle), the small town in eastern Francia where Charlemagne had been born, became his permanent capital. Aachen was famous for its hot springs, and Charlemagne had some of the water diverted into a huge marble swimming pool (it could hold one hundred people at a time). He swam there on a daily basis. He later built a palace and a basilica (chapel) of marble and granite, their design heavily influenced by Byzantine architecture. Within the palace were many large treasure rooms to store all the gold, silver and jewels he had acquired during his campaigns.

Charlemagne was concerned about the low level of literacy in his empire (even he didn't know how to read or write). How could his empire be a great one if its leaders were uneducated? So he established a school at the

The buildings at Aachen

palace for the training of his government officials. He offered huge rewards and unlimited support to any scholars who would come and teach there. The response was enthusiastic, and he soon gathered a group of extremely scholarly men, including Peter of Pisa (a grammarian), Paul the Deacon from Monte Cassino (a poet and historian), Theodulf, a Visigoth from Spain (a poet), and Einhard of eastern Francia (the historian who, we have learned earlier, became his secretary). But the most important scholar to come to Aachen was a Benedictine monk from Northumbria named Alcuin. A gifted teacher and writer, Alcuin had been taught by a student of Bede. He would become Charlemagne's chief advisor on diplomatic and religious affairs as well as his director of education. Once the faculty had been assembled, Charlemagne invited students from all over his empire to attend his school. Poor boys were enrolled as well as the sons of the nobles, and even a few girls were among them. Charlemagne's own sons also attended, of course.

Alcuin created what became the classic medieval curriculum consisting of the seven liberal arts. These were divided into two parts: the quadrivium (mathematics, geometry, astronomy, and music) and the trivium (rhetoric, grammar, and logic). As it turned out, the quadrivium was rather limited because the scientific works of the Greeks (they were masters in this area) were not yet available in Latin, and the trivium was basically a study of the Latin language and the writings of the Church Fathers. But despite these limitations, the students referred to Aachen as the second Rome, and even the second Athens, and they called each other by classical or Biblical names (Alcuin was known as Horace, the great Roman poet, and Charlemagne was called David, after the great king of the Old Testament).

Charlemagne was perhaps the most eager student at the palace school. He loved to visit the classrooms and become involved in what was going on there. He often criticized the laziness of the wealthy boys and praised the industry of those of humbler birth. He learned to speak Latin and Greek, and he slept with a tablet under his pillow so that he could practice the alphabet. Sadly enough, Charlemagne never mastered writing and had to dictate his thoughts and ideas to his secretary, Einhard. But he was skilled at reading aloud. He particularly loved the ancient histories and the writings of St. Augustine. He arranged for a book to be read aloud during the mid-day meal (just as the Benedictine monks did), and afterwards he and his dining companions discussed what they had heard. He ordered the long Frankish epics about Frankish heroes to be written down, but unfortunately, his son, Louis the Pious, later had them destroyed because of their pagan content.

Charlemagne loved music and he learned to play the lyre quite skillfully. He encouraged Italian music masters to refine the singing of the Frankish church choirs and had the Gregorian chant introduced to the services (more about the chants later). Theodulph wrote a number of hymns. One of them ("All Glory, Laud, and Honor") has come down to us and is sung in modern church services.

Charlemagne was pleased with his palace school, and he called upon the monasteries to establish similar schools to educate the clergy. Alcuin sent letters to many abbeys advising them about how to set up a curriculum. He counseled them to keep classes small and well supervised (an old idea that still has merit!). Some of the men educated at these schools went on to establish new centers of learning at other monasteries. New schools were also set up in villages, and any Christian could send his children there to learn to read and write. Fifteen years after the founding of his palace school at Aachen, Charlemagne could rightfully claim that he offered universal free education to his subjects. He was the first person in history to do so.

CAROLINGIAN WRITING

One of the major contributions made by the scholars of Aachen was the creation of a new type of writing. The earliest medieval manuscripts

Statue of Charlemagne in Aachen

were written on papyrus, a type of paper made from reeds growing along the Nile River in Egypt. The scribes (writers) used large Roman (capital) letters, and this form of writing remained standard in Europe for four hundred years. But when the Muslims gained control of the Mediterranean Sea, they cut off the supply of papyrus. This is when scholars began to write on parchment. But this material was much more expensive than papyrus, so, in order to fit more onto each sheet, smaller letters were used and no spaces were left between the words. The result was often rather sloppy writing that was difficult to read.

abcdefghijklm
nopqrstuvwxyz
ABCDEFGH
IJKLMNOPQ
RSTUVWXYZ

The alphabet in Carolingian script

Alcuin created a new, improved style of writing, known as Carolingian miniscule. It was a kind of script that was compact, graceful, and easy to write. Each letter was clearly formed, and the words were separated by spaces. Small letters were used (miniscule means "small letter"), and the large, capital letters appeared only at the beginning of proper nouns and sentences. Within two decades the Carolingian miniscule had replaced all other writing styles throughout the Frankish Empire. By the twelfth century it would be used everywhere in Europe. Our letters are derived from it. And, like the monks of Northumbria, the scribes living in Charlemagne's

empire illuminated each page they wrote with brightly colored pictures and designs.

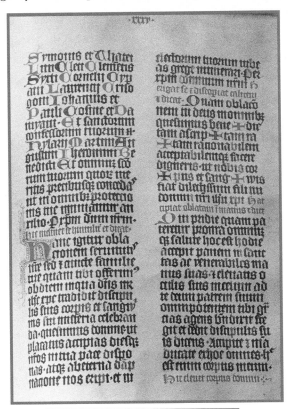

A page from a medieval Bible

Books were rare, so Charlemagne urged the monks to create new libraries by copying the ancient Latin manuscripts found in their abbeys. A trained scribe devoted from three to four months on the average text. It was hard work, and a monk often included on the last page a plea to treat the book with care (and sometimes added a curse upon any would-be thief!). By making multiple copies the monasteries could exchange texts with one another. Charlemagne had sparked a burst of enthusiasm for writing, and scholars throughout the Empire sought out rare ancient works and copied them. Nine-tenths of the Roman works that have come down to us were preserved as copies made by Carolingian monks! Alcuin once said, no doubt thinking about the huge vineyards of many monasteries:

"To write sacred books is better than to till the soil for the vine, for one nourishes the soul, and the other only the stomach." That wise old teacher personally prepared an accurate new edition of the Bible, and he saw to it that a new text of the Benedictine Rule was made and used in all the monasteries. Charlemagne also ordered copies to be made of Latin and German grammar books as well as poetry, biographies, and histories. This was the first major effort on the part of a monarch to establish a body of learning since the collapse of the Roman Empire.

Pages from a medieval hymn book

Because of all the many advances made in learning, writing, art, and architecture during the reign of Charlemagne, this period is known as the Carolingian Renaissance. (The word "Renaissance" refers to a period of intellectual and artistic achievement.) Alcuin, one of the most important contributors to this flowering of creative activity, eventually retired from Aachen to become the abbot of the monastery of St. Martin of Tours.

THE FINAL YEARS

Toward the end of his reign, Charlemagne's attention was drawn to the East, where Muslims were making attacks on the monasteries in the Holy Land. Hoping to end these hostilities by appealing to the enemy, Charlemagne established diplomatic relations with Baghdad. His negotiations led to a peace that lasted for many years. In 802 the Caliph of Baghdad sent him an elephant (named Abul Abbas) as a gift. The animal became a rather large household pet at the palace, and Charlemagne often took him along on expeditions as one would the family dog. The elephant thrived for eight years, thanks to the indulgent treatment of his owner, but the harsh northern winters finally proved too much for him.

Charlemagne himself died January 28, 814 at the age of seventy-two from complications following a winter cold. He was buried in his chapel at Aachen in a sarcophagus that had been taken from an ancient Roman site in Italy. A golden shrine with his image was placed over the tomb. He left eleven-twelfths of his treasure to the Church. Within a generation he had become a legend, and even today both Germans and Frenchmen claim the Frankish monarch as a national hero.

Charlemagne's empire was so large and unwieldy that it was impossible to keep it running without his strong personality. Two of his three sons died within a year of each other just before his own death, so his son Louis inherited everything. But Louis was a feeble ruler, and when he died in 840 at the age of seventy-one (the Carolingians were very long-lived), the empire was left to his eldest son Lothair. When Lothair's two brothers demanded part of the inheritance (remember, it had become a tradition for Frankish monarchs to split their kingdom among their sons), the Treaty of Verdun (843) divided the old empire in three. Louis gained eastern Francia (modern Germany), Charles the Bald obtained western Francia (modern France), and Lothair was left with a strip between the two running from Italy to the Netherlands (Lorraine).

Bust of Charlemagne

Within twelve years the middle region had collapsed into a group of small kingdoms, and the other two sections had become politically fragmented. So the old empire slowly disintegrated and, with no strong central government, the nobles increased their own powers and fortified their fortresses for protection. Eventually there were five duchies (Bavaria, Franconia, Saxony, Swabia, and Lorraine). Each one was ruled by a duke who reigned supreme, even though the Carolingian king was, technically, the ruler of them all. The powerful empire of Charlemagne was all but forgotten.

QUESTIONS

1. Who wrote *The Life of Charlemagne*, and is the work totally accurate?

2. Describe Charlemagne's physical appearance.

3. What was special about Charlemagne's army?

4. How did Charlemagne finally end the long wars against the Saxons?

5. How did Charlemagne feel about being crowned by the Pope?

6. How did Charlemagne organize his empire?

7. What improvements did he make in the economy?

8. Describe Alcuin's curriculum.

9. Why was the Carolingian miniscule a major improvement?

10. What happened to the empire after Charlemagne died?

FURTHER THOUGHTS

1. There was already a school in Aachen when Charlemagne began gathering scholars in his palace. It dated back to Charles Martel, but it was devoted solely to the art of war.

2. The concept of liberal arts employed by Alcuin was not new. It was derived from the ancient Romans. The subjects were called liberal arts because their study in Rome had been reserved for the *liberi* (the Latin term for "freemen").

3. One of the Gospel Books copied and illuminated at Aachen during the Carolingian Renaissance has survived and can be seen today in a museum in Charlemagne's capital city.

PROJECTS

1. Pepin was a strong monarch, but he was overshadowed by his even more successful son, Charlemagne. Can you think of other examples of famous fathers who were upstaged by their gifted offspring? Write a paragraph about one famous father and son.

2. For state occasions Charlemagne held an orb (a ball with cross on top) which represented the supremacy of God over his earthly kingdom. Find a picture of an orb, and then make a careful drawing of it. Put as much effort into your drawing as a medieval monk would have done.

Charlemagne's orb and cross would have been much more elaborate than this

3. It has been said that Charlemagne was a reformer, not an innovator. What does this mean? Do you agree with this statement or not? Give examples to back up your point of view. Present your conclusions to the class.

4. List five of the contributions that Charlemagne made to western civilization.

5. Read *Son of Charlemagne* (Living History Library) by Barbara Willard.

CHAPTER 4

THE NORSEMEN

During the ninth and tenth centuries, the emerging civilization of western Europe was nearly shattered by yet another long series of invasions. From the steppes of central Asia came the Magyars, nomadic horsemen who were so fierce that the Europeans called them Hungarians (meaning "Hun-like"). In the south Muslim pirates controlled the Mediterranean Sea and made frequent raids on European ports. And from Scandinavia to the north came tribes of ferocious warriors known as the Norsemen ("Northmen"). The Magyars were driven back before they had caused too much damage, and the Muslims did not take over any European territory beyond Spain. But the Norsemen seemed to be unstoppable, and they struck with such a vengeance that a popular prayer of the time called upon God to deliver the Christian kingdoms from their terrible fury.

LIFE IN EARLY SCANDINAVIA

Like the Franks, the Saxons, the Angles, and most of the other peoples we have studied so far, the Norsemen were Germanic tribesmen. Did you remember that all these tribes originated in Scandinavia? This being so, many aspects of the Nordic culture will seem familiar to you.

The Norsemen were tall, fair-skinned people. The men wore their blond hair shoulder length, and they often braided their beards to keep them out of the way while they were hunting or fighting. They were so proud of their beards (and mustaches) that to call someone "beardless" was a great insult! The women had very long hair, which had to be covered if they were married

with a scarf. The men wore long woolen tunics, trousers, and tall leather boots, while the women dressed in long, full tunics which they gathered at the waist. In cold weather they also wore fur-lined cloaks fastened at the shoulder with buckle-type brooches. Both men and women loved to wear jewelry, especially silver bracelets, necklaces, and pins. Recently, a sunken ship was discovered off the coast of Denmark. The rags (bits of discarded clothing) that had been used to fill up the seams between the planks of wood in the vessel provide invaluable clues about how the people dressed. Remnants of clothing have also been found in ancient grave sites.

A Norse village

The Norsemen lived in long thatch-roofed huts in small communities made up of several families. Most huts had a special sweating room, a forerunner of our modern sauna. The main room had raised platforms along each side. This is where the people slept. While the men hunted wild boar, deer, and bear, the women grew the crops (barley, oats, rye, peas, and cabbage). They also raised pigs, goats, sheep, and cattle. In later years, the men took over the farming. Norse women could own property, and they had a right to half of their husbands' wealth. (Such an arrangement was uncommon in those days.) The children loved to ice-skate during the long Scandinavian winters. Their skates were animal bones strapped to their shoes with strips of leather.

Bread was the staple of the Norsemen's diet, and it was often eaten with butter or cheese made from the milk of the family cow. The main beverage was mead (a sweet beer brewed with honey). This was often served in colorfully decorated drinking horns (cow horns). Since the horn had no flat bottom, it was passed around the table until it was empty. It was considered manly to drink the entire contents of a horn at one time!

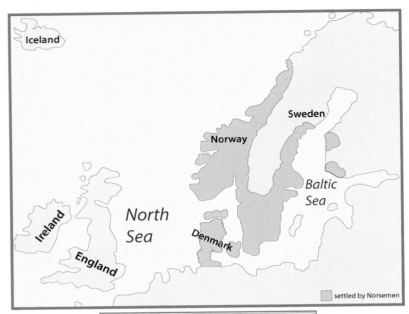

Scandinavia in the tenth century

A drinking horn

Farming conditions in Scandinavia were far from ideal, however. Norway was very mountainous and Sweden was covered with dense forests, so at first only the narrow river valleys and coastal plains could be cultivated. Much of Denmark was a vast, infertile heath. To make matters worse, the growing season was very short and much of the land in the northern regions was frozen half of the year. But since most people lived near the coast, there was always a bountiful supply of fish (such as cod, herring and salmon), and from earliest times the Norsemen were able shipbuilders and mariners.

Scandinavia was rich in iron, and its inhabitants eventually learned to use the ore to make tools to clear the forests and plow the fields. But as the population expanded, the amount of grain produced was insufficient to sustain it. So groups of kinsmen set sail in search of new farmland. Another factor that encouraged many people to leave their northern homes was the ancient tradition for a man to pass on his wealth and land to his eldest son when he died. This left nothing for the other sons to inherit, so they had to seek their fortunes elsewhere. While some Norsemen established new farms in more southern regions, others became traders.

Herring from the Baltic Sea

Piracy was the easiest way to acquire wealth, and many Norsemen were tempted to help themselves to other men's property. Stories have come down to us about the ships that would lay in wait at the entrance to the viks (a local word for the inlets or fjords along Norway's Atlantic coast). When an unsuspecting cargo vessel passed by, the lurking ship would suddenly rush out from the shadows to rob it. These attacks were the source of the expression "to go a-viking," which basically meant "to be a pirate." The term Viking was later applied to all the Norsemen by the other Europeans. We'll refer to them in that way from time to time.

A WRITTEN LANGUAGE

The Norsemen spoke a language known as Old Norse. (In later years it would evolve into separate languages—Norwegian, Swedish, and Danish). As early as the third century there was a Norse alphabet consisting of sixteen runes (characters). It is called the futhark after its first six characters (f, u, th, a, r, and k). Later, more runes were added. Having no paper, the people carved their messages on stone and sometimes on wood, metal, and animal bones. Since it was easier to carve straight lines than curves on these materials, the runes consisted almost entirely of straight strokes.

Thousands of rune stones have been found in Scandinavia. Originally the letters were decorated with paint (black, white, red and blue), but this was worn away long ago. The main functions of the stones were to establish a person's right to an inheritance or to record heroic deeds, but many were actually tombstones bearing memorial messages. Wandering Norsemen enjoyed carving messages on stones in the lands they visited, and this early form of graffiti helps us to determine many of the routes taken by Viking ships.

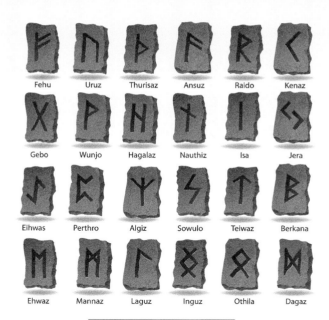

The Nordic alphabet

Fehu, Uruz, Thurisaz, Ansuz, Raido, Kenaz
Gebo, Wunjo, Hagalaz, Nauthiz, Isa, Jera
Eihwas, Perthro, Algiz, Sowulo, Teiwaz, Berkana
Ehwaz, Mannaz, Laguz, Inguz, Othila, Dagaz

A SYSTEM OF JUSTICE

Once or twice a year the warriors of a community would gather in an open-air assembly called a Thing to make local laws and dispense justice. (Thing is the Norse word for "court.") As we learned earlier, Germanic law grew out of tribal ties of kinship and personal loyalty. The Norsemen believed that the accusation of guilt was a stain upon a person's honor which had to be removed. Because blood feuds could go on for years, a system of justice was eventually devised to curtail the violence. (A similar system evolved in England.) This is how it worked. A person accused of a crime could plead his case by swearing an oath of innocence. The more important he was in the community, the greater was the value of his word. (However, if he hesitated, coughed, or stammered, it was considered a sign of guilt!) To strengthen his case, he could also call upon oath-helpers, neighbors who swore that he was telling the truth. Again, the more influential the oath-helper, the more valuable was his support.

But if, in spite of the oaths that were taken, a person's innocence was still in doubt, or if the evidence was contradictory, the court would employ a system of trial by ordeal. These ordeals were extremely unpleasant. An accused woman had to pick up a stone from the bottom of a cauldron of boiling water and carry it a certain number of paces. A man might be ordered to carry a red hot iron bar for nine feet or to hold his hand in a fire. If the defendant dropped the stone or the iron bar before covering the required distance (or pulled his hand out of the flames), he (or she) was pronounced guilty. Those who managed to complete the ordeal had their wounds bound. After three days the bandages were removed and the wounds were inspected. If they were healing cleanly, the person was declared innocent, but any sign of festering or infection was an indication of guilt. (In such cases, having a heavily calloused hand was a considerable advantage!)

Ancient runes carved on a piece of granite

And there were other ordeals. In a trial by cold water, the accused was bound and thrown into a lake. If he sank he was declared innocent, but if he floated he was considered guilty. The reasoning was that pure water would accept innocence and reject guilt. This was an especially risky ordeal, since an innocent man might drown before being fished out. (A smart person would expel his breath, sink, and hope for rescue before it was too late!) Many warriors chose trial by wager of battle to prove their innocence. In this case, two men would fight with wooden swords and sharp pikes until one surrendered. The victor would be proclaimed innocent of his crime. Of course, the opposite was true for the loser.

Someone found guilty by any of these means was sentenced by the Thing. If the crime was murder, he had to pay a fine (wergeld). As we learned in our study of the Anglo-Saxons in Chapter 1, wergeld was a person's value measured in the number of oxen, amount of grain, or sum of money that was paid to his relatives by anyone who killed him. If a convicted murderer would not pay the wergeld (or could not), the victim's family was free to take out their revenge on him however they wished. Someone found guilty of a lesser crime than murder might be fined, enslaved, or banished from the community (he could be killed if he didn't leave immediately). A particularly unpleasant punishment involved running between two rows of people who were throwing stones.

THE NORSE RELIGION

The rich mythology shared by the various Germanic tribes originated in Scandinavia. Norse poets called skalds went from village to village telling stories about the adventures and activities of the gods and goddesses. According to these myths (which were not written down until the twelfth century), the deities lived in a heavenly place called Asgard. Below was Midgard, the home of humans, which was connected to Asgard by a rainbow bridge called Bifrost. Midgard was surrounded by an ocean wherein dwelled a serpent (Jormungand). Beyond its waters were the mountains of the evil giants. (This region was called Utgard.)

Bifrost connected Midgard to Asgard

Dwarfs (ugly and exceedingly greedy creatures) lived in caves under these mountains. Directly below Midgard were Niflheim, the cold and dark land of the dead, and Muspellheim, the land of fire. Niflheim was ruled by the goddess Hel. She had the face and upper torso of a beautiful woman, but her body from the waist down was only a skeleton. Her companion was a dragon named Midhogg. Her palace (Eljundir) was guarded by a ferocious dog {Garni}. All three levels of the Norse universe (Asgard, Midgard, and Niflheim/Muspellheim) were held together by the roots of a huge ash tree, Yggdrasil.

The king of the gods was one-eyed Odin. According to legend, he had lost one eye in the pursuit of wisdom. Two ravens, called Hugin (Thought) and Munin (Memory), flew around Midgard during the hours of daylight; every evening they returned to perch on Odin's shoulders and to tell him what they had seen.

Two wolves (Geri and Freki) frequently crouched at his side. Odin was fierce as well as clever, and he had many battles with the evil giants. He had a magic spear (Gungnir), and he often caused wars among humans by flinging it down. The Norsemen believed that Odin rode an eight-legged grey horse named Sleipnir.

Odin and the two ravens

Odin riding Sleipnir

Thor, the son of Odin, had a fiery temper and loved to fight. He protected humans from the giants and dwarfs, as well as from cold and hunger. Considered the god of law and order, Thor always carried a huge stone hammer (Mjollnir). He drove a chariot drawn by two giant goats whose names meant toothgnasher and toothgrinder. When the Norsemen heard thunder, they thought that it was the sound of the wheels of Thor's chariot. When they saw a bolt of lightning strike the earth, they believed that Thor had flung down his hammer, Mjollnir.

Frigga, the wife of Odin, was the goddess of fertility. After planting new seeds, a Norse farmer always poured wine or beer on his fields as an offering to Frigga. (She also protected women and children.) Frey was the god of peace and fertility. His chariot was drawn by a giant boar named Gullinbursti. At harvest time in Sweden, a statue of Frey was pulled around from field to field in a cart as a gesture of thanks for his bountiful gifts. Freya, twin sister of Frey, was the goddess of love and death. She could predict the future. Her chariot was pulled by two great cats. Norse God Loki was a mischievous god, a practical joker, who could change his appearance at will. He was the son of two giants. Tyr was the god of truth (and, in some myths, of war). Several of our names of the days of the week are derived from the Norse nature gods: Tuesday is named for Tyr, Wednesday for Odin (later known as Woden in England), Thursday for Thor, and Friday for Frigga.

The Norsemen worshipped their gods in sacred groves and often sacrificed animals to them. In Uppsala, Sweden a gruesome ritual known as the Blot took place every nine years. On each of nine days, a man and many male animals (bulls, rams, horses, birds, and so on) were sacrificed. After they were decapitated with axes (the heads were offered to the gods), the bodies were hung on trees. Actually, the greatest sacrifice a Norseman could make was his own son. Earl Hakon, ruler of Norway in the late tenth century, sacrificed his son, Erling, to thank the gods for granting him a victory!

Woodcut of Thor, with Celtic border

THE LONGSHIPS

Sailing vessels were so important to the Norsemen that their language had over twenty ways of saying "ship". Viking warships are known as longships. They were narrow, swift, and extremely seaworthy. Overlapping planks of oak were lashed to the ribs (skeleton) of a longship with iron rivets. At the prow and stern the planks were tied on with leather thongs to give the ship better flexibility in a pounding sea. The shipbuilders stuffed the joints between the planks with rope or pieces of wool dipped in tar to make the vessels watertight (we heard about this earlier). The Viking ships were among the first to have a keel (from the Norse word quille). This was a long, narrow piece of oak attached to the underside of the ship and extending into the water along the center the entire length of the vessel. The keel reduced the rolling motion, making the ship more stable. It also improved the speed of the vessel and thus increased the distance it could travel without stopping for supplies. Despite its keel, a Viking warship could sail up a shallow river or land on a sloping beach, and this was a great advantage for a raiding party, as we will soon see.

A longship was propelled by as many as seventy oars (smaller vessels had only twenty-six). An oar was about eighteen feet long. Each oarsman sat on a sea chest which contained his extra clothing as well as a waterproof reindeer skin sleeping bag. The ship was equipped with a large square sail (about 330 square feet) made of homespun flax (called wadmal) and colored with stripes of blue, red, or yellow. The Vikings were the first northern Europeans to use sails. The mast was placed at the exact center of the ship. In bad weather the sail was lowered over the vessel and fastened down like a tent to protect the crew.

Model of a Viking longship

The longship was steered by a large rudder-shaped oar which was fixed on the right-hand side near the stern. The name for the steerboard side (from the Norse word styra, meaning "to steer") evolved into "starboard", our modern nautical term for the right side of a boat. When a longship entered a harbor, the warriors hung their shields around its sides. Each shield protected the rower sitting beside it.

A longship with shields hung

The high prow of a longship was carved in the shape of a dragon's head, and the stern was carved like its tail. With a little imagination, the square sails could be said to resemble the creature's wings, and the oars its feet. This explains why longships were often called serpents of the sea, and no doubt their ferocious appearance frightened most potential enemies. Because the heights of the prow and the stern were identical, and, as noted, the mast was in the center, a longship could easily withdraw without having to turn around. The warriors simply rowed in the opposite direction! The Vikings gave their vessels descriptive names, like Raven of the Wind, Wave Walker, and Sea Bird.

The Norse captains sailed by the sun, moon or pole star. Along the coast they looked for

Dragon head on the prow of a longship

table, they could make a sighting and estimate the ship's latitude. Longitude (distance east or west) was more difficult to assess. The captain could only make vague estimates based on the speed at which he thought he was traveling and such clues as the variation in the color of the water (which indicated its depth). Many captains noted the configurations of the coastlines they sailed along and kept records of such irregularities as shoals as well as the speed and direction of the currents in particular locations. This information was passed on to other mariners and contributed to the Vikings' ever-growing knowledge of the seas.

THE VIKING WARRIOR

The typical Viking warrior was a fierce-looking fellow. He wore a protective vest made of thick layers of animal hides (wealthy men wore shirts of iron mail) and a conical helmet of leather or iron with a metal bar extending over the nose. (The horns that appear on the helmets of Vikings in modern cartoons are inaccurate.) His basic weapon was the broad axe. It had a long handle and large flat blade with a curved cutting edge. A warrior used two hands to swing it at an enemy, lopping off arms and legs or crushing a skull. He might also carry a two-edged sword, a spear, or a bow made of yew rein-forced with leather (its string was allegedly made from the long tresses of a woman's hair).

Those horned helmets? There is no evidence, archaeological or otherwise, that Viking warriors wore any type of horns or wings on their helmets. What we do have is one single piece of evidence, the ninth century Oseberg tapestry, suggesting a rare ceremonial use (the figure on the tapestry may even be that of a god, rather than representative of real Vikings) and plenty of

landmarks for guidance. On the open sea, they were often aided by their knowledge of the habits of sea birds and mammals. For example, they knew that herring, cod and haddock feed on smaller marine creatures that gather above the continental shelf (a ridge in the ocean bed), and if they observed any of these fish they knew that they were not that far from the mainland. They also had learned that large black birds called ravens had an uncanny ability to find land. So if a captain was unsure of the direction of the land, he could release a raven and sail in the direction it flew. The symbol of the raven appeared on many Viking flags. The captains were also aware that certain species of birds were found at particular places at different times of the year. To determine their latitude (position north or south), the Norsemen consulted a table of figures that showed the sun's midday height for each week of the year. Then, using a measuring stick and the evidence for plain conical/domed helmets made mainly of leather.

Vikings had fearsome names like Ivar the Boneless, Eric Bloodaxe, and Harald Bluetooth. If they were surrounded in battle, the warriors formed a circle around their chief and made a wall with their shields. If he was killed, they were expected to fight to the death beside his body. A warrior always preferred to die in combat (or even by his own hand) than to be taken prisoner.

The berserkers were a special unit of warrior-fanatics who wore bearshirts and charged into battle with frantic speed, seemingly unaware of the pain of their wounds (as well as the commands of their leaders!). Some say the berserkers chewed on a type of toadstool that caused a hypnotic rage. They were quite terrifying to any enemy. Just before an assault they tried to control their excitement by nibbling on the edges of their shields! The berserker tradition sprang from a Norse myth about a fierce and reckless warrior named Berserk who fought for Odin. He and his twelve sons (the original Berserkers) entered battle dressed in bear or wolf skins.

Horned helmets like this were only used in religious rituals

Like other Germanic tribesmen we have studied, the Norsemen believed that Odin's palace (Gladsheim, or "Abode of Happiness") contained a great hall called Valhalla ("Hall of the Slain"). This was a sort of warrior's paradise, where days were spent in glorious combat, followed by long nights of feasting on wild boar and drinking mead. Valhalla was huge. It had 540 gates, each of which could be entered by eight hundred horsemen riding abreast. The walls were made of glittering spears, and the roof was composed of golden shields.

A helmet of a Viking warrior

The Norsemen believed that twelve war maidens called Valkyries ("Choosers of the Slain") decided who would die in battle. After the fighting was over they appeared, riding white winged horses, to take the souls of the fallen warriors from the battlefield to Valhalla. A warrior's greatest fear was that he would die in bed (this was called "a cow's death") and not on the field of battle. Those Vikings who were unfortunate enough to die from sickness or old age would never make it to Valhalla; instead, they would spend eternity in Niflheim, the cold, somber land of the dead beneath the earth.

A Valkyrie flies to the battle field

best clothing and jewelry and laid in a grave with his most precious possessions (which often included a favorite horse or dog, freshly sacrificed for the occasion). Some important leaders were buried with their possessions in a special longship. In 1903 a beautifully carved warship was found in Oseberg, Norway. It had been placed in a bed of clay in about 850 and covered with a thick layer of peat, which formed an airtight shell and prevented the vessel from disintegrating. Amidships was a large burial chamber. Although it had been broken into by thieves, many of its treasures had survived. The skeletons of two women were found near it. The arms and hands of one had been damaged when the thieves ripped off her rings and bracelets. The other skeleton was intact, presumably because this woman had worn no expensive jewelry. She was probably a servant. All sorts of furniture had been buried in the ship, including a beautifully carved wooden bed (complete with bedding, tapestries, and chests for storing valuables). There were kitchen items—cauldrons, pots, buckets, and a mill for grinding grain—as well as a four-wheeled cart and four sleighs (including leather harnesses).

And there were even the skeletons of ten horses. All these possessions were intended for use in the next life. Archaeologists puzzled for a long time over the identity of the damaged skeleton. Given the age and location of the burial ship, many concluded that she was the legendary Queen Asa who was described in a collection of Icelandic sagas entitled The Lives of the Norse Kings (Heimskringla). (Monks in Iceland were the first to write down the Viking sagas.) Supporting evidence for this theory comes from the name of the region in which the ship was found: Oseberg might be derived from the old Norse words meaning "Asa's berg" (barrow).

Some Viking leaders were not buried in the ground at all. Their bodies were placed on longships that were then set afire on giant funeral pyres or were simply pushed in flames out to sea. It was believed that the smoke would help the warrior's spirit to rise to Valhalla. Simpler graves of Viking warriors of humbler origin found in Denmark were marked by large stones arranged in the outline of a longship.

ATTACKS ON THE BRITISH ISLES

In 793, during the reign of Charlemagne, groups of Norsemen crossed the North Sea and raided the island monastery of Lindisfarne off the northeastern coast of England. Although the invading warriors had learned that the country's wealth could be found in the treasure rooms of its abbeys, they must have been astonished by the extraordinarily rich collections of gold and silver objects. These were theirs for the taking, being totally undefended (and so conveniently close to the sea).

The attack upon Lindisfarne marked the beginning of a long period of Viking raids in the

British Isles. The abbey had yielded such exceptional booty that in a short time the monasteries of Yarrow and Iona were attacked. In a typical assault the Vikings would burst open the doors of the abbey with their axes and snatch the silver and golden chalices, the jeweled crosses, the ivory croziers (ornamental staffs), and the golden books encrusted with jewels, often smashing the skulls of the cowering monks in the process. Many tried to hide their treasures from the invaders. A vast hoard of coins and jewelry was found in the floor of a church on Shetland Island. Its position was marked with a cross on the slab of stone just above it. The one shining example of successful resistance was the monastery of Monkwearmouth, where the brothers succeeded, with great difficulty, in repulsing a Viking raid.

A silver chalice

The Vikings are coming!

A jeweled cross

At first the raids were seasonal. The longships would appear in the springtime after the Norsemen had finished plowing and sowing their fields. The raiders often arrived under the cover of darkness or fog, and they would sail right onto the beach, break down the doors, load the ship with the treasure, and escape before a defense could be organized. In late summer they returned home to harvest their crops and to spend the winter repairing their boats and weapons. Beginning in 851, however, the raiding parties wintered in England rather than returning home. They seized local farms and established bases on the islands near their raiding grounds. The English referred to these intruders as sea-wolves. In the next chapter we'll learn how they dealt with them.

A Celtic cross beside a medieval church on the outskirts of Dublin

Meanwhile, other longships sailed to Ireland and brought to an end three centuries of the rich Celtic Christian culture we learned about in the last chapter. Turgeis, a Norwegian pirate chief, terrorized Ireland from 839 until 845. He founded the town of Dublin and used it as his headquarters. Other Viking towns, including Waterford and Limerick, were used as bases to raid inland territories and to launch attacks on England and France. They later became important trading centers. (Dublin, of course, is the capital of modern Ireland.) By the tenth century the Norsemen living in Ireland had become Christians and were living peacefully with the Irish Celts. In 865 Danish warriors invaded England and settled in the eastern half of the island. In the next chapter we'll find out how King Alfred dealt with them.

ATTACKS ON THE CONTINENT

The Vikings were no great threat to continental Europe while Charlemagne was alive, but in the late ninth century large groups of Danish warships sailed up the rivers of modern Germany, the Netherlands, and France. If they came to a series of rapids, they disembarked and dragged their ships ashore. Then they cut down trees and used them as rollers; they pushed their vessels on the rollers until they came to open water again. They plundered towns and monasteries, often taking captives who they sold as slaves. As in England, they proved to be masters of the surprise attack and quick retreat. In 836, hoping to minimize their losses, the monks of the monastery of Noirmoutier (near the mouth of the Loire River in France) dug up the bones of their founder, St. Philbert, removed them to a safe place, and then abandoned their home. While some Norsemen ventured up the French rivers to raid the abbeys in Rouen, Chartres, and Tours, others sailed up the Elbe to attack Hamburg.

On Easter Sunday in 845 (the Vikings often attacked on Sundays and religious holidays, when church treasures were on display), a fleet of longships sailed up the Seine and sacked Paris. Charles the Bald, the King of France, tried to prevent further damage by paying the invaders 7000 pounds of silver. This was the first payment in a series of bribes (known as Danegeld, or "Dane money") by the Frankish kings. Unfortunately, the Vikings soon returned and asked for more. In 857 Viking leader Bjorn Ironside and his army camped on an island in the Seine. Charles hired another Viking (Wetland) to kill Ironside and his men. But Ironside offered to split the Paris treasure with Wetland, and so the Norsemen joined forces and together they plundered the rich Seine Valley!

The Seine River flowing through modern Paris

The Swedes were more interested in trade than piracy. They sailed their ships up the Dneiper, Volga, and Vistula Rivers, making it to modern Russia and the Ukraine and even getting as far as the Black and Caspian Seas. They founded cities such as Kiev as fortresses. These Nordic warriors were called "Rus" by the peoples they encountered and this is how Russia got its name (Rus comes from the old Norse word for "route"). From the Black Sea the Norsemen sailed south to Constantinople where they traded with Arab and Byzantine merchants. Their cargo ships (called knaars) were wider than the longships, and they had no sails. The Norsemen transported otter pelts, amber (a hard yellow resin from the region of the Baltic Sea), walrus ivory, seal oil, reindeer antlers, glass from Germany, salt from western Europe, and weapons from northern France. They exchanged these wares for imported silks, spices, wines, and precious metals from the East. This trade made Hedeby, Denmark an important Scandinavian trading post. But, as we have learned, the Norsemen were also slave traders, and they captured so many Slavic tribesmen that the word slav became the origin of our word "slave".

Viking ships even penetrated the Mediterranean Sea. In 860 a fleet of Danish ships reached the western coast of Italy and sacked the city of Pisa. Then they moved on to the city of Luna, which the Viking leader (Halstein) mistakenly thought was Rome (Luna was several miles north of the old capital). Upon arriving at the city walls, Halstein pretended to be dying and begged to be baptized by the local priests. This wish was granted, and after the clergy left, the wily Norseman climbed into a wooden coffin which was carried inside the walls so that "the body" could be blessed in the church. When the coffin was placed inside the church, Halstein leapt out and struck down the bishop. Then the "mourners" drew their swords from under their cloaks and followed their leader on a rampage of the city.

As word spread of the prowess of the Viking warriors, many European leaders hired them as mercenaries (professional soldiers). One Byzantine Emperor organized an elite fighting force called the Varangian Guard (Viking Guard). Harald Hardrada ("the Ruthless") was a member of the Guard who later became the king of Norway (in 1047). He was killed when he tried to invade England in 1066. We'll learn more about him in the next chapter.

In 885 a huge armada of seven hundred ships (bearing over 30,000 warriors) again laid siege to Paris. By this time a huge stone wall had been built around the city, and an army of two hundred determined Frankish soldiers held out for ten months against the Viking warriors. The king, Charles the Fat, was in Italy at the time; when he returned to Paris, he paid the Norsemen a huge bribe to leave, which they did.

In 911 a Danish chief named Rollo invaded the northern shores of France. In the treaty of St. Clair-sur-Epte, King Charles (the Simple) offered Rollo the city of Rouen and its surrounding area on the condition that he convert to Christianity and promise not to attack other parts of France. The Norseman accepted the terms and became the first Duke of Normandy ("Norseland"). His people eventually adopted the language and customs of France. Today, Rouen is the capital of the French province of Normandy.

THE VIKINGS ARRIVE IN THE NEW WORLD

Vikings ships also sailed westward into the vast uncharted Atlantic Ocean, a feat that required a great deal of courage. The Norsemen traveled on these ocean voyages in knaars, the same broad-beamed, sturdy cargo ships that transported products to and from Constantinople. In 815 Floki of Rogaland, a Norwegian leader,

Normandy, France was first settled by the Norsemen

neared the island of Iceland. He threw instafar (wooden posts from disassembled houses in Scandinavia) into the sea and landed where the tide carried them to the beach. You might think that Iceland was not an appropriate location for a new colony, but the climate was somewhat milder in the north in those early times, and the island was also warmed by the Gulf Stream. Between 870 and 930, 10,000 Viking colonists arrived in Iceland to farm the coastal plains, and by the middle of the tenth century there were about 25,000 Norse settlers living there. In 930 an island-wide assembly known as the Althing was first convened to pass laws and punish criminals. Thirty-six chiefs and their entourage represented twelve Icelandic Things (district assemblies). The Althing met every year for fifteen days at the time of the summer solstice. Proceedings allegedly began on a Thursday in honor of Thor. This legislative body has lasted up to our times, making it the oldest parliamentary assembly in the western world.

As we've learned, the Viking sagas (tales about Icelandic and Scandinavian heroes) and eddas (stories about the gods and heroes of early

Germanic tribes) were first written down in Iceland in the twelfth century. (One of the great poets was Snorri Sturluson.) Perhaps the stories were influenced by the geography of Iceland—the fire and ice of mythology being derived from the volcanoes, hot springs, geysers, and glaciers of Iceland.

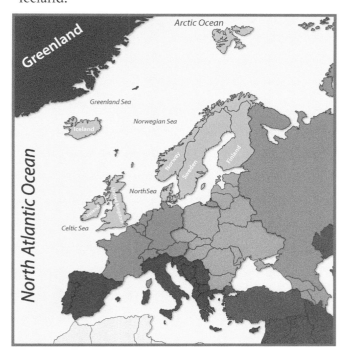

In time Iceland's communities grew crowded, so in 982 Eric the Red sailed west from Iceland to another large island he had heard about. (Actually, Eric had been accused of murder and exiled from Iceland for three years!) After exploring the coast he named the island Greenland, hoping that such a name would attract settlers from Iceland and Scandinavia. This was an early example of false advertising, given the fact that Greenland lay entirely in the Arctic circle, and of its 1,300,000 square miles (it is the world's largest island) only 236,000 are free of ice. The next spring twenty-five ships set sail from Iceland and headed for Greenland, carrying five hundred men, women, and children. It was a rough crossing, and ten ships perished in the ice flows and tempests. But in time villages of

Landscape of Iceland

sheep and goat herders were established on the island. Some of the new settlers hunted walruses for their tusks and arctic foxes for their fur. More enterprising men captured falcons to be trained to hunt for European nobles. However, conditions were poor for farming, and there was little timber.

In 985 Bjarni Herjolfsson set sail for Greenland from Iceland, but he was blown off course and ended up off the coast of Canada. He was amazed by the thick forests he saw along the coastline. When he finally got to Greenland, he

Remains of a Viking dwelling in Greenland

told everyone about what he had seen. In about 1000 Leif Erikson (son of Eric the Red) attempted to retrace the route taken by Herjolfsson with a crew of thirty-five men. He first sighted land at Baffin Island, which he called Helluland ("Rockland"). From there he sailed to the coast of Labrador, a land of low hills and dense forest, which he named Markland ("Woodland"). Then he sailed south and discovered a region he called Vinland (this was Newfoundland), possibly because of the wild grape vines he found there. He wintered in Vinland (he was the first European to land in America) and then returned to Greenland to tell everyone about his discovery. His brother Thorvald set out the next year, landed in Vinland, and encountered the local natives, whom he called Skraelings ("ugly men"). According to the sagas, Thorvold was killed and the others sailed home. Not long afterwards another leader named Thorfinn Karlsefni set out with three boats carrying men, women, and cattle. His son, Snorri, was the first child to be born to European colonists in America. They spent three long years in America, but they were in constant conflict with the Skraelings and they finally left. And so Vinland was forgotten.

Bust of Leif Ericson

We know that Vikings lived in America because the ruins of eight of their houses were discovered in 1960 in L'Anse aux Meadows, Newfoundland. Among them were many Viking objects, including a bronze pin used to fasten a cloak, a spindle whorl, a bone needle and a piece of smelted copper. This provides ample proof that Vikings were living in America nearly five centuries before the voyages of Christopher Columbus. Interestingly enough, the ruins were discovered by Helge Ingstad, a Norwegian archaeologist.

SETTLING DOWN

For about two hundred and fifty years the Norsemen were ever on the move, some greedily plundering European communities, others settling new lands or opening up trade routes. Those restless warriors sailed farther than any other Europeans. But as conditions changed at home, the wanderlust of the earlier warriors sputtered out. Trading cities brought prosperity to Scandinavia, and the widely scattered settlements were united under strong monarchs. In 965 Harald Bluetooth, the King of Denmark, became a Christian and by the eleventh century the Church had been established in most parts of northern Europe. The Norsemen ended up adopting the faith of the monks their ancestors had once victimized. But before everything settled down, Britain would have to sustain a few more attacks, not by pirates but by the armies of the new Nordic kings.

QUESTIONS

1. How did the Vikings get their name?

2. What was a Thing?

3. Describe two ordeals involved in the Norse system of justice.

4. Name and describe three of the Norse deities (gods).

5. How did the Norsemen design their longships to make them more stable?

6. Describe the berserkers.

7. What was Valhalla?

8. What were the main targets of Norse attacks on Britain?

9. What was the Varangian Guard?

10. Who was the first Duke of Normandy?

11. How did Greenland get its name?

12. Why wasn't the Viking settlement in America permanent?

FURTHER THOUGHTS

1. Around 1000 the Norwegian King Olaf (the Stout) attacked London. Olaf's men rowed their ships under a great bridge and tied ropes around the supporting posts. They tied the other ends of the ropes to their ships and rowed downstream as hard as possible. The posts were pulled loose and the bridge tumbled into the water. Many Anglo-Saxons fell into the Thames River and drowned. This is perhaps the derivation of the nursery rhyme, "London Bridge Is Falling Down'

2. In 1880 a burial ship was discovered in Gokstad, near Oslo. It had been in the ground since about 900. Because it was buried in blue clay, it was remarkably well preserved. The ship had held the bodies of a king, six dogs, twelve horses, and one peacock. A few years later an exact copy of the Gokstad ship was built and sailed from Norway to Newfoundland. The captain, Magnus Anderson, made the trip in twenty-eight days.

3. St. Cuthbert (634-87) was an Irish monk. He was buried at Lindisfarae. But when the abbey was attacked by the Vikings, his remains were unearthed and taken off with the fleeing monks. They were later buried at Durham Cathedral in 995. This grave was opened in 1827. The carved oak coffin held the bones of the saint as well as a portable altar, a cross of gold and garnet, a leather-bound book of Gospels, and a woven stole.

4. According to legend, Rollo was offended by the custom of kissing the foot of a king when swearing allegiance. So when he was commanded to swear allegiance to Charles the Simple of France, he lifted the king's foot to his mouth and then sent Charles tumbling backwards! Bad things were always happening to poor Charles, and in 923 he was deposed and fled to England, where he died.

5. To seal a bargain, the Norsemen struck palms together. It was called a handsala, and the tradition is still carried on by the descendants of the Vikings when completing business transactions. Our version of this is the "high five."

6. Every January the people of the Shetland Islands off the coast of Scotland celebrate a festival held in honor of their Viking ancestors. They dress in Viking costumes, and at the end of the day they burn a dragon-headed longship especially built for the event. As the vessel burns, the people sing songs about the Vikings of long ago.

A replica of a longship in a harbor of the Shetland Islands

7. Other Europeans landed in Iceland before the Vikings. Irish monks sailed there in skin-covered boats called curraghs. They established hermits' cells in the caves near the island's southern shore.

PROJECTS

1. When Olaf Trggvason, the king of Norway, was involved in a naval battle, he realized that he was badly outnumbered and facing defeat. So he leapt overboard, preferring to drown rather than be captured or defeated. Some say he survived and became a monk in Syria. In what ways was his behavior typical of Viking warriors? Do you think he was heroic or cowardly? Write a short essay to answer these questions.

2. Consult an Internet about farming in modern Scandinavia. How does it compare with farming in the days of the Vikings? Make a chart to illustrate the differences and similarities.

3. As we have learned, sagas are stories about famous battles and adventures of the Norsemen. They were passed on by word of mouth for generations and were finally written down by Christian monks in Iceland in the twelfth century. Find a book in your school library containing sagas of Scandinavia and read two of them. Then make a short report to the class.

4. Find out more about the longships. Consult the books in your classroom and library, or the Internet, and study the illustrations carefully. Then draw two diagrams of a vessel: one cross-section and one side view. Write a paragraph explaining why Viking longships were considered the finest vessels of the Middle Ages.

5. Eric the Red was accused of murder and banished from Norway. He fled to Iceland, where he apparently became involved in more murders. So he continued west to Greenland. Find out more about this fascinating Norseman. Was he hero or villain? Present your case to your classmates.

6. According to Norse mythology, the land of the dead was guarded by a ferocious dog. The ancient Greeks had a similar belief. Find out the name and function of the dog that guarded the entrance to the Greek land of the dead.

7. What does it mean today when someone "goes berserk?" Give three examples.

8. Make a map of the northern Atlantic, including Iceland, Greenland, and the Canadian coast. Then show the areas settled by the Vikings. Label them and indicate the approximate dates.

9. Read *The Story of Rolf* and the Viking Bow by Allen French or *Beorn the Proud* by Madeleine A. Polland. The first book is set in Iceland and the second is set in Ireland. Both are exciting tales that bring to life the culture and traditions of the courageous but often treacherous Viking warriors.

PART II
A FEUDAL SOCIETY

CHAPTER 5

THE BEGINNING OF NATION STATES

We learned earlier how Charlemagne's empire gradually crumbled in the decades following his death. As the nobles of France and Germany retreated to their strongholds and the farmers settled just beyond the high fortress walls, the concept of a strong central government was replaced by one based upon the authority of the wealthiest landowner in the territory. In England, however, the monarchy would actually be strengthened when the people united against a common enemy. But despite this difference, a new trend was gaining momentum both on the Continent and in Britain. The distinctions between regions and cultures were becoming more evident and a new group of independent nations were beginning to emerge.

ALFRED THE GREAT

In the middle of the ninth century large groups of Danes began building military bases on the islands near the mouths of rivers in Britain, and before long they were settling in the eastern regions of the island. At this time, England was divided into four major kingdoms: Northumbria in the north, Mercia in the midlands, East Anglia in the southeast, and Wessex in the southwest.

In 865 a huge fleet (known as the Great Army) landed in East Anglia and then moved north, capturing York, the capital city of Northumbria. The Northumbrian king (Aelle) had previously defended his land against Viking warrior Ragnar Lodbrok ("Hairy Breeches"). Aelle captured his opponent and had him thrown into a pit of poisonous snakes, where he died a terrible death. The Great Army was led by Lodbrok's son, and

he avidly sought out the king and captured him. (Remember the blood feuds?) King Aelle became the victim of the "blood eagle": His ribs and lungs were cut out and spread like an eagle's wings as an offering to Odin.

Within four years the Norsemen controlled all of Northumbria and East Anglia, as well as parts of Mercia. (The East Anglian king also suffered the "blood eagle", and the Mercian king fled to Rome.) The invaders demanded tribute from the local governments, threatening to kill anyone who wouldn't pay. As you know, such a bribe was called a Danegeld, and the invaders raked in tons of silver every year. As a further humiliation, they demanded that the English address any Norsemen they met as Lord Dane. If an Englishman and a Dane met on a narrow bridge, you can imagine who had to back up and wait for the other to cross!

The rolling hillside of Wessex

In 870 part of the Great Army, led by Guthrum, marched into Wessex, the most powerful kingdom in England at the time.

The king, a young man of twenty-one named Alfred, realized that he needed time to build up his forces, so he agreed to pay the Danegeld in order to temporarily keep the Norsemen at bay. Meanwhile, he systematically planned for the defense of Wessex. He reorganized the army (all free men had to serve) and built up a fleet of ships that were two times the size of the longships. He created new fortified towns (called burroughs). Many of these were built on the sites of old Roman towns (such as Winchester, Chichester, and Bath), where the old walls could be put to good use.

The Danes kept out of Wessex for a number of years, focusing their energies upon the conquest of the rest of Mercia. But in 878 Guthrum invaded Alfred's kingdom, forcing the young king and a small group of soldiers to seek refuge on the Isle of Athelney in a large swamp. The following spring Alfred gathered his forces and soundly defeated the Danes at the Battle of Edington. Guthrum and thirty of his chiefs agreed to be baptized as Christians and to withdraw from Alfred's kingdom. According to the Treaty of Wedmore, Watling Street (an old Roman road that ran from London to Chester) was established as the border between Wessex and the area occupied by the Danes (called the Danelaw). This was, in fact, a generous gesture on Alfred's part, since the Danelaw covered an entire third of English soil. (He could easily have demanded more.) Over the years, the Norsemen living there were assimilated into the English culture. However, the names of many of the modern towns in that region (those ending in -wick, -ness, -by, -dale, and -thorpe) are derived from the early language of the Danes and were originally settlements in the Danelaw.

The Treaty of Wedmore made Alfred the king of all of England except the Danelaw. He soon established a new, clarified national code of law, and had the laws written down in English (rather than Latin). He divided the land into districts called shires, each of which was run by an overseer called a reeve. The reeve collected taxes, enforced laws, called out soldiers in time of war, and informed the king about local issues. The title shire reeve was later shortened to sheriff. (Perhaps the most infamous sheriff in literature is the evil Sheriff of Nottingham in the legend of Robin Hood.) Certain regions in modern England maintain their old shire names. (Yorkshire, Devonshire, and Shropshire are some examples.)

The statue of King Alfred the Great in Winchester, UK

Alfred was anxious to revive the interest in learning that had distinguished seventh and eighth century Northumbria. The terrible pillaging of the Norsemen had destroyed many monasteries and schools, nearly snuffing out the intellectual spark of the past. Gone were the days of Bede, Boniface, and Alcuin. Many priests could not even read or write; they simply recited words during services that they had memorized but could not understand. To remedy the situation Alfred gathered scholars from many parts of Europe to teach Latin to the English clergy (just as Charlemagne had once done). He also saw to it that the priests as well as the sons of his lords were taught to read and write English. Alfred didn't learn to read Latin until he was forty, but he spent the last ten years of his life translating Latin works into English, including Bede's Ecclesiastical History and Pope Gregory's Pastoral Care. Alfred arranged for a record of English history to be compiled by his more learned monks, starting with the time of the Romans. The Anglo-Saxon Chronicle, which was begun at this time, was continued for two hundred and fifty years after Alfred's death. It, too, was written in the language of the Anglo-Saxons. Alfred even managed to retrieve some of the treasures stolen by the Norsemen from English churches, including the Codex Aureus (Gospels penned in England in the eighth century), which he purchased outright from the descendants of its Viking pillagers and returned to the clerics of Canterbury.

Alfred is credited with rebuilding London, making it England's leading city. He was a tireless worker with a practical mind: He allegedly marked off his candles to regulate the time he devoted to work, prayer, and sleep. (St. Benedict would have been impressed!) Because of his renown as a leader and scholar, he came to be known as Alfred the Great. He is the only English monarch to be so designated. After his death, tensions resumed between the English and the Danes. In 926 Alfred's grandson Athelstan defeated the Norsemen at the Battle of Brunanburgh. He seized the Danelaw and became the first king of all of England.

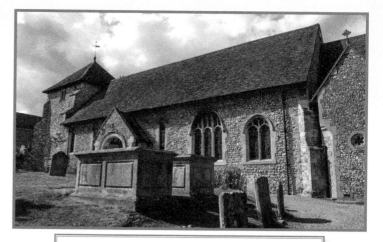

St Bartholomew in Winchester, Hampshire

Recent excavations have revealed bones believed to belong to the medieval King Alfred the Great.

WILLIAM THE CONQUEROR

In the middle of the eleventh century the Duke of Normandy was named William. He was a descendant of Rollo, the Norseman who had been bribed with that region in northwestern France by Louis the Simple. The King of England at the time was Edward the Confessor, a cousin of William's. Edward had previously spent many years in exile in Normandy (during the reign of Norseman Canute, see page 68), and he had gotten to know William quite well. Since he had no sons, Edward promised his Norman cousin the English throne upon his death. But when he died in 1066, the crown was grabbed by Harold Godwinsson, the Earl of Wessex. (He was Edward's brother-in-law and England's most powerful noble.)

There was also a third man who wanted the throne of England: Harald Hardrada, the King of Norway. He landed in England with an army, his banner embroidered with Odin's black raven. But after a fierce fight, Harald's army was defeated by the English troops at the Battle of Stamford Bridge. Harald, who died after being struck by an arrow in the throat, would be the last Viking warrior to invade British soil.

During the night of September 27, 1066 William crossed the English Channel with an army of 7,000 soldiers. The men, horses, and equipment were transported by a fleet of 777 ships. Harold (not to be confused with Harald!) had just finished fighting the Norsemen, and his men were exhausted. Nonetheless, he had no choice but to race south to fend off this new group of invaders.

The two armies met at Hastings (near London). William had the best trained horsemen in Europe, and they wore metal armor. The English troops, on the other hand, were mostly foot soldiers protected only with kite-shaped shields (each emblazoned with the dragon of Wessex). Harold established his position on the top of the hill. As William's knights advanced up the slope, the English soldiers made a solid wall with their shields. Undaunted, a group of Norman horsemen charged. They were immediately forced back by enemy arrows, but then some English soldiers made the mistake of racing downhill after them. This created a gap in the English line, which William spotted at once. He quickly devised an ingenious strategy. He ordered his knights to make a series of charges up the hill. Although the English repeatedly chased them down the hill, the Normans were able to kill a few of them each time, ever widening the gap. By nightfall, William had successfully broken through the English line. In the fighting that ensued Harold was killed by an arrow that lodged in his eye. What was left of his army fled.

William was crowned King of England on Christmas Day at Westminster Abbey. He was a highly intelligent man, and he established a strong personal monarchy. But his Norman followers were greatly outnumbered by the English (whose population was about one million), so he had to force his rule upon his new subjects. He rewarded his knights with small pieces of land that were scattered throughout the countryside. They built fortified castles to protect themselves from their rebellious neighbors. We'll learn more about castles in the next chapter.

Clifford's Tower, all that remains of York Castle, which was built by William the Conqueror

William established the Curia Regis (King's Council) to help him rule, drawing its members from his nobles and high churchmen. In 1086 he ordered a survey of his English lands to make sure he was getting all the rents and taxes that were due him. This was England's first census, and it took two years to complete. The survey is a very useful guide for modern scholars, since it provides a detailed portrait of life at that time: It lists how much land was cultivated, how many farm animals were owned, and what the people were doing (and, of course, how many people there were). According to the figures gathered by William's census officials, three quarters of

England's wealth (land and farm animals) was owned by the king and about three hundred nobles and churchmen. Among this group only two were English, so it's no mystery why the local people despised the Norman intruders!

Statue of William the Conqueror in Normandy

The findings of the survey were recorded in what is known as the Domesday Book. It was actually called the Doomsday Book (a different pronunciation in medieval times explains the change in spelling), and there are two possible explanations for its name. Many Englishmen complained that it was easier to escape Doomsday (the final Day of Judgment when God would encounter the forces of evil) than to avoid the royal data collectors. At the same time, those of William's subjects who lied about their holdings (fearing that they would be too heavily taxed)

were punished at court proceedings that seemed as harsh as the treatment sinners would receive on the Day of Judgment. But whatever the derivation of its name, the Domesday Book is an invaluable historical document. It is now in the Public Records Office in London.

William, of course, spoke French, as did his noblemen and soldiers. For a very long time, French would be the language of England's upper class (Norman descendants), while English remained the language of the people. Hie two eventually blended to form modern English. Did you know that nearly half of our English words are derived from Anglo-Saxon, about one third are of French (or Latin) origin, and the rest come from other sources, such as Greek and Arabic?

Under William's rule, England and northern France (Normandy) were technically one nation, and they remained so until the thirteenth century. But during that time, as we will see, the conflict arising from questions of the ownership of the French land would cause all kinds of hostility between the kings of England and France.

THE PLANTAGENETS

William was succeeded by his sons, William II and Henry I. Although they were harsh rulers, they maintained peace and order throughout the kingdom. But after Henry I died in 1135, the crown was due to pass to his daughter Matilda (his son, William, having drowned in the English Channel). However, the Norman nobles were convinced that a woman was incapable of running the country and so they proposed that Henry's nephew Stephen be crowned instead. They had their way, and Stephen became king. But Matilda, who was married to Geoffrey of Anjou (a county in France), refused to accept the nobles' decision. She crossed the Channel with an army and challenged Stephen for the throne, claiming it for her infant son, Henry. The result was eighteen long years of civil war, during which time the Norman nobles took advantage of the royal disorder by helping themselves to more land and building greater castles. In the process, they became extremely powerful.

In 1153 Stephen's son and heir (Eustace) died. Geoffrey of Anjou had died two years previously, and Matilda's son Henry was now the Duke of Normandy and Count of Anjou. When he married Eleanor of Aquitaine and added

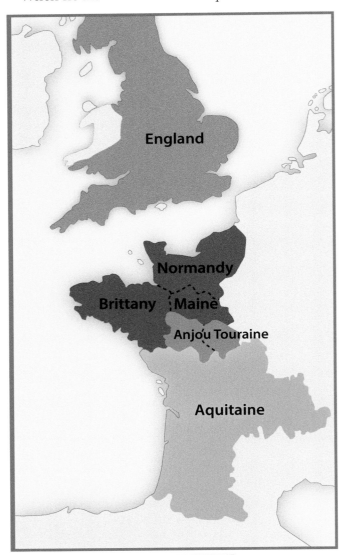

The Angevin Empire

her sizeable kingdom to his holdings he gained control of the entire western part of modern France. (Eleanor had previously been married to King Louis VII of France, but their marriage had ended in divorce. We'll hear more about this intriguing woman later.) Henry was a broad-shouldered, strapping youth with shortly cropped red hair and freckles. He loved nothing more than to hunt in the thick forests of France. He had tremendous energy and a keen mind (it was said that he never forgot a face or an important fact), and he seemed the perfect candidate to rule England. So Stephen, who was not in good health, agreed to sign a document naming Henry as his heir. One year later (in December 1154) Stephen died.

Henry was only twenty-one when he added England to his domain in France. Historians call his territory the Angevin Empire because Henry was descended from the counts of Anjou. Henry's family name was Plantagenet. It was derived from the name of a yellow flower that Henry's father (Geoffrey) wore when he went on a pilgrimage to the Holy Land. The French version of the Latin name of the plant (planta genista) was plantagent. The Plantagenet dynasty would rule England until 1399.

Henry II turned out to be an excellent monarch. He instituted many reforms and created a new class of government bureaucrats. During his long reign (he ruled for thirty-five years) his administration grew in complexity and efficiency. He radically improved the court system, abolishing the old procedures of trial by ordeal and duel and replacing them with a more reasonable system of trial by jury. Judges appointed by the king traveled from place to place throughout the kingdom. When a crime was reported, they gathered together "twelve good men and true" from the area to investigate the facts. These men had to swear to tell the truth. Since the French word jurer means "to swear," they became known as the jury. Their final report was known as the verdict (meaning "the truly spoken"). Punishments could be harsh: A thief was hanged, a traitor was blinded, and people found guilty of other crimes could be mutilated.

Engraving of Henry II

The system of royal justice devised by Henry is known as Common Law, since the same laws were common throughout the kingdom (previously laws had varied from shire to shire). It would become the basis of the legal systems of many modern English-speaking peoples. However, when Henry challenged the power of the Church courts, he ran into a great deal of trouble. We'll learn more about this in Chapter 10.

THE CAPETIANS OF FRANCE

Let's turn back to see what was happening in France at the end of the tenth century. As we have learned, the western third of Charlemagne's empire became the country we know as France. But for many years the French kings controlled only a small territory between Paris and Orleans (known as the Ile de France) while large regions such as Normandy, Brittany, Anjou, Flanders, Burgundy, and Aquitaine were ruled by powerful nobles. The king technically reigned over all of France, but in reality he had very little power beyond the borders of the lie de France.

In 987 the last of the Carolingian kings died, and Charles of Lorraine, an uncle of the dead king, demanded that he should become the next monarch. However, the Archbishop of Rheims, believing Charles to be a poor choice, proposed instead the name of nobleman Hugh Capet. The Archbishop had his way, and Capet was crowned, establishing a new dynasty—the Capetians.

Like their predecessors, the first Capetians had relatively little power beyond their own domain in central France. They had no organized government administration, no means of raising money, and no army. The nobles, on the other hand, continued to make their own laws, coin their own money, and command their own armies. But at least in theory the Capetians were the overlords of the nobility, and their position was strengthened by the fact that Hugh had been selected and crowned by an important leader in the Church. Furthermore, the Capetians did not dilute the family power, nominal though it was, as the Carolingians had done by dividing their kingdom among several sons. They established a new tradition of the eldest son inheriting the crown, and, to insure his claim to power, his coronation took place when his father was still alive.

When Louis VI (Louis the Fat) came to the throne in 1108, he strengthened the power of the monarchy in the He de France by discharging those nobles who were not loyal to him and replacing them with others he could depend upon. It was Louis' son (Louis VII) who married Eleanor of Aquitaine. When they divorced, he lost her rich parcel of land. However, France was fast becoming the most populous region in Europe, and it would soon be considered the heart of medieval culture.

Fleur de lis, symbol of France

THE HOLY ROMAN EMPIRE

Meanwhile, let's see what was happening further east at this time. We learned in Chapter 3 that the eastern part of Charlemagne's empire (modern Germany) was broken into the five duchies of Bavaria, Franconia, Saxony, Swabia, and Lorraine, all ruled by powerful dukes but technically under the authority of the German king. When the last Carolingian of Germany (King Louis the Child) died in 911, the nobles and clergy elected Conrad, Duke of Franconia, as the new king. Conrad, however, was a weak ruler; when he was about to die, the crown was passed on to a man who seemed more likely to succeed: Henry, Duke of Saxony. The messengers who carried Henry the news of his election found him hunting with hawks, and for this reason he became known as King Henry the Fowler.

Henry turned out to be a good choice. He succeeded in uniting the duchies of Saxony, Franconia, and Lorraine. In 924 he managed to convince the leader of hordes of marauding Magyar tribesmen to agree to a truce. This gave him time to build up his own defenses and train his soldiers (does this remind you of Alfred?). When the Magyars attacked again in 933, Henry defeated them handily at the Battle of Riade. He also drove back an army of invading Danes in 934, and he was planning an expedition to Italy when he suddenly died.

Henry's son was Otto I (936-973). He was later known as Otto the Great. When he came to power northern Italy was broken up into a group of small kingdoms, and two strong rivals were fighting for control of much of the region. When one was killed his widow, Adelaide, sought refuge with Otto. Their relationship soon led to marriage. In 951 Otto marched his army into northern Italy, conquered it, and made it a part of his own kingdom.

Otto's army consisted totally of mounted knights. His decisive victory over the Magyars at Lechfeld in 955 made him the most powerful European monarch since Charlemagne. As we learned earlier, the Magyars were called Hungarians because they seemed as ferocious as

Flag of the Holy Roman Empire

of irony, Otto the Saxon was spreading Christianity to the primitive people living on his borders just as Charlemagne had once done in Otto's native Saxony.) He even convinced the Roman Cardinals to swear not to elect a new Pope without the advice of the Holy Roman Emperor. This gave him and his successors an influence over the papacy that was unknown to even Charlemagne.

Otto inspired an intellectual revival that continued through his two successors. Among the scholars who were summoned to the royal court, the greatest was Gerbert of Aurillac (later Pope Sylvester II). This learned monk had visited Spain, and he brought the knowledge of Arab scientific discoveries to eastern Europe.

When the Saxon dynasty died out in 1024 it was succeeded by a line of Franconian monarchs known as the Salian Dynasty. They became even more powerful than Otto. Henry III, for example, appointed popes as freely as he did bishops and abbots, and he even deposed those he considered unsatisfactory!

SPAIN

We learned in Chapter 2 how the Moors (Muslims) settled in Spain and built many beautiful towns and cities. By the tenth century their capital, Cordova, was Europe's largest and richest city. It had a population of about 250,000 people, and it was filled with beautiful palaces, public baths with hot and cold running water, and handsome mosques with delicate minarets. The city was also a center of learning (that's where Gerbert of Aurillac visited and studied).

In the eleventh century, Spain was divided into two regions: Christian kingdoms were established in the mountainous northern regions

the Huns. After their defeat by Otto, they finally settled on the plains of modern Hungary.

Soon afterwards a Lombard leader seized the throne from his king and threatened the Pope (John XII). John sent an urgent message to Otto begging for his protection. So the German king marched his men into Italy and recovered the throne of Lombardy, driving off its usurper. In gratitude, the Pope declared Otto the Roman Emperor and placed the imperial crown upon his head (962). The adjective "Holy" was later added to the title. For the next thousand years German kings would rule the Holy Roman Empire.

This empire, however, was certainly not a restoration of Charlemagne's vast and diverse former realm. Otto ruled mostly Germans who shared a common language and customs. He had no jurisdiction over France, and he expressed little interest in the government affairs of Italy. And unlike Charlemagne, he allowed local rulers to make and maintain their own laws. He did, however, strengthen his authority in the Church. He saw to it that only men loyal to him were appointed bishops and abbots, and he established new churches in the eastern and northern frontiers of his empire. (In an interesting twist

Courtyard of Moorish Palace of Alhambra in Granada

QUESTIONS

1. What did Alfred do after he paid the Danegeld?

2. Where was the Danelaw?

3. Name three good things that Alfred did for England.

4. How did William defeat Harold?

5. Describe the Domesday Book.

6. What is the origin of the name Plantagenet?

7. How did Henry II change the legal system in England?

8. How did Louis VI strengthen the French monarchy?

9. Why was Otto crowned Roman Emperor?

10. What was the Moorish capital in the early Middle Ages?

FURTHER THOUGHTS

1. The Danegeld was collected for many years. Archaeologists recently discovered in a site in Sweden over 30,000 English coins dating from the period of the Norse invasion of Britain.

2. Alfred probably never expected to become king. He had three elder brothers, and all served as monarchs before him. When the last one died (during the Danish invasion), Alfred became king. He was not terribly well prepared. His education was poor (his training had been in hunting and warfare). Furthermore, he was in chronic poor health most of his life. There are no details about his afflictions, except that he seldom complained about his frequent bouts with illness.

There is a famous story that bears telling here. When Alfred was driven by the Danes into the marshes, he took refuge in the hut of a peasant. As he sat by the fire, tending his bow and arrows,

of the Iberian peninsula, while the Moorish civilization flourished in the south. In 1085, the Christian kingdom of Castile attacked and captured the Moorish city of Toledo. Rodrigo Diaz de Vivar (1043-1099) was a Christian knight who fought in the so-called Reconquest of Spain, a long series of conflicts between the Christian and Muslim soldiers. He was medieval Spain's greatest hero and was known as El Cid (Spanish for "The Lord"). His story has come down to us in the *Poem of El Cid* (written in the twelfth century).

In 1140 the kingdom of Aragon, joined by the county of Barcelona, launched another assault against the Moors, but they met with little success. In the following century the King of Castile won a decisive victory. After Cordova fell in 1236, the Moors were confined to the small southern kingdom of Granada, where they remained until 1492. Meanwhile, the rest of the peninsula was controlled by three large Christian kingdoms: Castile, Aragon, and Portugal.

several loaves of bread (in some versions they were cakes) that were baking above the fire began to burn. The peasant woman rushed over and grabbed the bread, scolding the king, "Can't you see that they're burning? You did nothing to rescue them, and yet you'd probably be the first to eat them!" This humiliating situation shows the depths to which a great man can be reduced when he falls upon hard times. Alfred, by the way, apologized for his inattentiveness.

3.   The actual spot where William fought Harold is marked today by a small village named Battle. Some reports indicate that it existed in 1066. William's victory is officially named after the larger town of Hastings, located nearby. But, technically speaking, we could say that William the Conqueror defeated Harold of England at the Battle of Battle!

4.   The Bayeux Tapestry is a 231-foot long piece of linen upon which were embroidered a series of seventy pictures relating to the events that occurred at Hastings in 1066. Each section has a separate Latin caption. Eight colors of yarn were used to outline ships, knights, horses, and even castles. The tapestry, which looks something like a giant cartoon strip, might have been stitched by Henry IPs mother Matilda (it is extremely pro-Norman). It can be viewed in the Bayeux Cathedral in Normandy.

5.   In April, 1066, a "long-haired star" (Halley's Comet) was visible in England for seven days. Harold was told it was a bad omen. It was!

6.   Harald Hardrada (the Ruthless) had a very interesting life. He left Norway after his brother, King Olaf, was killed. He sailed to the Mediterranean, where he led a number of raids. He then joined the Viking guard (the Varangians) of the Emperor at Constantinople. In 1047 he returned to Norway and claimed the throne. When he heard of the death of Edward the Confessor in 1066, he decided to add England to his kingdom. But, as we have seen, King Harold's army was superior to that of the invading Norsemen. According to legend, Harald tried to bolster his men's courage by marching in front of them and cutting a path through the English soldiers with his sword. Perhaps this is how he was fatally wounded. His army's defeat marked the end of the Viking Age.

7.   Henry I of England had twenty children; only one was a boy. As we've learned, he drowned before he could inherit the throne.

A section of the Bayeux Tapestry

8. The name of El Cid's horse was Babieca (Spanish for "stupid"). Apparently his godfather once told the young Cid to choose a horse, and the boy selected what seemed to be the ugliest, clumsiest steed in the herd. The man must have shouted out, "What a stupid choice!" and the name stuck. As it turned out, the boy had chosen an excellent mount.

PROJECTS

1. After the death of King Ethelred, a Danish king named Sven Forkbeard conquered England. His successor, Canute (Knut), ruled England from 1016 until 1035. (This is the period when Edward the Confessor was in exile in Normandy.) Upon his death, the crown returned to the Anglo-Saxons. During Canute's reign, England was part of a larger kingdom that included Scandinavia (he also conquered Norway). Find out more about this fascinating Norseman, particularly his philosophy about ruling the English people. Write a short report.

2. During the Second World War, the Allies came ashore to defeat the German invading army at the same place where William the Conqueror waited for a favorable tide to set out for England. Find out more about D-Day. Then write a short report comparing the invasion of England in 1066 with the invasion of Normandy in this century. Illustrate it with a map.

3. Compare Henry II to President John Fitzgerald Kennedy. (For starters, both were handsome, charismatic, and ambitious, and they died young.) Write a short report.

4. Many books have been written about the life of Eleanor of Aquitaine. An excellent work geared for middle schoolers by E.L. Konigsburg, *A Proud Taste for Scarlet and Miniver*, describes what happens when Eleanor and Henry II are reunited in Heaven. Read it, and present a report to the class.

Normandy Beach

5. Henry was a very common name among medieval royalty. Make a list of all the men named Henry who ruled in Germany, France, and England from the early Middle Ages until the end of the Renaissance.

6. The French philosopher Voltaire (eighteenth century) once mocked Otto's empire, saying that it was not holy, not Roman, and not an empire. What do you think he meant by this statement? Think about what you've learned about medieval history thus far, and then write a paragraph explaining what Voltaire had in mind when he made his remark.

7. The Last Judgment is described in the Book of Revelations in the Bible. Read it (it's not very long). Then find out about what an encyclopedia has to say about the Apocalypse. Write a report about medieval views on Doomsday.

8. We have learned that many English words are derived from French. How many words can you think of that are used by English speakers and that come from French? (Examples: croissant, "boulevard, café, ballet, clique, and unique"). Consult a dictionary for word origins, and then make a list of English words of French origin (not necessarily from medieval times).

"Bouquet" is a French word

CHAPTER 6

LORDS AND VASSALS

When the nobles of continental Europe fortified their estates against the Viking invaders, the local peasants offered them tracts of their own land and promised to work the fields in exchange for their protection. At first each nobleman retained heavily armed horsemen (knights) in his household. However, these fighters could be boisterous and crude (we'll learn more about them in the next chapter), and over time it became customary for a lord to grant (lease) each of his knights a part of his land. The knights, in turn, promised to be loyal to the noble and to come to his aid in times of war. This arrangement kept the peace in the lord's living quarters and gave the knights significant power and social prestige. The crops produced on the land by the peasants provided the knights with an income to pay for their horses and weapons.

HOW THE SYSTEM WORKED

The concept of exchanging land for military service had its roots in earlier times. You will remember how the Germanic chieftains rewarded their warriors with a share of the plunder and a piece of land. Similarly, the early Frankish kings provided their nobles with large estates for their service and loyalty.

By the tenth century an orderly system of land usage had been worked out which defined the duties and obligations of all levels of society. Of course, the system varied somewhat from one region to another, but this is how it basically worked. A knight who leased some land from a noble (called a lord) was known as a vassal (from the Latin vassalus, which means "military retainer"). The more vassals a lord had the better,

since a large number of loyal knights made him powerful. Only the members of the upper class (the nobility) could be vassals; the vast majority of the population were peasants. The plot of land leased in exchange for military service was called a fief (it rhymes with beef). It was generally passed on from father to eldest son. Land was plentiful in those days, and so it became the chief source of wealth. A landless nobleman was rare indeed, and he would be pitied and even regarded as a danger to the community.

The relationship between lords and vassals is known as the feudal system or feudalism (from feudum, the Latin word for fief). By the eleventh century thousands of small communities were flourishing around the fortresses of the nobles of western Europe, although a number of free farms continued to prosper among the feudal estates. Even the Church was part of the system; it would later become the largest landowner in Europe. In a time of disorder and danger, feudalism was a useful plan. It provided a structure of government, a system of justice (as we'll soon see), and a means of protection. It changed little until the development of towns in the twelfth century.

A medieval writer once compared the classes of his society as the parts of a human body: the priests and monks (the spiritual guides) were the head and eyes; the nobles (the protectors and defenders) were the hands and arms; and the peasants (whose labor supported the others) were the feet and legs.

THE VASSAL'S OBLIGATIONS

The king owned all the land in his kingdom and was owed obedience and support by all of his subjects. In fact, apart from the king, everyone in medieval society owed some kind of service to someone higher up. At the highest level of the feudal system were the tenants-in-chief (counts and barons who possessed huge tracts of land); they leased part of their land to lesser tenants (knights and other nobles), who thus became their vassals. These, in turn, might lease part of their land to less affluent peers. When summoned by the king, a tenant-in-chief had to appear on a field of battle with a fighting force made up of his vassals. But, apart from the Viking raids, most wars during this period were private fights between feudal lords over land, and in such cases

a tenant counted upon the support of his vassals to defeat his opponent.

As you can see, a nobleman might be both a vassal of a greater lord and a lord of lesser vassals. (William the Conqueror was King of England, and yet, as Duke of Normandy, he was also the vassal of the King of France.) In later years, a knight might be given land by two different lords. In such cases, he would have to choose between them if they both became involved in a dispute. As you can imagine, this could lead to some bad feelings. When he received a fief, a vassal was required to participate in a ceremony known as doing homage. Kneeling before his lord, bareheaded and unarmed, he placed his right hand on the Bible and promised to be one of the lord's "men" on the battlefield whenever called upon to fight (homage comes from the French word homme, meaning "man"). This was known as the oath of fealty ("loyalty").

Failure to keep such a vow was considered a crime (it was called a felony). In fact, breaking an oath or being disloyal to one's lord were considered among the worst crimes during the Middle Ages. After the oath was taken, the lord took the vassal's hands between his own and raised him to his feet. He then presented him with an object (usually a twig or a clod of earth) which symbolized the land he was leasing to him. Even bishops and abbots, as land owners, had to swear oaths of fealty to the king, and, as we will see in the next chapter, many a clergyman appeared on the field of battle.

Apart from owing military service to his lord (usually forty days a year) and supplying military protection for the peasants who lived on and farmed his land, a vassal had numerous lesser obligations. He was expected to 1) ransom his lord from captivity if he was taken as a prisoner of war; 2) pay the expenses of making the lord's eldest son a knight and provide a dowry for his eldest daughter; 3) attend the lord's court whenever summoned; and 4) entertain the lord when called upon (even placing his own castle at the lord's disposal). Although a fief was inherited by the lord's eldest son, but if a vassal died and his heir was a daughter, the lord had her married to a man of his choice. The new husband would become his vassal. Medieval women had few rights or privileges!

A lord was duty-bound to protect his vassals' land from invading armies. In addition, he collected taxes (mostly paid in wheat) and presided over the local court. He was required to consider the advice of his vassals before making laws, and he could not impose extra taxes without their consent. When a vassal died, his heir paid the lord a sum equal to a year's income of his fief.

William the Conqueror brought the feudal system to England. To discourage his nobles from uniting against him, he gave them small fiefs that were widely scattered across the countryside. Each of his lords had to swear allegiance directly to him as well as to the man who leased him his land. In this way, William strengthened his authority and laid the foundation for a centralized government.

In the twelfth century, during the reign of Henry II of England, a new practice known as scutage was introduced to the feudal system. The term comes from the Latin scutum (meaning "shield"), and it refers to the practice of paying money instead of providing military service to a lord. Henry used his scutage payments to hire soldiers—particularly archers and other footsoldiers who were recruited among the common people. Scutage changed the character of the feudal system, weakening it in the process, and it ultimately led to the development of national armies made up entirely of professional soldiers.

THE MANOR

The estate of a lesser tenant was called a manor. Many lords had several manors, and they spent some time at each of them. (This was particularly true on the Continent; most English lords owned only one manor.) The earliest manor houses were tall wooden structures surrounded by wooden palisades. A building contained one large multi-purpose room. At night the lord and his family slept there on sacks stuffed with hay, covered by woolen blankets or animal skins. There was an open hearth, but no chimney, so it must have been very smoky. By the twelfth century manor houses were larger and were built of stone.

The average manor covered between 900 and 3000 acres and was worked by two or three dozen families of peasants. In the center of the land was the lord's house, the church (and the priest's dwelling), a mill (beside a stream whose water was a source of power), pastures, woodlands, fields, and a village of peasant huts. The typical hut had a timber frame that was covered with wattle and daub. The roof was made of thatch (bunches of dried grass). A hut usually had two rooms, a dirt floor, and an open hearth (with a hole in the roof just above it). There were few if any windows, and those that existed were covered with oiled animal skins to let in light but keep out drafts. One room was used for the family. The only furniture was a trestle table (a board resting across two saw horses), a wooden chest, and some three-legged stools. The family slept on the floor on mattresses stuffed with straw. Dried herbs hung from the ceiling, ready to be used for seasoning or medicinal purposes. The second room of the hut was used for storage. Cattle and other animals were sometimes stabled there. A peasant's dwelling was not very comfortable, so he was only inside to eat, sleep, or find shelter from bad weather. Nearly all work was done out of doors.

A thatch-roofed hut

THE LIFE OF THE PEASANTS

The lord kept about one third of the land for himself. This was called his domain (demesne). Peasants paid for the use of the rest of the land by giving him a portion of their harvested crops (usually wheat grown for this purpose) and working on his land. The fields were divided into strips, and a peasant was given strips in each field so that everyone could share the good and the bad land. All the strips in a given field were used to grow the same crop.

Because the soil in northern Europe is moist and thick, the peasants had to use a heavy plow with an iron blade. (Lighter plows were used in the thin, dry soil of southern Europe.) The plow was drawn by teams of oxen (usually two but sometimes as many as eight). Since animals and equipment were expensive, the peasants shared what they had with their neighbors. Each strip in the fields was a furlong in length, which was the

distance a team of oxen could plow before having to rest. The long strips were preferable to squares because turning a team of oxen was difficult and cumbersome. In the tenth century some farmers began to use horses in the fields. This was made possible by the invention of the horse collar. First developed in central Asia, the collar gave an animal five times more pulling power than the earlier, more primitive chest harness, which constricted his windpipe. Horses cost more money to feed, but they drew the plow many times faster than a team of oxen ever could.

By the thirteenth century the European farmers were using a three field system. The first field was planted in the fall with winter wheat and rye. The wheat was grown to make white bread for the nobility; rye was the basic grain for everyone else. A second field was sown with other grains, such as barley and oats. The barley was brewed to make ale, and the oats were used to feed the animals in winter. A third field would lie fallow (be unused). Cows, sheep, and horses were grazed there, and their manure fertilized the soil. Vegetables (onions, garlic, peas, lentils, cabbage and beans) were grown in small garden plots. In the summer all the crops were harvested. This was a cooperative effort by all the peasants in the local village. After they harvested their own crops, they had to put in more time (called Boon Time) in the lord's strips.

A team of modern horses wearing horse collars

The next year the use of each field rotated: The first was sown in the spring, the second lay fallow, and the third was be planted in the fall. As the three-year cycle continued, a given field being used in a different way each year, the farmers produced more crops per season than ever before.

In England there were two types of peasant. Freemen paid the lord rent and could move about whenever they wished. Serfs, on the other hand, were the lord's property. They had few rights. In fact, the word serf comes from the Latin servus (which means "slave"). On the Continent most peasants were serfs. Their average life expectancy was less than forty years. Most of them died in the same village where they had been bora, their world limited to about two square miles. Sometimes a lord would give a hard-working serf his freedom. (The Church said that such an act would counter-balance some of a man's sins when his soul was in purgatory.)

As was mentioned earlier, rye and barley were the staples of the peasant diet. From these grains could be made a coarse dark bread, porridge, puddings, and ale. Cheese, eggs, and cabbage supplemented the meals. (No nobleman would even think of eating cabbage, since it was a symbol of the peasantry.) Pigs were slaughtered in the fall, because there wasn't much food to get them through the winter. But even when it was salted, the meat didn't stay fresh very long, and its rancid taste had to be disguised with onion and garlic sauce. Apart from ale, the peasants drank milk (from a goat or ewe) and mead (made from honey). At the year's end there was always a big feast at the manor (the people of the Middle Ages celebrated all twelve days of Christmas). At this time some animals were slaughtered, and their bones were burned in a huge fire. This "bone fire" is the origin of our bonfire.

A serf was obligated to have his flour ground in the lord's mill. Because of this, the miller

became an unpopular member of medieval society. He paid the lord for the right to operate his mill, and the peasants had to pay him one-sixteenth of the flour he made from their grain. Since the miller did the measuring, he might be

White bread for the nobility, brown bread for everyone else

tempted to cheat on the weight of the grain or to substitute bad grain for good. This led to the creation of a popular medieval riddle: What is the boldest thing in the world? The answer: A miller's shirt—it clasps a thief by the throat every day! A serf also was required to have his bread baked in the lord's oven and to have his grapes squeezed at the lord's wine press, both services for which he had to pay a fair sum. On the other hand, he did possess the right to pasture a certain number of his animals (cattle, sheep, pigs, and goats) on the lord's land, and he could gather fuel in the local woodlands^. A typical annual payment of a serf

Five eggs at Easter

to his lord in England was one bushel of wheat, eighteen sheaves of oats, three hens and one rooster, plus five eggs at Easter. (This is the origin of the giving of Easter eggs!)

Poor modes of transportation and communication as well as the continual warfare forced the manors to be independent and self-sufficient. Apart from the field laborers, each manor had a small community of smiths, coopers, carpenters, tanners, and other craftsmen. Certain materials, such as iron, salt, and tar had to be obtained from traveling merchants. The manor was run by special officials, the most important being the Steward and Bailiff. And, as we have seen, every manor had its own court over which the lord presided. In many regions the serfs were divided into groups of ten (a group was called a tithing). Each man was bound to observe the others in his group to make sure that they followed the laws. If someone broke the law, the other nine were responsible for bringing him to court.

CASTLES

The typical fortress constructed by the wealthy nobles (the tenants-in-chief) in the ninth century was a tall wooden tower similar to the early manor houses of the lesser lords described earlier in this chapter. The ideal location of such a tower was a hill or cliff, but if there was no natural elevation a huge mound of earth (called a motte) was made by digging a circular ditch (a moat), piling the earth in the center, and then packing it down. The tower and an enclosed courtyard, called a bailey, were surrounded by a wooden palisade. A sentry walk built along the inside of the palisade allowed soldiers to keep watch. The moat could be filled with water or left dry. This type of fortress, called a mottle and bailey, was the earliest version of a castle. (The word castle comes from the Latin castrum, meaning "closed fort or stronghold.")

Blacksmith at work

Reconstruction of a wooden keep

The tower of a castle was known as a keep (so-called because lord and men were kept there in times of war). The French called the tower a donjon. It had no door on the ground floor. A ladder led to the first level above ground, and it was drawn up after use. The keep had one large room where the lord and the household ate, lived, and slept during an attack or a siege. Within the confines of the bailey were a kitchen, a wooden hall for meals and sleeping, bakehouses, brewhouses, barns and pens, storehouses, workshops, and usually a chapel.

In later years, the lord lived in the keep all the time. It was somewhat larger now. Its main room was called the Great Hall. At one end was a raised platform (called a dais) where the lord sat to conduct business and eat his meals. At dinner time trestle tables were set up at right angles to the dais for members of the household. These were thick oaken boards resting on wooden frames (saw horses), a larger version of the tables the peasants had in their huts. The tables were easily dismantled after the meal, so that the inhabitants of the castle could sleep on straw mats placed on the floor. When William the Conqueror arrived in England, his men put together a motte and bailey castle in one day using precut timbers that he had brought over from Normandy. The sections were fitted together and held with wooden pegs. It was one of the three prefabricated castles which were reassembled near Hastings to serve as his headquarters and as places to which his men could retreat from a battle if the need arose.

Once William became king, similar castles were built throughout England to protect the Norman nobles from their English subjects. Any houses standing on the site chosen for a castle were demolished. (In the town of Lincoln 166 English dwellings were torn down for this purpose, further increasing the native hatred for the Norman intruders.) But wood was highly

The White Tower of London

flammable and an entire castle could easily be destroyed by one flaming arrow. Furthermore, the damp English climate caused the wood to rot. So the Normans began making castles of stone. (Stone castles had existed in France since the ninth century.) Gradually, the old wooden palisades were replaced by thick stone walls which surrounded a square stone keep. The White Tower that stands at the heart of the Tower of London (the name for the entire castle) was one of the first stone keeps in England. It was designed by William the Conqueror and contains some stones that were brought over from Normandy.

By the twelfth century there were thousands of massive stone fortresses throughout Europe. In Germany alone, over ten thousand were constructed during the Middle Ages. Six thousand were built in France, of which six hundred remain (at least, in part). A lord's castle became the symbol of his independence and his power to protect and defend his vassals.

The drawbridge leading to the raised portcullis

holes" cut in the ceiling of the gatehouse passageway between the two portcullises enable the defenders of the castle to shoot arrows and pour boiling liquids down on their enemies.

The crenellated wall of a castle

A TYPICAL STONE CASTLE OF THE MIDDLE PERIOD

Over the centuries the design of stone castles slowly changed. Let's look more closely at a typical castle of the late twelfth century. It is encircled by a moat which is crossed by a drawbridge that can be raised or lowered at a moment's notice. The drawbridge leads to a gatehouse. It has a heavy door of oak covered with iron grating hung on chains, which slides up and down vertical grooves in the gatehouse walls. This is called the portcullis (from a French term meaning "sliding door"). At the bottom of the portcullis is a row of metal points. The door is controlled by a winch, a pulley-like mechanism. Many castles of this period have two portcullises, one on either side of the gatehouse. If an enemy advances through the first one, both doors can be dropped, trapping him between them. "Murder

A tall stone wall (called the curtain) surrounds the castle itself. The surface of the wall consists of smooth cut stones; the core contains rubble and mortar. Along the inside edge of the wall is a sentry walk, and the top is crenelated (it has a toothy appearance). A crenel is a gap in the wall where a soldier can stand and shoot an arrow or throw stones, while a merlon is a solid part of the wall behind which he can duck for cover. Wooden platforms called hoards project outwards

Square towers of an early castle

just below the sentry walk. Holes cut into the floors of the hoards enable soldiers to dump hot water, liquid tar, or molten metal on their enemies. The inner ward (the old bailey) includes the barracks for the knights, stables, quarters for grooms, kennels, crafts shops for the armorer, smith, and carpenter, a garden, and a well. It is a bustling center of activity.

Norman keep

The heart of the castle is the square keep, which has towers (square ones) at each corner. The ground floor is used to store food and weapons. It also has a dungeon for holding prisoners. The first floor contains the Great Hall. As in earlier times, a dais is raised a step or two above the main floor and bears the table of the lord and his family; and, as before, trestle tables and benches are set up at right angles to it during meals. Wood paneling covers the walls of the Great Hall, and it is decorated with shields and lances as well as deer antlers and boars' heads.

Above are rafters of dark solid oak. The floor is flagged with large stones and strewn with rushes and sweet-smelling herbs, such as basil, lavender, mint, and fennel. Although fragrant and pleasant when fresh, the floor covering is quickly fouled by bits of food and dog droppings. The windows are small, and the thickness of the walls allows very little light to penetrate the interior. They have no glass (it is extremely expensive), and when the shutters are closed on a cold day the room becomes very dark. The only artificial lighting is provided by tallow (animal fat) candles and oil lamps. A fireplace lined with tiles is built into one of the walls, and the smoke escapes through slanting vents which lead to holes in the outer wall. Each night a cover (the couvre feu which is French for "fire cover") is put over the hearth to reduce the fire hazard.

Medieval kitchen fireplace

Beside the great hall is the chapel (services are held daily for the lord and his family). The third level of the keep is the lord's living quarters. The latrine can be reached at the end of a corridor on the second floor. It consists of a stone seat placed above a drainage shaft that leads to a hole in the ground. Bits of hay are used as toilet paper! The latrine is also known as a guardrobe (clothes closet), because winter clothing is hung there during the summer. Why? Because the draft that is constantly blowing up the drainage shaft (as well as the unpleasant smell) seems to keep the moths away from the wool! Sometimes a latrine shaft leads to an outside castle wall, perhaps draining into the moat. This can be dangerous. In the Chateau Gaillard in France an attacker once climbed up the latrine shaft and entered the castle unobserved!

The kitchen is located in a building next to the keep. It is a large room with big ovens for baking bread and huge open fireplaces where whole deer or sheep are hung on spits and turned before the fire. Large copper cauldrons are suspended by chains just above the fire. Along one wall are long tables for the preparation of food. Just outside the kitchen door are an herb garden, a vegetable garden, and fruit trees. Water is brought in from the well dug just within the castle walls.

LATER CASTLES

Many of the knights who fought in the First Crusade (we'll learn about this in the next chapter) remained in the Holy Land and built huge castles, using the technology of the Greeks and Turks. These became models for the castles that were built in Europe in the years that followed. By the thirteenth century towers were placed at intervals along the curtain wall and at the corners. Archers could fire from arrow slits cut into them down at the enemy without being seen.

The old square towers of the earlier castles had many disadvantages. A corner could be easily undermined (an enemy could dig under it to make it collapse), and defenders could only see in one direction (there was a blind spot at the corners, where enemy soldiers could lurk unobserved). Round towers did not have these

Castle drawbridge being lowered and portcullis raised to admit returning knight

disadvantages, and they also deflected missiles more effectively. So little by little the square towers were replaced by round ones. (For a short time the builders experimented; some constructed castles that were circular on the outside and square on the inside.)

The towers that strengthened the curtain wall contained staircases that spiraled counterclockwise. These were designed so that an enemy climbing up and carrying a shield in his

A castle with round towers

Belvoir Castle is a concentric castle

left hand could not easily see who was around the corner just above. The defending soldier carried his sword in the hand away from the inner wall, and this gave him greater mobility. By this time the hoards were built of stone and were an integral part of the wall. They were called machicolations. A small building called a barbican was built in front of the gatehouse to prevent an enemy from rushing at the entrance.

The interior of the castle was more comfortable than in earlier times. Fireplaces now had chimneys, and the hearth was often large enough to burn an entire tree trunk. Tapestries and silk wall hangings decorated the walls and cut down on the drafts. (We'll learn more about these eastern luxuries in the next chapter.) Most of the windows contained greenish glass. There was a large tank on the upper level, and pipes conducted water to the floors below. Sometimes a large wooden tub was filled in the living quarters and placed next the fire so that the lord and his family could bathe in winter. (In the summer, it was more pleasant to get clean by taking a dip in the local pond!)

By the end of the thirteenth century concentric castles were being built in France, England, and Wales. A concentric castle had one set of walls inside another, making an inner and an outer ward. Each wall contained living spaces in its towers, so there was no need of a separate keep. It was like having two castles in one. The walls were up to twenty feet thick. The inner wall was higher than the outer one so that the castle defenders on the inner wall could shoot over the heads of those on the outer one.

THE CASTLE IS ATTACKED

A castle was built for defense and could withstand a siege of many months. Every castle had a well to supply drinking needs as well as stockpiles of wheat, ale, and salted meat. And, of course, there were gardens and farm animals in the inner ward. A lord was not officially defeated until his flag had fallen from the main tower of his castle. (Capture the Flag is a modern game derived from that medieval tradition.)

Replica of a battering ram

When a lord planned an attack upon someone's castle, he hired professional siege engineers to help him. In fact, the term engineer originally referred to someone who could construct and man siege machines (he needed to be a carpenter and a soldier at the same time). Many devices were used to attack a castle. Most of them had been used centuries earlier by the Greeks and Romans, but they had been forgotten and weren't rediscovered until about the eleventh century. Medieval engineers then improved upon the ancient technology.

The battering ram was a heavy beam of wood with an iron point at one end (which was often molded in the shape of a ram's head). It was slung from the roof of a long shed-like structure that was covered with ox hides to make it relatively fireproof (the castle defenders would often hurl hot pitch at the shed hoping to set it ablaze). The shed was pushed to the edge of a castle moat on wheels or rollers; once a section of the ditch had been filled with earth, tree trunks, and stones, the shed was rolled over it and positioned against the castle wall. Protected from the objects and arrows fired from above by the roof of the shed, teams of soldiers swung the ram repeatedly against a wall or a gate until it finally caved in.

A siege tower was a huge structure, also built on wheels, that was as tall as the castle wall. It was covered with ox hides and could be pushed across a dam of earth and rock placed in the moat. Once the tower was in position, a drawbridge opened onto the top of the wall and the attacking soldiers came out with their swords drawn.

Siege weapons included a wooden catapult, called a trebuchet. It looked like a giant slingshot. Its wooden framework supported a long beam with a sling (made of twisted animal sinews) on the long end and a heavy weight on the short end. To fire the catapult, a soldier would pull down the sling (which had been armed with a boulder) against the weight, then suddenly release it. The weight would crash down, and the sling would fling the boulder with tremendous force. Later, winches were used to wind down the long end of the beam. Besides boulders, barrels of boiling tar and buckets of burning oil-soaked rags (a primitive fire bomb) could be hurled by the trebuchet. Sometimes dead horses were shot into the castle, so that their decaying bodies would make the defenders ill. The mangonel was a smaller catapult whose power came from the tension produced by tightly twisted ropes. It was used for hurling stones or bolts of red-hot iron over walls. An even smaller catapult was the ballista. It was a giant crossbow mounted on a stand, and it could fire rocks a considerable distance.

An enemy army often placed scaling ladders against the castle wall and soldiers tried to climb to the top before they were knocked off by missiles hurled from above. Defenders could respond to the assault by throwing down scaling forks, which were huge hooks that could drag a soldier off a ladder.

Model of a trebuchet

A basic procedure used by many attacking armies has already been alluded to. This involved digging a tunnel under a wall, removing the foundation stones, and then supporting the tunnel with timber beams. (Think about how a modern coal mine is constructed.) When the tunnel was complete, it was filled with straw and brush and then set afire. When the beams collapsed, the stone wall often collapsed on top of it.

A siege could be a long, drawn out affair. Sometimes it might seem as though it would never end. Sometimes it never did, and the besiegers had to pack up and go home. A long siege was a real problem for the attacking lord, since his vassals were only obligated to serve in his army for forty days a year. If an army managed to get inside a castle (by the late Middle Ages this was very difficult to do), they usually vented their pent up anger and frustration by killing everyone in sight.

QUESTIONS

1. What problems did the feudal system solve?

2. What were the obligations of the lord to his vassals?

3. What were the obligations of a vassal to his lord?

4. What was scutage?

5. Describe a typical peasant's hut.

6. What was the three-field system?

7. Why were the millers so unpopular?

8. What was a motte?

9. What were the weaknesses of a square tower?

10. What was a concentric castle?

11. What was a trebuchet?

12. How did many besieging armies try to weaken a castle's defenses?

FURTHER THOUGHTS

1. Cadbury Castle in England was occupied from 470 until 500. Many people think that it belonged to the legendary King Arthur. It had a wooden hall built on four level banks, which rose like concentric rings, one on top of the other. The top bank was surrounded by a stone and wooden wall. Little remains of it today.

2. A well was essential to the survival of the occupants of a castle under siege. But there is a story of one castle whose well went dry after a very long siege. So the defenders resorted to using wine in place of water. They made bread with it, boiled their food in it, and even used it to douse fires started by torches and burning missiles that had been thrown over walls. But once the wine was used up, the castle had to surrender.

A restored castle overlooks the Rhine River

3. Some castles were built at mountain passes and along rivers, where they collected tolls from those passing by. Many castles constructed along the Rhine River were built for this purpose. Their German owners became immensely rich with the growth of trade!

4. In 1446 Lord Cormac McCarthy completed his castle in Ireland at Blarney, near Cork. Set into its walls is a limestone rock. According to legend the stone can confer the gift of speech (blarney) on all who kiss it. In about 1600 the castle's owner (another Cormac McCarthy) used his "gift" by making numerous convincing excuses to delay surrendering the castle to an English army. Today, tourists in Ireland go out of their way to kiss the famous Blarney Stone.

5. Serfs did have some fun. When the field work was done, they played soccer, using the inflated bladder of a pig!

PROJECTS

1. When a serf died, his eldest son gave his best animal to the lord. This gift was called a heriot. It had to be paid before the son could take over his father's strips of land. James Herriot is the pen name of a well known English author who writes about animals. Do you think he chose his name from the medieval term? Find out the names of Herriot's books. (They're well worth reading!)

2. A feudal system also existed in Japan during the Middle Ages. Find out more about it. Then write a short report, comparing and contrasting European and Japanese feudalism.

3. Read *Castle* by David Macaulay (or see the video).

4. Make a castle of out of cardboard. Use the rolls from paper towels for the towers.

5. Draw a diagram of a twelfth or thirteenth century castle. Consult the books in your classroom for ideas.

6. Read *The Castle in the Attic* by Elizabeth Winthrop. Make an oral report to your class

CHAPTER 7

KNIGHTHOOD

The waves of barbarians who first crossed the Roman borders fought on foot. In later years, after the Goths, Franks, and other tribes had settled in western Europe, they were often hard put to hold their own against such mounted warriors as the Huns and the Arabs. So they adopted their enemies' greatest weapon: the horse. Charles Martel was the first Frankish leader to include armed horsemen in his army, and, as we have learned, Charlemagne used his paladins (knights) to form the model medieval fighting force. Armored knights soon became the major soldiers of the Middle Ages. Indeed, a mass of mounted warriors charging across a field at a full gallop must have been a frightening sight! Otto owed his victory over the Magyars to an army made up entirely of knights.

MEN OF ACTION

As we've seen, the feudal system required a lord to appear on the battlefield with a group of fighting men (his own vassals) whenever summoned by the king. These knights formed a new class of warriors who devoted their lives to training for battle. As lesser tenants, many could afford to be single-minded, since their manors were run by bailiffs and worked by serfs. But because land was passed on to the eldest son, a younger brother had no property and had to make a choice between two options: He could join the clergy or become a knight errant, a wandering fighter who made his living by offering his services to whomever required them.

The average knight was less than 5' 6" tall. He was in his twenties (his life expectancy was about thirty-five, if he was lucky in battle). He was, of course, in good physical condition and highly skilled in hunting and the art of warfare. But the image many people have today of a gallant knight in shining armor who seeks out and destroys evil and injustice (and dragons!) is far from reality. The earliest knights were, in fact, brutal and savage warriors who showed their opponents no mercy. In later years, as we shall see, knights did become somewhat courteous, but only toward members of their own class.

A KNIGHT'S ARMOR

The barbarians wore armor made of leather or cloth that was thickly padded and quilted. The soldiers in Charlemagne's army wore leather tunics reinforced by heavy, overlapping iron plates (scale armor). By the eleventh century, Norman knights wore vests made of many small, interlinking rings (chain mail). This type of armor could be traced back to their Viking ancestors. The fashion soon spread throughout Europe, the vest evolving into a knee-length tunic (called a hauberk) made of as many as 30,000 iron rings and weighing as much as thirty pounds. Each ring had four others linked through it. A hauberk was flexible and easy to put on. More importantly,

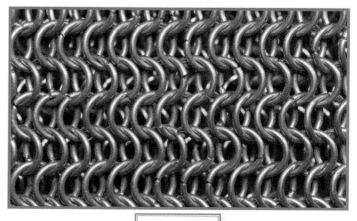

Chain mail

it offered excellent protection against the point of a spear or sword. The metal rings were often painted with varnish to prevent rusting. They could be cleaned by placing them in a leather sack with mixture of sand and vinegar and tossing the sack vigorously.

A hauberk was worn over a quilted or leather garment called a gambeson, which kept the metal from chafing the wearer's skin and prevented a certain amount of bruising. A knight also wore a hood of mail and a conical helmet of leather or metal, which was padded to absorb the blows of an enemy's weapon (like a modern crash helmet). Because a hauberk and helmet were rather expensive, they were passed down from father to son. They were often removed from dead bodies on the battlefield for reuse by other knights.

Man modeling a hauberk and hood of chain main over a helmet

And yet, chain mail had its disadvantages. If a knight received a hard blow from a hammer or axe, the armor might tear his flesh, making

rough, jagged wounds that were hard to heal. So for further protection armorers of the thirteenth century designed plates of steel which were attached to the mail at such vulnerable parts of the body as the shoulders, elbows, thighs, and knees. A knight of this period wore a heavy metal helmet that might weigh as much as twenty-five pounds. Since it covered much of his face, it was hard for him to hear, speak or even see while he was wearing it. (This explains why a knight put on his helmet at the last possible moment!) Sometimes a helmet was adorned with a crest in the shape of an animal or weapon. This was made of wood or leather that had been boiled a long time so that it could be molded.

Knight wearing mail and plate armor

By the fifteenth century knights wore entire suits of armor made of overlapping steel plates connected with iron rivets. This armor was so strong that scarcely any weapon could pierce it, but it was incredibly heavy (it weighed from forty to sixty pounds). Hinges enabled the knight to move his arms and legs, but these had to be oiled frequently. The knight's head was now protected by a steel helmet with a visor that could be pulled down over his face; small slits enabled him to see (sort of) and breathe. He still wore a shirt of mail underneath the plate armor to protect any exposed areas, like armpits, elbows, and other joints. Assisted by his squire, he had to spend about an hour putting on his equipment.

Each suit of armor was molded for an individual knight by a team of craftsmen. A hammerer shaped the metal places, another fitted the rivets and hinges, another engraved the plates. The best armor was made in Germany and northern Italy (Milan), and it was in great demand throughout Europe. Certain armor makers signed their works (an early example of "name brands"). Ironically, the finest examples were made in the sixteenth century, when knighthood was on the wane.

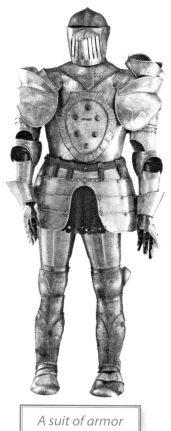

A suit of armor

Plate armor was heavy, hot, and uncomfortable. If a knight was unhorsed, he was about as agile as a turtle on his back. An enemy could easily pin him down with one foot, lift his visor, and stab him in the face. However, in the later Middle Ages, more knights died from heat stroke or suffocation due to the weight of their own armor than were killed in battle.

A KNIGHT'S WEAPONS

Back in the tenth century, a knight's main weapon was his steel sword, which he wore in a scabbard (holder) on his left side. The sword was double edged, and it was designed for cutting and slashing, not thrusting. It was about thirty-two inches long, weighed two pounds, and might be elaborately engraved. The best blades were made in Toledo, Spain. The sword's handle was often covered with soft velvet or satin, which was held in place by leather strips. The handle might contain a sacred relic (a bit of hair or clothing of a saint). A transverse bar below the handle gave the sword the shape of the cross. A dying knight would lift his sword to his eyes so that the cross would be his last worldly vision. The sword was a knight's most prized possession. It symbolized his high rank in medieval society and was proudly passed on from father to son.

Apart from his sword, a knight was armed with a dagger, which he carried on his right side and used to deliver the death blow to a fallen enemy. Other weapons designed for battle included the battle axe, the war hammer, and the mace (a wooden club with a metal head). A particularly gruesome instrument was the war flail (also known as the morningstar). It consisted of

A knight's sword

Knight swordsmen

A morningstar

a wooden ball studded with metal spikes, and attached to a wooden handle by a chain. Its function was to bludgeon an opponent.

Since Church lands were part of the feudal system, even bishops were expected to supply soldiers in times of war, and some clergy actually took part in the fighting. Because the Church forbade the spilling of blood, these warriors did not carry swords and daggers. However, they felt free to batter their enemies with maces and flails. Observers of the time revealed their sense of humor by referring to the mace as "a holy water sprinkler!"

Medical practices during the Middle Ages were generally quite primitive. If a knight was injured in battle, his wound was seared

A mace

with a hot iron to stop the bleeding, but he would probably die from blood poisoning. If the wound was particularly bad, he would call upon his fellow knights to slit his throat.

THE KNIGHT'S HORSE

A war horse was called a destrier. The name comes from the Latin dexter meaning «right hand"; just like today, a horse was always led by a person's right hand. A destrier was bred for strength, stamina, and courage. He was trained to charge fearlessly into battle, guided only by the pressure of his rider's knees. (Remember, a knight's hands were occupied holding his sword and shield.) Needless to say, a destrier was very expensive. During the early Middle Ages a good horse cost the equivalent of six cows.

Mounted knights could never have been an effective force were it not for two important inventions: the horseshoe and the stirrup. Primitive horseshoes had been used by the Romans (they were called horse sandals and were easily removable), but medieval smiths devised practical pieces of iron that could be hammered directly to the bottom of the hoof (which is like a fingernail so the horse experienced no pain). It could be replaced as the hoof grew. The horseshoe

Knights and horses in plate armor

made it possible for the animal to bear heavy weights and to travel over rough terrain without splitting its hooves (which would make it lame).

Modern man and horse in medieval armor

The stirrup was probably invented in China in the fifth century. The first European soldiers to use it were members of Charles Martel's army (the Frankish leader learned about the device from the Arabs he battled at Tours). Stirrups enabled a rider to brace himself and maintain his balance in the saddle; with his feet in the stirrups he could not be easily knocked off his horse by the impact of a sword or spear.

The stirrups were attached to a wooden saddle with a high front and back designed to keep the knight upright. It somewhat resembles a western saddle, which is actually a modern version of the saddles brought to America by the Spanish conquistadors in the sixteenth century. Horses often wore flowing robes called caparisons bearing the knight's colors or coat of arms (more about that later). In the fifteenth century, when suits of plate armor were commonly used by knights, the destrier was also protected by leather or metal plates. Imagine how heavy the combined weight of mounted knight and horse armor must have been! This explains why the horses of this period were very powerfully built, resembling modern draft horses like Clydesdales. And they no longer galloped into battle; they trotted. The knight must have had an uncomfortable ride!

A modern draft horse

Usually a knight owned three horses. Two of them (called hacks) were for everyday riding. The third was his destrier. Of course, horses were trained for other uses during the Middle

Ages. Some horses were trained for jousting in tournaments; they were called coursers. A palfrey was a horse used for hunting and traveling. A jennet was a small spirited horse ridden by a lady (the side saddle was invented to accommodate her long dress in the fourteenth century). And don't forget the hardworking horses that pulled a farmer's plow.

HERALDRY

In the next chapter we will learn about the Crusades. For now, we need only know that the European knights who fought in the Holy Land were subjected to very hot weather conditions. To decrease the terrible discomfort of burning hot armor, a knight would wear a surcoat (a long sleeveless tunic) over his hauberk and a mantling (cloth) over his helmet. The surcoat eventually became a standard part of a knight's attire, and it was often embroidered with a distinctive mark or device referring to his family and position. The tunic came to be known as the knight's coat of arms. In later years, when a knight in plate armor

Knight wearing his coat of arms

was not easily recognizable, he had his personal symbol painted on his shield.

The earliest shield designs were arrangements of straight lines (crosses, zigzags, and so forth). Then animals (mythical and real) were added, each one symbolizing a particular character trait. For example, a lion stood for power and courage; a boar symbolized ferocity, as would a dragon and a griffin (half eagle, half dragon); a unicorn (a white horse with a horn on its forehead) suggested purity and innocence. Sometimes an object was depicted because its name sounded something like the family name. For example, Sir Roger de Trumpinton had a trumpet on his shield, for obvious reasons! The device of Sir Robert de Setvans included seven fans (sept fans in French, which sounds a lot like his family name). Depictions of animals or objects that echo a name in this manner were called canting arms.

Medieval shields

Eventually the nobles had paintings made that included the shield, helmet, mantling, and crest worn by the knights in their families, as well as their war cry. The shield was supported by two animals, real or mythical. This became known as the family coat of arms (although the coat no longer existed). The oldest surviving example appears in an enamel funeral portrait of Count Geoffrey of Anjou, the father of Henry Plantagenet. Geoffrey himself is depicted, holding a shield decorated with golden lions. It is now in a museum in Le Mans, France.

A coat of arms with quartered shield

A coat of arms was, of course, hereditary. As the symbols became increasingly elaborate, officials known as heralds regulated the designs and kept track of them. Only certain colors and designs could be used, and copying someone else's family crest was forbidden. By the fourteenth century it became customary for a woman of particularly high birth who married to join her family symbols with those of her husband. This led to a configuration known as quartering in which the shield was divided into four sections (two were his and two were hers).

Today coats of arms are no longer limited to the families of European aristocrats. You will often see them displayed as the symbol of a country, school, or even a manufacturing company.

Coat of arms of the city of London

PREPARATION FOR KNIGHTHOOD

During medieval times, a boy of noble birth had to pass through many years of training before he could become a knight. At the age of seven, he was sent to live at the castle of a lord, usually a friend of his family. Every important noble had several young lads living in his household for this purpose. They served as pages and received much of their training from the ladies of the castle. The pages learned to sing and dance, to compose music and play a harp, and to behave in a polite manner (a page was supposed to stand as still as a stone and bow his head when answering). They delivered messages, set the table, lit the evening candles, and learned the stories of famous knights and heroes of the past.

An important part of a page's training, of course, involved the fundamentals of warfare. He learned to ride a horse and to use a spear, sword, and lance. A popular training activity was called tilting at the quintain. The quintain was a wooden figure of a knight holding a shield in one hand and a club in the other; it was attached to a large willow post on a pivot so that it would swing around when any part except the shield was hit. The page galloped up to the quintain and tried to strike the dummy's shield with his lance (a long wooden pole with a metal point at the end). If he missed his target and struck the dummy instead, it would whirl around and strike him with its club—much to the amusement of the other pages!

A modern model of a quintain

Upon completing his years as a page, a young man became a squire to a knight. He wore silver spurs as a sign of his new status. He polished and oiled the knight's armor, helped care for his horses, waited upon him at meal time, helped him dress and undress, and made his bed. Each night he took the knight a glass of spiced wine and then lay down across the threshold of his bedchamber, so that he could defend the knight from any nocturnal attack. A squire rode with his knight to the site of a battle, carrying his sword, lance and shield. In fact, the word squire comes from the French ecuyer meaning "shield bearer." If the knight was wounded, his squire cared for him; if he fell off his horse, his faithful servant helped him on again. But most of the squire's time was devoted to the mastery of horsemanship and the use of weapons.

At the age of twenty, the squire was ready for knighthood. In the later years of the Middle Ages, this milestone was marked by an elaborate ceremony. Things had certainly changed from earlier times when a Germanic warrior was simply given his weapons to mark his entry into manhood! The night before the ceremony, the squire took a bath to cleanse himself of the blemishes of his past. He shaved his beard or cut his hair short as a sign that he would honor God. Then he lay down for a moment upon a bed to signify the rest God grants to his special servants (namely, the brave knights). Afterwards, he put on a white tunic, signifying that he was pure in spirit; over the tunic he wore a scarlet robe, to indicate that he was willing to shed blood in battle; finally he put on black stockings, black shoes, and a black coat, whose somber shades showed that he was not afraid to die.

He skipped supper and spent the night alone in a dark church, where the only light was a small lamp. He knelt in prayer before the high altar on which he had placed his weapons and armor thereby consecrating them to God's cause. Remaining in that awkward position for hours and hours (he was not allowed to sit or lie down) was certainly a rigorous test of self-discipline! At daybreak he partook of the Holy Sacrament (Communion) and was instructed by a priest in the duties of a true knight. Then he took the solemn vows of chivalry, promising to be brave and honorable, to maintain what is right, to redress wrong, to protect women, to give help to those in trouble, and to show mercy to the weak and defenseless. These were certainly fine goals, even if they were seldom achieved.

Later in the morning the young knight-to-be went to the castle courtyard. It was a festive atmosphere, with music playing and flags flying. Here the dubbing ceremony took place: The lord of the castle presented his protegé with his shield, belted on his sword, and buckled on his golden spurs (always the right foot first). Ever since those early times, winning one's spurs has meant to achieve something important. Having received his arms, the squire fell upon his knees before his lord, who, striking him lightly on the shoulder with the flat of his sword, uttered these words: "In the name of God, St Michael, and St George, I dub thee knight. Be loyal, brave, and true." This procedure was known as the accolade. (In the early Middle Ages, a squire was simply given a brisk, open-handed blow to his neck, followed by the warning to conduct himself with bravery, loyalty, and skill; the slap on the neck was supposedly the last blow he'd receive without taking revenge.) Once formally dubbed, the new knight was given the title of Sir.

A well groomed steed awaited him, its bridle ornamented with silver, gold, and jewels. He swiftly mounted the horse and charged across the field, tilting with his lance at a straw-stuffed dummy (the symbol of his future opponents). It was a glorious day.

Sometimes a squire became a knight without the many ceremonies just described. If, for example, there is a great need for more warriors during the heat of battle, a squire might be called aside by the man he was serving and instructed, "Be thou a Knight." And he was one! On other occasions, a squire exhibiting particular bravery while serving his knight might be elevated to the highest rank on the field of battle. (As we will see, this happened to the Black Prince of England.) Being a knight was an expensive proposition, however, and it was open only to those who had enough land or money to pay for horses, equipment, and the various knightly duties. Many a squire remained in that subservient position for his entire lifetime.

If a knight broke his vows or was guilty of some grave crime, he was publicly disgraced. His shield was smeared with paint and hung upside down on a post. Then he was led forth and stripped of his armor, piece by piece, and his sword was broken over his head. After this terrible humiliation, he was laid in a coffin which was dragged to the church, where priests chanted a funeral service over him as if he were dead. (In many ways, he was.)

TOURNAMENTS

Knights practiced for battle or simply showed off their skill in mock battles called jousts. A series of jousts made up a tournament (just as today a tennis tournament consists of a series of matches). In the early Middle Ages, however, such a mock battle was little more than a free-for-all that took place on certain saints' days in a field near a castle. Two groups of mounted knights lined up behind ropes stretched across the opposite sides of the field. One group might have as many as one hundred knights. When the ropes were cut, the horses charged at a full gallop towards the opposing line of warriors. This event was called a melee (a very appropriate term which means "mixed up" in French). The knights clashed head on, and if someone was thrown from his horse, he fought on foot. Since there were no rules, a melee was an extremely dangerous and bloody event. The winners were

Two knights ready to joust

those who survived intact! In 1240 sixty knights were killed in a single melee in England; the following year eighty knights were lost in similar circumstances in Neuss, Germany. This was certainly not a very practical way for knights to train, and the Church violently opposed it.

By the twelfth century a system of elaborate rules were drawn up and practice combat became less deadly. In fact, as knights became less important on the battlefield (we will see how bowmen later played the critical role in a battle), tournaments became festive occasions organized by lords for their friends as a means of showing off their wealth. They lasted about a week and drew jugglers, musicians, and merchants as well as the local people.

A tournament took place within an oblong enclosure known as the lists. A special official called the steward of the field rolled and flattened the surface with a wooden roller and had any stones carried away. Then the ground was covered with a layer of sand, which would give the horses better traction. At the sound of trumpets, the knights who were the challengers entered at one end of the lists, and the champions who opposed them at the other. As was mentioned, an individual match between two opponents was called a joust. After the rules were read, the

trumpet sounded again and the first joust began. A pair of horsemen rode along the sides of a four-foot high fence, both armed in heavy armor specially designed for jousting. Each knight aimed an eight-foot lance (with a blunted end) across the neck of his horse toward his opponent. He received three points for knocking his opponent off his horse; two points for breaking his lance on his opponent's shoulder or helmet; and one point for hitting him above the waist. But he could also receive deductions for missing his target completely, wounding his opponent's horse, or hitting beneath the waist.

Reenactment of knights jousting

There were usually six or eight rounds in one joust. The winning knight got the horse and armor of the loser. An English baron named William Marshall won twelve horses (and suits of armor) in one tournament. Occasionally a loser was allowed to keep his possessions and pay a sum equivalent to their value. Some knights became professional jousters, traveling from tournament to tournament just as a modern professional golfer does. At each gate of the lists heralds were stationed to identify the coats of arms and to keep records of the results of the jousts. They drew in the appropriate designs of the victorious knights on the blank shields imprinted on long rolls of parchment.

The joust just described was called a jouste a plaisance ("friendly contest"). Most jousts were of this type. However, a joust a Voutrance ("fight to the death") was sometimes arranged to settle disputes. On such occasions the knights used real weapons rather than blunted lances. Outside the lists were the tents of the competing knights. On each tent was hung the shield of the occupant. A knight issued a challenge by riding up to a rival's shield and hitting it with his lance: If he hit it with the butt end of the lance, he wanted a jouste a plaisance; a blow with the pointed end meant that he wanted a jouste a l'outrance.

They loved to fight and were often bored unless they were on the battlefield, participating in a tournament, or hunting for wild game. The Church tried to limit their fighting by issuing decrees. In the eleventh century, for example, it issued the Peace of God to ban fighting in certain places (like churches!). Nearly two centuries later the Truce of God forbade fighting during Lent, on holy days, at harvest time, and from Wednesday evening until Monday morning of every week. That left just eighty days a year in which combat was sanctioned. The decrees were a good idea, but does it surprise you that they were frequently ignored?

Surrounding the lists were galleries set up for the occasion. They were covered with brightly colored carpets and tapestries, and there were soft cushions on the seats. These galleries were intended for the ladies and noblemen who had come to watch the tournament. (The seats to the rear were occupied by the squires.) Often there was a central seat in the gallery that resembled a throne with a canopy above it. Here sat the fairest of all the ladies, who had been chosen the Queen of Beauty and Love for the tournament. Anyone who was not a member of the nobility stood behind ropes that surrounded the lists to watch the jousts.

THE IDEALS OF CHIVALRY

Despite their high ideals, knights could be (and usually were) crude, rough, and cruel.

The code of chivalry arose in the twelfth century, largely in response to the coarse behavior of the knights. The word chivalry comes from the French word chevalier (meaning "horseman"). Until this time, knights had sworn an oath to honor and defend their lords, but they gave little heed to aiding the helpless, fighting injustice, or even acting civilized. But, as we shall see in the next chapter, the European nobles were greatly influenced by the more refined Muslims they encountered in Asia during the Crusades. This led them to incorporate into their oaths of loyalty many loftier ideals. Although few knights lived up to code, at least they gave it some thought, and it became the source of the western concept of good manners. Chivalrous behavior in medieval times, however, was basically restricted to members of the upper class. Serfs and other laborers had good reason to fear the approach of a hungry or bored knight.

THE TROUBADOURS

The process of civilizing the European knights was greatly enhanced by a literary movement that flourished in France in the twelfth and thirteenth centuries. It all started in southern France (called Provence). In those times the culture of Provence was different than that of the northern section. Its people spoke a language that has nearly disappeared. It is known as the Langue d'Oc (the language of the south), as opposed to the Langue d'Oil (the language of the north, which evolved into modern French). Provence was a sunny land with rich soil, warm temperatures, and lots of beautiful flowers. It had been spared the attacks of the Vikings, and life was less stressful than in the north.

A troubadour

Aquitaine was a major region in Provence that had retained much of the Roman culture of earlier times, particularly in areas of literature and art. As you will recall, it was the birthplace of

Eleanor, wife of Henry II. Eleanor's grandfather, William IX (Duke of Aquitaine), had gathered many poets about him in his court. They were known as the troubadours, and they wrote music and verses about knights who performed heroic deeds—not for power or prestige but simply to win the love of a beautiful lady. The word troubadour means "found or invented songs." The poets (who were always noblemen) hired minstrels to sing their creations at court and at tournaments to the accompaniment of a lute. Even William composed a number of ballads, and his are the oldest troubadour works to have survived. When Eleanor married Henry she took a group of troubadours to England.

The northern version of the troubadour was the trouvere. He was less aristocratic than his southern counterpart, and his poems dealt with the more traditional themes of courage and valor on the battlefield. The epic poems of the trouveres, called chansons de geste, were based upon the deeds of Charlemagne, his court, and his successors. The most famous example is *The Song of Roland*. It was the first great epic in French literature. As we learned in Chapter III, the rearguard of Charlemagne's army was ambushed by local Christians (Basques) in 776 when the king was returning from Spain to Francia. This occurred at the Pass at Roncesvalles in the Pyrenees. A member of the rearguard was a duke named Roland. He did not play a very important part in the ambush, but as the story was told by future generations, the details changed significantly. Roland became the most important knight in his unit, and the Christian Basques were transformed into Muslims. The resulting epic was a romantic episode in which a Christian force struggled against the infidels (and eventually triumphed). As for Roland, he became the model of the ideal European knight: He was brave, honest, and proud (so proud, in fact, that he wouldn't summon aid until it was too late to save himself!). His Spanish counterpart was El Cid.

Marie, Countess of Champagne, was the eldest daughter of Eleanor of Aquitaine and King Louis VII of France. She, too, patronized poets in her court, particularly a trouvere named Chretien de Troyes, who composed romans (legends) in verse. Chretien brought the story of King Arthur and his knights to France. As we have learned, the figure of Arthur was derived from a sixth century Briton chieftain. His legend grew and evolved over the centuries to the point where he would have been unrecognizable to his own warriors. Arthur was now portrayed as a skilled and refined medieval king, who, with the aid of his famous knights of the Round Table, spent much of his time fighting dragons and rescuing damsels in distress. The stories were first written down in England by Geoffrey of Monmouth. Chretien de Troyes introduced new themes, such as the love of Sir Lancelot for Arthur's wife, Queen Guinevere. He invented Camelot, Arthur's castle, and his knights' code of honor based upon generosity, loyalty, and dedication to God and the Church. He also added the theme of the quest of the Holy Grail which pervades much of the epic. The grail was the chalice used at the Last Supper in which Joseph of Arimathea later caught the blood of Christ dripping from the cross. According to the poet, the grail had the magical ability to supply food and drink when it was held by human hands. It was also a source of healing, so it had a spiritual dimension. Only a pure knight could hope to find the grail. In the fifteenth century, Sir Thomas Mallory would offer yet another version of the legends of Arthur in his work, *The Death of Arthur*.

A modern Queen Guinevere

Although the greatest literature of this period was produced by the French, there were also German bards called minnesingers who composed love poems (minne means "love" in old German) and Italian poets called trovatori.

They composed their works in the languages of their native countries.

THE COURT OF LOVE

Let's return to Marie of Champagne. The poets she gathered at her court went beyond the code of chivalry by formulating a new code of love. *De amore* (About Love) by Andreas Capellanus is a book written at the time which answers a series of questions about love. For example, in response to the query, "Does true love have any place in marriage?" the answer is an unequivocal "No!" The reasoning offered is that marriage is an arranged relationship with a contract and a list of duties, and this leaves no room for romantic love.

In fact, the ideal love of this period was that which a knight had for an older woman who was married to someone else! The fact that she was unavailable made him dream of her all the more, and he would spend hours thinking of ways that he could get her to smile at him! In this way, flirtation became a part of chivalry, and love was viewed as a diversion, a pastime, and an art (like swordsmanship!).

Marie even established a private "court of love" where judges (all ladies) decided whether a knight was treating his beloved well enough. According to the new way of thinking, women (the ladies) were the overlords of men (the knights), whose main purpose in life was to amuse them. This led to a a new form of homage: A knight knelt before lady, his two hands joined between hers, and swore to defend her and to serve her faithfully. If she accepted him, she put a ring on his finger, kissed him, and raised him to his feet. She then gave him a trifle—a sleeve from her dress, a ribbon, or a kerchief—which he would wear on his arm as proof that he was first in her affections. She might even ask him to play chess or backgammon after supper. A lady collected as many suitors as she could, sometimes stealing them from her rivals. It was better for a knight to be the second among the suitors of a popular beauty than the first choice of someone considered unattractive or unfavorable in society. But if a knight tried to kiss his special lady, she would probably scream. She might even have him executed!

It wasn't hard for this new cult of love to go from the sublime to the ridiculous. Knights made personal sacrifices, such as keeping their hair extremely short (a crewcut was definitely out of style in those days), refusing to eat, or wearing a patch over one eye until he had performed a deed of bravery that was applauded by his lady. A knight once fought in a tournament wearing the dress of his beloved! He didn't survive. The most common penalties for a knight whose behavior was deemed unchivalrous were to write a love song on the spot or to be pelted by the ladies of the court with roses!

The most famous love poem of the period was *The Romance of the Rose*, which was composed in the thirteenth century by Guillaume de Lords. The poet died before completing his work, so the last part was written forty years later by Jean de Meun. The main part of the poem is a somewhat tedious allegory in which Love strives to win his Lady. He is alternately encouraged and frustrated by such characters as Welcome, Shame, Reason, Danger, and Pity. De Meun's section of the poem is strikingly different, being a violent satire against love and women. French poetess Christine de Pisan later defended women against these attacks in her own poem, *Epistle to the Good of Love*.

The stories and poems of the troubadours and their successors, artificial and silly as some of them might have been, glorified many of the attributes we value today, including sensitivity, loyalty, and resourcefulness. Thanks to the poets and ladies of the aristocratic courts of France, the model knight was now well garbed (and bathed), witty, and capable of composing a song (and singing it) on the spot about his beloved. This was certainly an improvement over the rough and tumble warriors of earlier centuries!

ORDERS OF CHIVALRY

In the later Middle Ages exclusive clubs of knights were founded by kings. Their members took an oath to support each other in all kinds of circumstances. Each of these clubs, called an order, had its own elaborate robes, badges, and rules. The leader of an order was called the Grand Master. Meetings were called chapters. A chapter could act as a court of law and expel any knights who acted inappropriately.

The first order was established by Edward III of England in 1347. Called the Order of the Garter, it was made up of twenty-five of Edward's best knights, with himself as Grand Master. But why a garter? According to legend, Edward was once dancing with a lady when her garter worked loose and dropped to the floor. To cover her embarrassment, he gallantly picked it up and,

raising it high, uttered the words, Honi soit qui mal y pense (French for "shame on him who thinks evil thoughts about this"). Then he vowed to the lady that he would make her a garter the most honorable one ever worn. As we have just seen, it was common for knights to wear "favors" of their ladies in the form of ribbons, kerchiefs, and sleeves, so it was not too strange to found a new order of chivalry whose symbol was a lady's garter!

A lady's garter

King Jean of France founded the Order of the Star in 1351, Philip (the Good) of Burgundy established the Order of the Golden Fleece in 1430, and Louis XI of France created the Order of St. Michael in the fifteenth century. And there were many others, including the Spanish orders of Calatrava, Santiago, and Alcantara, all of whose members fought against the Moors. In the next chapter we'll learn about a different kind of knightly order.

QUESTIONS

1. What is a hauberk?
2. What were the advantages and disadvantages of plate armor?
3. What was a flail?
4. What two inventions dramatically improved the usefulness of a warhorse?
5. What was the use of a surcoat?

6. Why did a knight-to-be wear white, red, and black clothing for his dubbing?

7. What was a joust a plaisance?

8. Why did the code of chivalry arise?

9. What did the troubadours write about?

10. Who was Chretien de Troyes and why was he important?

11. Describe the two parts of THE ROMANCE OF THE ROSE.

12. What was the first order of knighthood established in England?

FURTHER THOUGHTS

1. A tremendous amount of labor was involved in the manufacture of chain mail. Here's how it was done. A smith worked on a piece of hot iron for hours over a fire, getting it soft. Then he drew it through a hole in a metal plate with pincers several times, each time through a smaller hole. The result was a long piece of wire, which he cut into lengths and then sold to an armorer. The armorer pounded the wire around a bar making rings, leaving a slight opening in each one. The rings were then beaten until they were flat. A hole was made on each end for a rivet. A special craftsman then joined the links together, riveting each one shut.

2. Jousting could be dangerous. In the sixteenth century King Henry II of France insisted upon participating in a joust during the festivities following his daughter's wedding. The spear of his opponent splintered, and the jagged end passed through Henry's visor, penetrating his brain. He suffered grievously for two days before he died.

3. During the Hundred Years War (see Chapter 14), a French squire named Regnault captured the English Earl of Suffolk. When the Earl realized that Regnault was not a knight, he quickly dubbed him. Why? Because only a knight could properly capture another knight!

4. As William the Conqueror rode towards Hastings, his minstrel accompanied him singing The Song of Roland to inspire his Norman knights.

5. *The Book of Chivalry* by Ramon Lull written in the thirteenth century offers his version of the origin and rationale of knighthood. The Book of Chivalry written by Geoffrey de Charney in the following century (1356) is a more down-to-earth work describing the practical aspects of knighthood.

6. The Order of the Garter still exists. To become a member is one of the greatest honors offered by English society. The chapter meetings take place every year at Windsor Castle.

7. Rodrigo Diaz, the hero of the Christian wars against the Moors in Spain, was depicted as the ideal knight in the medieval *Poeme del Cid* (see Chapter 5). However, although he was courageous and brave, and he did lead a dazzling campaign against the Moors, he was also a knave who stole, lied, and cheated. Nor was he generous. When he captured

Valencia he had the city's governor burned alive and many citizens massacred. According to legend, after he was killed in battle his body, armed and armored, was strapped upright on his white horse. This sight so terrified the Moorish army that they beat a hasty retreat!

PROJECTS

1. There were three basic types of plate armor: those designed for battle, tournament, and parade. Learn more about these three types of armor using the Internet. Then select one type. Draw a picture of a suit of this kind of armor, labeling the parts. Make an oral report to the class about this type of armor, using your drawing as an illustration.

2. Make your own coat of arms. There are many books available on heraldry. Choose one that presents all the rules about types of helmet, colors, and so forth. You can choose to be anyone you want: a nobleman, a king (or queen), or an untitled person.

3. In 1605 Spanish author Cervantes wrote a book about *Don Quixote*, an old knight who wanders across the countryside, charging at windmills that he mistakes for an enemy. Find a copy of the book and read the first few chapters. Did Cervantes admire or disdain the concept of knighthood? What makes you think so?

Statue of Don Quixote and his sidekick, Sancho Panza

4. A popular legend of the Middle Ages concerned St. George, who killed a dragon and rescued a princess. St. George seemed so much the ideal knight that in the fourteenth century he became England's patron saint. Read the story about his adventures, and then make a report to the class.

St George and the dragon

5. After being ignored for centuries, the culture of the Middle Ages was "rediscovered" by the English romantics of the nineteenth century. In 1839 the Earl of Eglington held a huge, festive reenactment of a medieval tournament, complete with pavilions, horses, and costumes. The poet Tennyson penned a memorable work about King Arthur entitled *The Idylls of the King*. Sir Walter Scott wrote a number of novels that take place during the Middle Ages. One of them (*Ivanhoe*) was made into a movie. Even though a bit dated, it is still fun to catch on a DVD.

6. Even today people are knighted in England. Find out more about this procedure. Then make a list of ten famous Englishmen who have been knighted in this century.

7.   According to the legends of King Arthur, only three knights ever saw the grail. Find out who they were.

8.   Legendary knights often gave names to their swords. Roland's sword was called Durandal. What was the name of Arthur's sword? Where did he get it? Report your findings to the class.

9.   Find out more about *The Song of Roland.* Then answer these questions. Who was Roland's best friend? Why wouldn't Roland blow his horn? What did Charlemagne do about the massacre at the mountain pass?

CHAPTER 8

THE CRUSADES

Palestine, the Holy Land of the Christians, lay at the center of the known medieval world. It was in that bleak desert land that Christ had been born (in Bethlehem), lived (in Nazareth) and died (in Jerusalem). Christians from all over the ancient world trekked for hundreds and even thousands of miles to visit the Holy Sepulcher in Jerusalem, the site of Christ's burial. As we have learned, the Arabic Muslims conquered Palestine in the seventh century (638). Since their religion recognized Jesus as one of the world's great prophets, they did not interfere with the Christian pilgrimages made to Jerusalem.

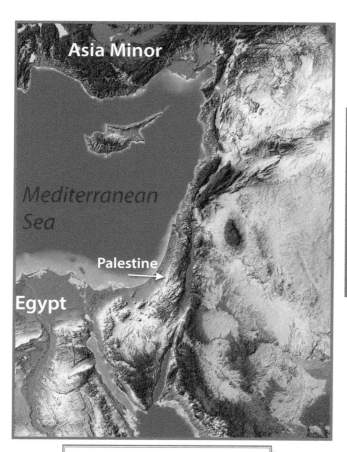

The bleak landscape of Palestine

THE POPE MAKES AN APPEAL

In the eleventh century (1076) Palestine was conquered by the Seljuk Turks, a warlike tribe from the steppes of Asia (Turkistan) that had adopted the Muslim faith. The Turks were far less tolerant than the Arabs. They treated the Christians harshly and prevented them from visiting the Holy Sepulcher. In fact, they killed many Christian pilgrims and captured others as slaves. The Turks conquered most of Asia Minor (modern Turkey) and posed a great threat to the city of Constantinople, which lay just across the narrow Dardanelles. The Byzantine people referred to these invaders as Sarakenos (a Greek word meaning "Easterners"), and they came to be known to most Europeans as the Saracens.

Region of Palestine near Bethleham

Alexius I, the ruler of the Byzantine Empire, was so worried about an invasion of Constantinople that he appealed to the western Church for aid. Pope Urban II enthusiastically took on the cause. The Church had been involved in earlier holy wars, such as those against the Moors in Spain so dramatically described in

The *Song of Roland and El Cid*. So in 1095 at the Council of Clermont in central France Urban made a dramatic speech that would affect Europe for the next two centuries. Dressed in white and standing on a cloth of gold, he addressed a crowd of 2000 priests, nobles, soldiers and peasants. He told them to stop warring among themselves and to join together in a Crusade to drive the infidels (nonbelievers) out of Jerusalem. France was already overcrowded, he continued, while Palestine, a vast land of "milk and honey," awaited them.

Urban guaranteed that the Church would protect the property and family of anyone willing to go on the Crusade. All debts and taxes were to be canceled, and criminals were to be pardoned. As a further incentive he promised an indulgence of everlasting absolution: The soul of anyone killed on the Holy War would go directly to heaven, all sins forgiven. The Pope also had personal motives. He hoped that in return for his help, the Orthodox Church of Constantinople would reunite with the Roman Catholic Church under his leadership (the two churches had split in 1054).

The response at Clermont was an enthusiastic. These words would become the soldiers' battle cry. Word quickly spread throughout France, and soon thousands were preparing to leave for the Holy Land. Calling themselves the soldiers of Christ, the knights wore a cross of red material stitched to their tunics. We know them as the Crusaders, a word derived from the Latin cruciata (meaning "marked with a cross"). Many responded to the call for religious purposes (they considered it their mission to liberate the Holy City), while younger sons of nobility saw a chance to increase their power, territory, and wealth. Merchants joined up to search for new markets. Peasants set out in hopes of escaping the long hours of hard labor in the fields of their manor, and others were simply drawn by the promise of adventure. There were to be many Crusades during the next two hundred years.

The Red Cross of the Crusader

THE PEOPLE'S CRUSADE

The movement did not get off to a very good start. A fanatical French monk called Peter the Hermit and a poor knight known as Walter the Penniless convinced hordes of peasants to set out on a People's Crusade, promising them that God would guide them to the Holy Land. Peter had previously attempted a pilgrimage to Jerusalem, but the Turks had prevented him from entering the city. He was a small, thin man, with a beard falling to his waist and long, unkempt hair. Some said he resembled his own donkey! But despite his frail (and bizarre) appearance he was a passionate and convincing speaker.

In the spring of 1096 thousands of people, many of whom were old men, women, and children, set out from France on their three-

An engraving of Peter the Hermit preaching

of the peasants (Rainald) offered to surrender if he and his closest friends would be spared. The Turks agreed, but when the castle gates were opened, they rushed inside and attacked everyone in sight. Those not slain were sold as slaves. A smaller group of Crusaders escaped the massacre, but they were later picked off by other Turkish troops. Peter was one of the few to escape with his life.

THE FIRST CRUSADE (1096-1099)

The same year another very different expedition set out. This was the first proper Crusade. Four nobles (Godfrey of Bouillon, Raymond of Toulouse, Robert of Normandy, and Bohemond of Sicily) led their armies by different routes to Constantinople. Godfrey de Bouillon was an honorable man who fervently desired to free the Holy Land, but the other three leaders were more interested in satisfying their own ambitions.

The soldiers brought along their wives and children, cooks, blacksmiths, and anyone else who might prove useful on the long march. In fact, of the 40,000 people who set out, only 4,000 were knights. Throughout the many Crusades most participants would be foot soldiers and a motley collection of artisans, merchants, and peasants. When Alexius saw the huge numbers arrive, he remembered Peter's masses and worried (and rightly so) that they might plunder his city. So, after having the knights swear an oath of fealty to him, he immediately loaded the travelers on ships and sent them off to Asia Minor.

But no one was prepared for the long, hot march across that rugged terrain to the Holy Land, and many people suffered terribly. The Crusaders besieged Nicaea, the capital of the

thousand-mile journey. They traveled on foot and in two-wheeled carts drawn by slow-moving oxen. They had little idea of how long the journey would take, and at nearly every town they would ask, "Is this Jerusalem?" Since they had few supplies or weapons, a large number of them died of hunger or were killed by bandits. The survivors relied upon the goodwill of people along the way, but when their needs were not met, they started plundering the countryside. They also attacked many Jewish communities in France and Germany and demanded that the inhabitants either convert to Christianity or be killed.

At last they arrived in Constantinople. The Emperor was aghast. This bedraggled crew was going to defend his mighty city? When they started plundering Constantinople, Alexius quickly shipped them across the Dardenelles to Asia Minor. The major group of travelers found an empty castle at Exorogorgon and settled in. One night, while they were sleeping, Turkish soldiers crept up and surrounded them. After an eight-day siege with no water or food, the leader

Turks, and after a week they entered its walls, subdued the people, and helped themselves to whatever struck their fancy. Then they proceeded south. As they marched along they were often short of food, so they split into two columns traveling several miles apart in order to have a better chance of finding supplies. One of the columns was attacked by the Turks. Although the knights fought bravely and managed to drive off the enemy, their horses became weary. The Turks took advantage of this and returned, once again attacking the knights, who by now had dismounted and were standing with the foot soldiers. It was a desperate situation, but at the last moment the other column of knights galloped into sight. To the soldiers of the first column this must have seemed like a miracle. Together the two groups soundly defeated the Turks at the battle of Dorylaeum, greatly restoring their sagging morale.

Moving south, the Crusaders laid siege to Antioch, a rich city surrounded by high walls that stretched for miles and were reinforced at intervals by four hundred towers. They waited outside the walls for months. At first they feasted on the fruit from the local orchards and vineyards, but as the siege continued they ran short of supplies. Many were reduced to killing and eating their own horses. It was a discouraging time, and it reached a low ebb when a Byzantine bishop was lowered down the side of the city wall in a cage. Finally, after seven months, the Turkish commander was successfully bribed to open the gates. As they rushed through them, the knights were dazzled by the city's network of wide streets bordered by

handsome stone buildings. Paris and the other European cities, with their wooden houses crowded along narrow, twisting roads must have seemed like primitive villages in comparison. However, the beauty of the city did not deter the soldiers from killing many of its citizens.

Three days later, the Crusaders found themselves besieged in Antioch by the army of the emir of Mosul. Now the tables had turned. As usual, they had few supplies and little food. It was a desperate time, until someone found a relic

Engraving of ancient Antioch

The Old City of Jerusalem

in the Church of St. Peter. It was supposedly the iron head of the lance that had pierced Jesus' side. Believing that this find would bring them luck (and God's support), the knights marched out of the city, shouting "God wills it!" They fought with such determination and gusto that they chased off the Turks!

As the Crusaders continued their march south, the leaders quarreled frequently among themselves. Some even left the army to set up feudal territories, while large numbers of knights suddenly disappeared to plunder villages and seize pieces of land. As the rest of the people trudged on, they remarked that the country they were passing through was no promised land of milk and honey! It was incredibly hot, and there were no trees to provide shade. Many horses died, and the surviving sheep, goats, and even dogs had to be used as beasts of burden. The relentless sun heated the metal helmets and heavy mail of the knights, making them miserable. A few of them discovered the practicality of wearing cloth over their helmets and mail. (This is how the

surcoat and mantling later became an integral part of a knight's attire.)

On June 7, 1099 the 12,000 surviving Crusaders finally reached Jerusalem and camped outside its walls. The holy city of Christians, Jews, and Muslims was the strongest fortress in the ancient world, rising high above the hot, dusty plain. Immediately the engineers began constructing siege towers and battering rams from the few pieces of wood they could find. The Turks had blocked up or poisoned all the wells around the city, and so many of the people died of thirst. But after about six weeks the Crusaders made their final assault and entered the city. What followed was a terrible massacre of thousands of Muslim and Jewish inhabitants— men, women, and children. The Christians shot their victims with arrows, slashed their throats with swords, or tortured them by casting them into the flames. Heads, hands, and feet were piled up in the streets of the city. The Soldiers of the Cross, who were supposedly fighting in the name of Jesus, the Prince of Peace, showed little compassion or mercy. A witness wrote that the

Crusaders slaughtered their victims until they "waded in blood up to their ankles." At the end of the day, their hands still covered with blood, the triumphant warriors prayed at the altar of the Holy Sepulcher.

OUTREMER

Godfrey of Bouillon was elected ruler of Jerusalem. He refused to be crowned king, remarking that he could hardly wear a golden crown in the city where Christ had worn a crown of thorns. Instead, he took the title of Defender of the Holy Sepulcher. Most of the army returned home, their mission accomplished. Those who remained in Palestine organized four feudal territories which together were known as Outremer (the Kingdom beyond the Sea). These included the County of Edessa, the Principality of Antioch, the County of Tripoli, and the Kingdom of Jerusalem. They formed a long strip along the coast of the Mediterranean, five hundred miles long and fifty miles wide. The four regions were subdivided into fiefs.

Peace was restored in Palestine and the pilgrimages resumed. The local Muslims had to pay taxes and give half their crops to the Crusaders. Over the years that followed, many of the knights married local girls and became friendly with the Muslims. They learned Arabic and had their children educated by Arab tutors. They adopted the desert dress of the East—turbans and long, loose robes for the men, long silken gowns and veils for the women. The knights who had once been so uncouth and rowdy now trimmed and perfumed their hair and beards, and they even learned to bathe on a daily basis (something unheard of in Europe!). French and German soldiers who arrived after the Crusader territories had been established were allegedly shocked and even appalled by the changes they observed in their countrymen!

The pace of life was slower in Outremer than it had been in Europe, and many luxuries imported from the East were readily available at the local markets. (Palestine was a major trading crossroads.) The new homes of the Crusaders were decorated with beautiful tapestries and brocaded wall hangings, and they were furnished with exquisite tables inlaid with mother-of-pearl, upholstered chairs, and handsome wooden

Stained glass window in Brittany depicting knights of the First Crusade

Byblos, a Crusader castle in Lebanon

The Arabs introduced the Crusaders to the fork

chests. The floors were covered with brightly colored mosaic tiles. The Europeans enjoyed meals that were light and refreshing, seasoned with the eastern spices (such as pepper, nutmeg, and cinnamon) that produced new and intriguing flavors. Desserts included a variety of exotic fruits—apricots, figs, dates, lemons, and water melons. The Arabs even taught their new neighbors how to eat with forks!

Fruits from the East

In order to protect their vast land holdings in Outremer, the Crusaders built gigantic castles, using the construction techniques they learned from the Byzantines and Arabs. These were the concentric castles we learned about in Chapter 6.

THE MILITARY ORDERS

In about 1070, a group of Italian merchants founded the Hospice of St. John near the Church of the Holy Sepulcher. A hospice was like an inn where pilgrims could rest and obtain food. This one was run by Benedictine monks and nuns. After the Crusaders liberated Jerusalem, a hospital was set up at the same site to care for the sick. Over the years, a great deal of money and land was given to the monks to create other hospitals, so that by the early twelfth century there was a chain of them stretching across the Holy Land.

In 1113 a papal bull established the Knights of St. John (known as the Hospitallers) as an independent religious order. According to their new charter, the monks were instructed to take up arms in defense of pilgrims traveling to Jerusalem or to protect the hospitals and even the holy city itself. These warrior monks took the usual monastic vows of poverty, chastity, and obedience, and they followed the Benedictine Rule. But when they gave up their worldly possessions to the order, they were presented with weapons and horses. Their leader was known as the Grand Master and he was accountable only to the Pope. A Hospitaller was easily identified by the black tunic embroidered with a white star that he wore over his armor.

A Knight of St. John

Krak des Chevaliers

The Hospitallers acquired many castles in the Holy Land, the greatest one being Krak des Chevaliers in Syria. Its storehouses and water reservoir could sustain about 2,000 fighting men for a long period of time. Krak withstood twelve sieges and was not taken until 1271, and then only by ruse. (This is how it was lost. A letter was delivered to the knights defending the castle that was supposedly written by the Grand Master. It ordered them to surrender. Only later did the defenders discover the letter was a forgery!)

When the Hospitallers were driven from the Holy Land in later centuries, they established new headquarters on the island of Rhodes. There they built up a fleet of ships to protect pilgrims sailing from Europe to Jerusalem. The order of Hospitallers exists today as a charity organization.

The order of the Poor Knights of Christ (known as the Templars) was founded in 1118 by nine French knights. The name Templars was derived from their first monastery, which was built beside the Temple of Solomon in Jerusalem. The aim of this order was to protect pilgrims by fighting off their attackers, but in time this narrow goal expanded into a mission to attack Muslims anytime anywhere. Templars took strict military vows, pledging themselves to battle the infidel to the death; to refuse to be ransomed if defeated; to accept every combat, no matter what the odds; to refuse ransom to an infidel; and, of course, to defend any Christian who was molested by Muslims. The Templars claimed that they slept fully armed; no knight removed his white surcoat (emblazoned with a red cross) until it rotted or was slashed away by a Saracen's sword. Their determination to fight to the death made the Templars the most feared of all the Christian knights. In later years, the Muslims automatically executed any Templars they took in battle.

Many feudal lords in Europe contributed funds for the Templars to arm themselves and to build castles in the Holy Land. Eventually, the order established outposts in Europe and Africa as well as Asia to recruit and train new members. In the second half of the twelfth century the Templars were among the leading landowners in Syria and Palestine, where some of their castles are still standing. They also created one of the largest and most efficient banking systems in Europe (in spite of a Church ban on money-lending by Christians). Pilgrims could deposit money at a Templar castle in Europe and withdraw it, using letters of credit, upon arrival in Jerusalem. The Templars even had their own ships to transport pilgrims from Italian seaports to the Holy Land.

The Hospitallers and Templars became the backbone of the army of the kingdom of Jerusalem after the first Crusade. They earned a reputation for courage and valiance, and in time they would supply about half the total number of knights available in the Holy Land. Recognized as the best fighters, they were always given the position of honor in a battle formation, the Templars on the right wing, the Hospitallers on the left.

Engraving of Knights Templar

But unlike the Hospitallers, many Templars became more interested in becoming wealthy than in keeping their vows, and this caused a decline in their military strength. After the last Crusade, the Templars moved to the island of Cyprus and the order deteriorated into an organization of bankers and money lenders. But the idea of a religious order being so involved in money-lending was offensive to many Christians.

In October 1307 Philip IV of France ordered all Templars to be arrested and executed, and other European rulers followed suit. In 1310 forty-five Templars were burned to death on one day in Paris. The order was dissolved, and much of its vast wealth was grabbed up by Philip. (What does that tell you about his true motives?) Some went to the Hospitallers, and the rest disappeared. There is a legend about Jacques de Molay, the last Grand Master of the Templars who was burned at the stake in Paris in 1314. Just before he died he called upon his accusers (Philip IV and Pope Clement V) to meet with him before God. Within a year, both men were dead.

THE SECOND CRUSADE (1147-1149)

For half a century the Crusaders occupied Outremer. Trade flourished as Italian cargo ships carried products between Europe and Asia. However, the federation was weakened by the constant quarreling among its rulers. In 1145 the County of Edessa was captured by the Turks. French King Louis VII, inspired by the preaching of Bernard, the Abbot of the Clairvaux Monastery (more about him later), decided to lead a Second Crusade. He was joined by Conrad HI of the Holy Roman Empire. Louis was married at the time to Eleanor of Aquitaine. (Do you remember who her second husband was?) Eleanor joined Louis on the Crusade, accompanied by a troop of troubadours as well as wagons stuffed with clothes, furs, jewels, cosmetics, cookware, glasses, carpets, and other articles she considered necessary for her rather elegant life style. After the caravan was attacked by the Turks, the survivors made their way to Antioch, which lay in the Crusader kingdom currently ruled by Eleanor's uncle, Prince Raymond. The queen was impressed with the manner in which Muslims and Christians lived together so peacefully. Louis, however, was shocked that his countrymen should be consorting with the infidel.

Tapestry image of a Crusader

The French and German armies had agreed to attack Damascus, even though it was a Muslim ally of the Christian states. But when a storm of arrows was suddenly released from the walls of that city, killing hundreds of French soldiers, Louis promptly retreated. He continued south to Jerusalem, where Eleanor thoroughly enjoyed sightseeing. After two years the crusading army returned home and Edessa remained under Muslim control. Many scholars attribute the failure of this Crusade to the half-hearted support given by the knights of Outremer. They had become so friendly with the Muslims that they were reluctant to attack them.

THE THIRD CRUSADE (1189-1192)

In 1174 Saladin, the ruler of Egypt, united the Muslims throughout the Near East and started a jihad against the Christians. His army was made up of groups of warriors led by emirs (Arab chieftains). They rode swift ponies and used short bows. Although less well armored than the European knights, the Muslims depended upon their speed and skills of horsemanship as well as their superior numbers to strike down their opponents. In 1187 Saladin captured Jerusalem. But unlike the Christian knights, he treated his captives well, exhibiting great generosity and mercy. He maintained order in the city and forbade any acts of violence towards its inhabitants.

Responding to the loss of Jerusalem, three powerful kings of Europe decided to join forces to drive out the infidel. Leading the Third Crusade were Richard I of England, Philip Augustus of France, and Frederick I (known as Barbarossa, or Red Beard) of the Holy Roman Empire. Richard was a tall, athletic monarch who loved warfare but who also wrote tender love poems and played the lute with skill. He was in many ways the ideal knight (The ladies of the French courts must have adored him!). Although he could hardly speak English (he was raised by his mother, Eleanor of Aquitaine, in France) and spent only six months of his ten-year reign in England, he was much loved by his subjects and even today is considered a great hero in England. Philip was very different. He was a slight, frail, man who hated taking risks and loved plotting against his enemies. The two kings could not have been more opposite. As for Frederick, he was one of the greatest of the Holy Roman Emperors (we'll learn more about him in a later chapter), but at the time of the Third Crusade he was seventy years old.

Stained glass image of King Richard

From the beginning of the campaign there were problems. Richard's ships were blown off course, ending up in Cyprus, and Frederick drowned while crossing the River Salef near Antioch. Richard and Philip finally came together with their armies at the port city of Acre (north of Jerusalem), which had been under siege by the Christians for a long time. Richard used his fleet to blockade the port in order to keep supplies from the city. According to legend, one ship laden with supplies for the Muslims also carried two hundred poisonous snakes, which were intended to be released against the Crusaders. Fortunately for the Christians, who didn't find out about the deadly cargo until later, the ship was sunk. Richard, a far better military leader than Philip, set up an array of siege towers, catapults, and battering rams and ultimately led his soldiers over the crumbling walls of the city. In the burning heat of July, the Muslims finally surrendered.

During the siege of Acre a group of German merchants had set up a tented hospital outside the city gates to care for the wounded. By the time the siege was finally ended, the hospital had become a permanent institution. It evolved into the order of Teutonic knights, similar in many ways to the Hospitallers and Templars. Teutonic knights wore a white mantle with a black cross. The order was recognized by the Pope in 1199.

When Acre fell, the kings of England and France set up their standards (banners) near the gates to signal their victory. Duke Leopold of Austria also raised his, but it was pulled down and even trodden upon in the mud by English soldiers, who were outraged by his impudence. When Leopold protested, Richard kicked him in the stomach. A few days later Leopold left for Austria. This is not the last we will hear of him.

Richard and Philip never got on well, and soon after Acre surrendered, Philip lost interest in the Crusade and returned with most of his troops to France, where he began plotting with Richard's brother John against his former ally (John and Richard were sons of Henry II.). Richard tried to negotiate with Saladin, but to no avail, and three years of intermittent fighting ensued. When the Crusaders approached Jaffa, the port for Jerusalem, hoping to establish a base there with access to the sea, Saladin tore down the city walls and destroyed the harbor.

While the Muslim engineers were busy at Jaffa, a battle was fought at Arsuf, a village fifteen miles to the north. It was here that Richard earned his nickname, Coeur de Lion (the Lion-hearted). This is how it happened. After routing a group of Muslims, Richard's knights broke formation and scattered into little groups around the banners of the English nobles and barons. The Muslims took advantage of the disorder and charged once again. The Crusaders were caught completely off guard, but Richard, determined to win the day, went from one group of knights to another, entreating them to follow him against the infidel. All the while, he had to fight off Muslim swords. His men responded to his pleas and rallied behind him. A fierce cavalry charge spearheaded by the English monarch drove back the Muslims and defeated them once and for all. Richard's horse was killed under him, but he continued to fight valiantly. According to legend, when Saladin heard about this he sent Richard a groom and two fresh horses. This is but one example of the mutual respect that was growing between the two rival leaders.

After the battle, Richard fell ill. Messengers went back and forth between him and Saladin, and it was reported that the English king's fever caused him to long for fruit and a cool drink. Saladin immediately sent him pears, peaches, and snow carried down from the heights of Mt. Hermon.

The Crusaders now had no leader: Frederick was dead, Philip was gone, and Richard was ill. But in time Richard did recover, only to receive word that his brother John and King Philip were plotting to seize the English throne. So on September 2, 1192, he signed a truce with Saladin. Many scholars believe that he might have won Jerusalem by diplomacy if he hadn't had such a love of fighting or been so anxious to leave.

Richard wouldn't allow himself to look upon the holy city that he had failed to liberate. According to the truce, Jerusalem would remain in the hands of Saladin, but both Muslim and Christian pilgrims were to be allowed to visit the city in safety (provided they were unarmed). The Christians gave up Palestine except for a thin strip of land along the coast between Tyre and Jaffa that was one hundred miles long. The cost of the Third Crusade was high: Many thousands of men lost their lives.

Richard left Jerusalem and sailed for England. But once again he was shipwrecked, this time on lands belonging to Holy Roman Emperor Henry IV. He was disguised as a poor Knight Templar, but he neglected to remove his large ruby ring. This led to his being discovered and taken prisoner. Henry passed his captive on to Leopold of Austria. (Do you remember what Richard had done to him?) Leopold had Richard imprisoned in the Castle of Durnstein in Germany and held for a ransom of 150,000 silver marks. Although his brother John, ruling England as regent while Richard was away, allegedly remarked, "Let him rot!" 100,000 silver marks were raised among the English subjects (the equivalent of $6 million). Richard's mother Eleanor went to Germany to personally pay the ransom. So after two years of imprisonment, the king was released. Soon afterwards, Leopold had his foot crushed by a fall from his horse and died from the infection that resulted (gangrene).

Arriving in England, Richard took back the throne from a petulant John and punished those who had plotted against him. Two months later he sailed back to France, where Philip had confiscated much of his land. While attacking a

castle in 1199, Richard was mortally wounded by a bolt from a crossbow. He died in the arms of his mother Eleanor, who was now eighty years old. Richard had forgiven the soldier who had wounded him, but after his death the man was hanged.

THE FOURTH CRUSADE (1204)

After the third Crusade, enthusiasm for a mission to liberate Jerusalem dwindled. The religious zeal of earlier times was gone, and apart from pilgrims, most people who set out for the Holy Land were drawn purely by hopes of material profit.

The Fourth Crusade began in 1204 when Pope Innocent III persuaded an army of European knights to attack Egypt, the center of Muslim power. When the army reached Venice, they didn't have enough money to pay for the sea passage to Egypt. So Dandola, the elderly Doge (Duke) of Venice, dreaming of the day when his city would control the lucrative trade of the Mediterranean Sea, came up with a plan that would benefit him as well as the Crusaders. He offered to cut the costs of transporting the 30,000 men and 4,500 horses to Egypt if the knights would first attack Zara. This was a city in Dalmatia on the Adriatic coast that was a major commercial rival of Venice. The Crusaders agreed to the deal and captured Zara, much to the despair of Pope Innocent. (Zara was a Christian city!) The Pope promptly excommunicated the entire army of Crusaders, but it doesn't seem to have mattered to them as they greedily divided the spoils with Dandolo. In fact, they were easily convinced by the wily Venetians to attack Constantinople, supposedly to restore the deposed Emperor to his throne, but really to obtain more loot.

Hagia Sophia, a Christian basilica later converted into a mosque, towered over Constantinople

In April of 1204 the assault of the Byzantine capital began. For many centuries Constantinople had been the largest and finest city in Europe as well as a center of classical learning. All this was to change. The churches and palaces were robbed and stripped of everything, and many valuable objects and manuscripts were taken to Venice or destroyed or simply lost. Rather than restoring the Emperor to his throne, the Crusaders took him to the top of a tall marble column and

fascinating details concerning the infamous Fourth Crusade.

The Crusaders never made it to Egypt but instead set up a feudal kingdom where they were. The Venetians were perhaps the greatest victors, since the destruction of Constantinople gave their own city the trading monopoly that they had hoped for. We'll learn more about Venetian commerce in Chapter 11.

Constantinople (modern Istanbul) lay on both sides of the Bosphorus Strait that separates Europe from Asia

pushed him off! After months of looting the city, the local Byzantine land holdings were divided up between the invaders. Geoffroi de Villehardouin, a nobleman from Champagne, participated in the sack of Constantinople. He later wrote an account of his adventures in his native French. It is a literary masterpiece that contains many

LATER CRUSADES

There were several more Crusades during the thirteenth century, but not much was accomplished by them. The saddest event took place in 1212 when two expeditions, jointly known as the Children's Crusade, set out for the Holy Land. Stephen of Cloyes, a twelve-year-old

French shepherd boy, and Nicolas, a German lad, assembled groups of children to march to the Holy Land, not to fight, but to convert the infidel. They were convinced that angels would guide them and that the sea would part for them, just as it had for Moses and the Israelites. The German children made it as far as Italy, where most were killed by thieves or died of hunger. Stephen's group managed to get to the port city of Marseilles. Since the sea did not part for them as expected, they accepted the offer of two ship captains to transport them to the Holy Land free of charge. As you might have guessed, the greedy men did not keep their word; instead, they sailed to North Africa and sold the children to Arab slave dealers.

In 1228 Holy Roman Emperor Frederick II (grandson of Barbarossa) led an army to Palestine. He had been excommunicated by the Pope because, after agreeing to lead the Crusade, he seemed indecisive about actually setting out. By this time, neither the Muslims nor the Europeans who had settled in the Holy Land wanted warfare, so once he arrived there Frederick was able to negotiate a treaty. Without a drop of blood being spilled, the Muslims presented him with Bethlehem, Nazareth, and Jerusalem. The Pope, who should have been pleased, was furious that the Crusaders had not attacked the infidels. He even called for a crusade against Frederick! Unfazed by such ignoble behavior, Frederick placed the first two cities in the hands of the Teutonic Knights for safekeeping and arranged to be crowned King of Jerusalem. Unfortunately, he quarreled with the Templars and Hospitallers as well as his own barons. So he left Jerusalem, still on extremely friendly terms with the Muslims living there. Near the end of his life, he sent a letter to the Sultan warning him that another Crusade was about to begin.

Statue of Louis IX in Sainte Chapelle, Paris

And he was right. Louis IX of France (St. Louis) had previously led an army to Egypt. After capturing Damietta, he and his men got bogged down in the swampy upriver country just south of the fortress and became the prisoners of the Sultan Mansourah. The French had to pay a ransom to free the king and his army. (The Sultan allegedly first demanded 500,000 livres, but when Louis immediately agreed to the sum, he knocked off 100,000, complaining, "By Allah, this Frank does not haggle!") The money was raised by the Templars. In 1249 Louis, now an old man, led the Eighth Crusade. His plan was to attack Tunis on his way to Egypt, but he fell ill in that city and died. (He later became the patron saint of France.) Louis had been accompanied on his campaigns by Jean de Joinville, a steward from Champagne. His memoirs, like those of de Villehardouin, are an invaluable source of information about those early times.

The age of the Crusaders was over. One by one, the Christian territories were lost. Antioch fell in 1268, Krak des Chevaliers was taken in 1271, and in 1291 the Muslims took back Acre, the last Christian stronghold. After two hundred years of terrible bloodshed, the Muslims still ruled the Holy Land.

THE EFFECTS OF THE CRUSADES

From a military standpoint, the Crusades were an absolute failure. Only the first one achieved its goal, and the terrible slaughter did little for the cause of Christianity. In the end the political situation in the Holy Land had changed very little. And yet, the development of western civilization had been greatly influenced. We have already learned how the knights settling in Outremer were drawn to the Muslim culture and how their life style improved as a result. Many of the new trends were imported back to Europe. Contact with the Byzantines and Muslims also created a new interest in learning: The vast accumulation of writings of the ancient Greeks and Romans, which had been translated and thus preserved by the Arabs, became available to European scholars. The West also benefitted from the advances made by the Arabs in the areas of mathematics and science.

Italian cities like Venice became the major ports through which the products of the East as well as new technologies reached Europe. Before long gold coins from Byzantium were being used throughout the Mediterranean world, while Venetians adapted the glassmaking techniques of the Asian port city of Tyre, French villagers cultivated silkworms from China, and Spanish farmers planted plum trees from Damascus and sugar cane from Tripoli.

All the fighting in the East actually preserved peace at home. Those knights who longed for battle took out their aggressions on the Muslims, enabling the communities of Europe to grow and prosper. And while the feudal lords were off crusading, the kings were able to increase their power. A growing sense of nationalism is shown by the fact that while the knights of the First Crusade all wore a red cross, among those of the Third Crusade only the French wore red crosses (the English wore white ones, and soldiers from Flanders and Lorraine wore blue). As nationalism slowly grew, feudalism steadily weakened.

Damascus plum tree

QUESTIONS

1. What does the word Saracen mean?
2. What incentives did Pope Urban offer the Crusaders?
3. Describe Peter the Hermit.

4. Why was the march to the Holy Land difficult for the people of the First Crusade (not the Peoples' Crusade)?

5. How did the Crusaders treat the citizens of Jerusalem?

6. What aspects of the Muslim culture appealed to the knights who settled in Outremer?

7. How did the Hospitallers differ from the Templars?

8. What famous queen went on the Second Crusade?

9. Why did Leopold hold Richard captive?

10. Who was Richard's younger brother?

11. Why did the Venetians want the Crusaders to attack Constantinople?

12. What happened to the participants in the Childrens' Crusade?

13. Why was the Pope angry (twice) at Frederick, grandson of Barbarossa?

14. Who raised the money to pay Louis' ransom?

15. Name three ways that the Crusades positively affected western culture.

FURTHER THOUGHTS

1. As we have seen, the Crusading knights were often cruel to anyone who didn't share their faith. They lumped all non-believers together as infidels. And despite rampant anti-Semitism on their part, they forced Jewish bankers to help finance the Crusades (they had to pay for the crimes of all the infidels).

2. Terrible atrocities were committed by the Crusaders. Some soldiers sawed open the dead bodies of Muslims looking for gold. Sometimes they even ate the flesh, finding the taste "better than spiced peacock," according to a chronicler of the time.

3. An interesting order of knights that sprang up during the Crusades was the Knights of St. Lazarus, founded in the twelfth century. This order was originally a leper hospital. Templars or Hospitallers who contracted leprosy had to leave their own order and join brothers of St. Lazarus. In 1147 members of St. Lazarus were known as the Leper Brothers of Jerusalem,

4. The Crusaders brought to Europe the new art of dyeing cloth bright colors. (Until the Crusades, most cloth was dyed somber earth colors.) In fact, the words crimson, lilac, and azure come from eastern languages. Other words that entered the English language via Arab traders are bazaar, jar, magazine, taffeta, tariff, artichoke, tarragon, orange, muslin, gauze, sugar, and saffron.

PROJECTS

1. King Richard, the favorite son of Eleanor of Aquitaine, got along poorly with his father, Henry II of England. Consult three sources about the lion-hearted king. The English consider Richard a great hero. Do you? Was he a good ruler? Was he an able general? What kind of a person was he? Why did he quarrel with and plot against his father? Write a short biography about him.

2. Find out more about the early history of Jerusalem (before the Crusades). Write a short report. Illustrate it with a map of the region.

3. Make a map showing the routes of the various Crusades.

4. Krak des Chevaliers still stands in Syria. Find out more about it. Then write a report, and illustrate it with a pencil or pen drawing of the famous fortress.

5. According to legend, King Richard's place of imprisonment was discovered by Blondel, his favorite minstrel. Blondel rode from castle to castle, singing a song that only he and Richard knew. When Richard heard the minstrel sing the first lines, he sang back the refrain. This episode is contained in Sir Walter Scott's novel *Ivanhoe* (already referred to in Chapter 7). Read the book, or see the video.

6. Find a collection of pictures in magazines and make a collage of some of the products that the Crusades made available to Europeans. (Suggestions: spices, fruit, almonds, rice, silk, tapestries, glass—and there are many more.)

7. Pope Urban gave the European knights a license to kill in the name of God. Think about this statement. Does it upset you? Do you agree that this is true or do you disagree? Write a paragraph or two describing your reactions to the statement.

8. Some scholars say that the Holy Land was ultimately lost because of the constant quarreling between the Templars and the Hospitallers. Do some research on the subject and decide whether you think this is an accurate statement. Write a short report explaining your views.

9. Make a drawing of three men—a Hospitaller, a Templar, and a Teutonic knight. Consult the books in your classroom for important detail

CHAPTER 9

A DAY IN THE LIFE OF A LORD

So far, we have been learning about how particular groups or classes of people lived. Now let's take a little time to focus on the life of one individual lord living in England in the mid-thirteenth century. We'll call him Sir Cedric Farnsworth.

THE MORNING HOURS

Sir Cedric awakens at dawn in his solar (sleeping chamber) above the Great Hall of his castle. The large bed he shares with his wife, Lady Anne, has a wooden frame and springs made from interlaced strips of leather. The soft mattress of goose down feathers is covered with a linen sheet. (Goose feathers are also the filling of the lord's puffy pillows.) A quilt and fur cover provide warmth on a cold night. Attached to the bed are woolen curtains that can be drawn at night to provide privacy and keep out drafts.

Tapestries woven in Persia cover the grey stone walls of the solar, adding color and making the room seem warmer. The windows have green glass, another recent import from the East. The lord and lady's personal belongings are kept in two intricately carved wooden chests. There are no other pieces of furniture in the room, although a window seat in the deep recess of the wall has a number of soft cushions. This is where Lady Anne enjoys doing her embroidery. The floor is covered with grasses and sweet smelling herbs.

Slipping out of bed, Sir Cedric puts on a long-sleeved cotton tunic over the linen underclothing he wears all the time. (It is washed every week or two.) The tunic reaches his mid-calf and he

Carved chest

belts it at the waist. Then he pulls on his wool stockings and slips into his soft leather shoes. Over his tunic he wears a sleeveless woolen surcoat which has been dyed a deep purple and is embroidered with gold thread. In these times, a nobleman wears a purse around his waist, so the surcoat is slit on one side to allow easy access to it. (This is the origin of our modern pockets.) If it were cooler, Sir Cedric would put his mantle over his shoulders. A mantle is a circular piece of brightly colored cloth lined with fur and fastened at the neck with a brooch. But it's a warm morning, and there is no need for such a cloak.

Lady Anne also dons a cotton tunic; hers falls to her ankles and has long sleeves that are laced from the wrist to the elbow. Over this she wears a long surcoat of finely woven crimson wool, gathered at the waist by a leather belt. Buttons have not been invented yet, so she uses elegant gold pins to hold her dress together. Then, holding up a mirror of polished steel, she applies white makeup to her face. (It's made from sheep fat.) A fair complexion is the sign of wealth, since the faces of the lower classes are deeply tanned from working outside in the fields. She parts her hair in the middle and braids it into two long plaits, which she pins up on her head. Then she puts on a white linen wimple, which covers her hair and neck. Medieval nobility cover up well, even in summer. They consider nakedness ugly and degrading, and so they try not to show even the smallest patch of skin except on their hands and faces.

Nobleman and noblewoman

Since the days of the Crusades, bathing has become more common, and Lord Cedric takes a bath every week. During the cold weather a wooden tub is placed in the solar and filled with water that has been heated in the hearth. The tub water helps to take the itch out of the bites of fleas and lice, common creatures in these times even among the rich. (In fact, combs are used more for picking them out than arranging one's hair!)

Once they are dressed the lord and lady enter the private chapel that adjoins the solar and say their morning prayers. Sir Cedric is proud of the beautiful gold cross that hangs above the altar.

It was brought back from the Holy Land by his grandfather. Breakfast is a simple meal of bread, cheese, and ale. Lady Anne quickly finishes hers and then gives special instructions to some of the household servants. The seneschal (steward) oversees the large staff of domestic workers to keep the castle functioning and recruits new servants from among the serfs if the need arises.

Once the servants go about their chores, Lady Anne gets to work on the piece of cloth she has been embroidering. Medieval women spend much of each day making clothing for the family. This is true of even the highest classes, who spin wool from their own sheep, dye it, weave it on a loom, and then fashion the cloth into an article of clothing. When the sewing is done the cloth can be embroidered.

As she stitches, Lady Anne thinks of her children, Charles and Elizabeth. She sees little of them these days. Charles is a page in the castle of a neighboring lord, Sir Oliver. Elizabeth is living on the estate of her Uncle William, where she is learning how to run a household. Three other children were born to Lady Anne, but one was stillborn and the others died in infancy. She has accepted the loss as God's will.

Sir Cedric takes a last sip of ale and then sets out to spend the morning inspecting the fields with his bailiff. As they ride along, the bailiff will tell him about the court case that will be held next week dealing with a serf who has been growing crops in a strip leased to someone else. The bailiff is also in charge of the lord's military staff: the knights that are on guard duty, the watchman, and the squires.

At least once a year Sir Cedric is supposed to go to war as a vassal for the lord who leases him his fief, but he has recently arranged to pay a scutage fee instead. This pleases Lady Anne, because it can be difficult for her to run the castle while her husband is away.

Tables in the Great Hall

A silver salt cellar

THE MAIN MEAL

The main meal is served about midday in the Great Hall. Lord Cedric and Lady Anne sit on one side of the high table facing the center of the hall. They are joined by several knights. The table is covered with a white cloth that falls to the ground on the side where they are sitting, doubling as a communal napkin. There is a centerpiece called a subtlety, a piece of pastry molded in the shape of a unicorn (subtleties are usually made in the shapes of castles, ships, or animals). An elaborate silver salt cellar stands beside the subtlety. Smaller salt cellars have been placed in the middle of each of the two trestle tables arranged along the walls at right angles to the high table. People of higher status sit on the side of these tables that is "above the salt" (or closer to the high table); servants and craftsmen sit below the salt. Even today the expression "to sit above the salt" is used. Can you explain what it means in modern times?

The dinner plates are trenchers: thick slices of stale bread from the previous day. The bread absorbs the meat and vegetable juices that are spooned onto it. After the meal they will be collected and distributed to the serfs. In some castles wooden plates are used, and on special occasions the nobles dine on plates of gold or silver. To the left of the places of Lord Cedric and Lady Anne are two small ornamental dishes in the shape of a ship. Each one (it's called a nef) contains a knife, spoon, and napkin. Other male diners bring their own knives to the table, usually carrying them on their belts. Forks will not be in general use until the fourteenth century. Actually, most of the food is eaten with the fingers. Pages occasionally carry around bowls of perfumed water so diners can wash off some of the grease. Two people commonly share a dish, one helping himself and his partner to pieces of food and placing them on the trenchers. They also share a winecup and an ecuelle (a two-handled bowl used to serve stew or soup).

Medieval table rules are not terribly different than our own. Elbows are not allowed on the table, burping is discouraged, the mouth is to be wiped before drinking anything (remember, people share wine cups!), one shouldn't talk or drink with one's mouth full, and it is considered poor manners to serve food with the same fingers that have been used to scratch at flea bites! It is also considered rude to pick one's nose, teeth, or nails at the table, to bite off a piece of bread

Birds roasting on the spit

is the only one that includes sweets such as fruit pies, pastries, and spiced wine.

Sir Cedric loves meat. In the warm seasons his table is filled with many dishes made from fresh pork, mutton, venison, and rabbit. Often the meat is cooked in a pie, but an entire animal can be roasted on a spit in one of the huge fireplaces in the kitchen. Thick stews are cooked in huge cauldrons that are suspended on chains above the fire.

Pigs are the most common animal raised for the table, since they eat almost anything (they especially love acorns) and can be fattened quickly. However, medieval pigs are lean, razor-backed beasts with long tusks (resembling wild boars), and their meat is quite tough. Roasted brawn (pig's head) is a special treat at Sir Cedric's table. Chickens and geese are fattened in coops within the castle walls (their feathers are used for pillows and feather beds), and there are special roosts where pigeons are raised. When Sir Cedric goes hunting he often brings back ducks, pheasants, and quail. And the fish that is always served on Friday (this is a Christian tradition) comes from the artificial fish pond near the castle that is kept stocked with trout, carp, and pike.

rather than breaking it, and to dip food in the salt cellar. It is acceptable, however, to throw bones to the dogs, once the meat had been chewed off, and to wipe one's fingers on a piece of bread.

Wine is served at the high table, and the people sitting at the others tables drink ale. Water from local streams is seldom used for drinking purposes because it seems to cause illness, but occasionally spring water is served, flavored with honey or licorice. The castle's supply of wine and ale are kept in the buttery (a word derived from the French term bouteillerie, meaning "bottlery"). The butler is in charge, and he orders new bottles each year. In addition to wine cups, drinking horns are still used. One cow horn holds a fair amount of wine or ale, and since the horn cannot be set down, its contents must be consumed right away. (Does this remind you of the Vikings?)

Dinner consists of three courses, but they are not like our modern first course (an appetizer or soup), second course (meat and vegetables), and third course (dessert). Each medieval course is a mixture of meat, vegetable, and pastry. While one is being eaten, the next batch (or course) is being prepared in the kitchen. The last course, however,

The meat prepared during the winter has usually been salted, smoked, or preserved in verjuice (vinegar made from unripe grapes). This is because, as we learned earlier, most of the castle's animals are slaughtered in the fall to avoid the heavy cost of feeding them hay throughout the winter months. The salt used for preserving comes from the coast where seawater is kept in metal pans until it evaporates (leaving behind the salty residue). Salted meat has to be soaked and thoroughly rinsed before it is used. Then it is cut up, mashed, drowned in spices (to disguise its rancid taste), and cooked with dried peas and beans. It looks a lot like mush when it is served.

Sometimes the strongly flavored meat mingles with spices and honey in a mince pie.

A hearty stew cooking in the cauldron

The cooks in Sir Cedric's kitchen are skillful at pounding meat into a paste, mixing it with other ingredients, and serving it as a custard. Blackmanger is a dish made from a paste of chicken mixed with rice, boiled in almond milk, and served with sugar. A quenelle is a dumpling of fish or meat that has been pounded, mixed with bread crumbs, chicken stock and eggs, and then poached. (This is a French recipe.)

The spices, of course, are imported from the East. Pepper is one of the most highly prized. In fact, lords have been known to accept rent payments in pepper. Saffron is an expensive yellow seasoning produced in Spain from the stamens of crocuses. It is more than worth its weight in gold! Medieval cooks often experiment with combinations of spices, and they have found

that cloves added to cinnamon produce a curry taste. Despite their high cost, great quantities of spices are added to each dish, and we would probably find the food on Sir Cedric's table much too spicy for our modern tastes.

Peppercorns come in many colors

Few vegetables are served, and they are always cooked until they are soft and mushy. They're usually added to stew for flavoring (especially carrots and onions). Raw vegetables (called worts) are considered unhealthy because they produce "wind" (gas). A bowl of thick vegetable soup (called pottage) is often served at the beginning of a course. It is made of cabbage, carrots, onions, and leeks. Mushrooms are threaded on long strings to dry and then added to meat dishes. There is an herb garden outside the kitchen door where Sir Cedric's servants grow mustard, parsley, sage, garlic, basil, thyme, rosemary, marjoram, and fennel.

Bread is the staple food for all classes (the average peasant eats over a pound of bread each day). The finest bread is the wastel (a white loaf) made from finely ground wheat flour. It is served at the high table. Whole wheat bread is served at the other tables. Although most people eat the bread plain or dip it in stew, butter and cheese are also available to eat with it. There is a special room off the kitchen where the bread is baked. This is called the pantry (from the French word pain meaning "bread").

Cooked apples, pears, plums and cherries, usually served in pies, are a favorite dessert. Like the vegetables, raw fruit is not eaten. Sugar is very expensive (it, too, comes from the East), but the honey produced in the castle beehive is an excellent sweetener.

When visitors of noble rank arrive at the castle, Lady Anne arranges for a special banquet to be served. Her cooks and bakers spend long hours preparing elaborate dishes, such as roast cygnets (baby swans) and stuffed suckling pig. An unusual banquet dish is a cockatrice, a combination of a suckling pig and a pheasant (the front half is a pig, and the back half is a bird, or vice versa). Another special feature is a pheasant, swan, or peacock served with all its feathers intact. This is done by skinning the bird (feathers and all) and then roasting the carcass. (Of course, the internal organs have been removed.) After the bird is cooked, the skin and feathers are replaced. When it is served, this dish is bound to impress any visitor! Do you remember the Nursery Rhyme in which "four and twenty blackbirds were baked in a pie?" Such things actually do happen. A pie crust is baked and, at the very last moment before it is placed before a guest, one or several small

birds are slipped beneath the upper crust. As the guest cuts into the crust, the birds fly out! This dish is only for show. No one would want to eat that pie crust!

THE HUNT

Life can be boring in the thirteenth century, even for a nobleman. So since there are no interesting visitors at the castle and no court procedures to oversee today, Sir Cedric decides to spend the afternoon hunting. He has a kennel of keen-nosed hunting dogs who are always ready to chase after a deer or wild boar, game which is far tastier than the skinny sheep, pigs, and chickens that are usually served for dinner. He even has several swift greyhounds (imported from Egypt) who dash after hares and rabbits at break-neck speed. Large tracts of woodland have been set aside expressly for the lord to hunt in. Any peasants who are caught trespassing there are severely fined. A poacher might even be killed.

But this particular day Sir Cedric feels like hunting wild birds. This is done with the use of a trained bird of prey, such as a hawk or falcon. It is known as falconry, an ancient sport that originated in Persia. Falcons are the world's fastest birds, darting through the air at speeds as high as 100 miles per hour. The best falcons are the gyrfalcon and peregrine (many of which are imported from Iceland). Does it surprise you that the hens are better hunters than their male counterparts? Dark-eyed and long-winged, these spectacular fliers love to knock their quarry out of the sky with a headlong swoop or dive.

Falcons are very expensive and difficult to train. They are taken from a tree or cliff as nestlings or captured in nets as young birds that have just left the nest. The lord's falconer has a full-time job, and he receives a piece of land and a cottage in payment for his efforts. Only a nobleman can own a falcon, and a well-trained bird is often treasured next to his war horse. Anyone caught stealing a falcon is to be bound and tied while the bird eats six ounces of flesh from his chest! Pilgrimages have been made to the shrines of saints to pray for the recovery of a sick falcon. Sir Cedric often carries his favorite bird around with him, placing her on a chair behind him when he eats. Every castle has a one-room building in its courtyard called a mews. This is where the hunting birds roost.

Modern falcon on a falconer's arm

It's time for the hunt. After mounting a horse, Sir Cedric is handed his bird by the falconer. He places her on his forearm, which is protected by a heavy glove (the falcon has sharp talons). The bird's head is hooded so that she cannot see. On each leg is a leather strip (called a jess) with a bell and a ring on the end. The bell makes it easier to find a bird that has been released, and it bears Sir Cedric's name in case she is lost. A leather leash is attached to the rings, and the lord winds this around his arm. Thinking about a dog's collar and leash might help you to envision the leather jesses and leash used on the falcon.

A hooded falcon

Once the bird seems settled on his arm, Sir Cedric spurs his horse and gallops off into the woods in search of herons, ducks, cranes, pheasants, and partridges. As soon as a prey is spotted, he removes the bird's hood and unties the leash from the rings. The falcon immediately takes off with lightning speed and knocks a duck out of the air. When the bird falls to the ground, it is retrieved by one of the dogs. Now Sir Cedric twirls a piece of leather (called a lure) to which is attached a chunk of raw meat. The falcon has been trained to respond to the sound of the leather cutting through the air, and she flies back and lands on the lord's glove. He quickly ties the leash to the rings of the jesses, gives the bird the meat, and then replaces her hood. He smiles to himself, and decides to compliment his falconer on the fine work he has done with the bird when he returns to the castle.

There is a strict hierarchy of birds that can be used in hunting. It is based upon social status. As was noted earlier, only a wealthy lord is allowed to own a peregrine falcon. Knights (lesser lords) use smaller falcons called merlins, and squires hunt with even smaller birds (lannerets). Everyone else hunts with hawks. Unlike falcons, hawks have short broad wings that are designed for brief bursts of speed in horizontal flight. These birds are scorned by the nobility because they fly lower and slower than the falcons. However, they are better for hunting in thick woods. But even among the hawks there is a caste system. The best hunter among the hawks is the goshawk; it is flown by a yeomen (a prosperous freeman). The sparrow hawk, the bird of the village priest, is too small to take a quarry much larger than a mouse!

THE ROLE OF WOMEN

Marriage in the upper classes has little to do with love. Parents of marriageable children are concerned with finding a spouse who possesses or stands to inherit a sizeable piece of land. A woman spends her life under the guardianship of men: first her father and then her husband. If a young girl's father dies before she has married, she becomes the ward of her father's lord. Most noble girls are married by the age of fourteen. Gracia, the daughter of Thomas of Sakeby was married at the age of four! If a young woman reaches the age of twenty-one and is still single, she is considered a spinster (someone who has nothing to do but spin wool). Her only option at this stage is to spend the rest of her life in a convent. By the age of twenty the typical noblewoman has borne many children. Several

of them will probably not make it to adulthood, given the poor medical treatment of the times. As we have learned, this is the case with Lady Anne. By the age of thirty a noblewoman will probably be a grandmother!

The Church has traditionally considered women inferior to men, branding them as evil temptresses. According to canon law, women were put on the earth to be the servants of their husbands, who have the right to beat them (their wives), provided they don't kill them! In recent years, however, the cult of the Virgin Mary has improved the image of women.

Lady Anne's daughter Elizabeth is learning to behave politely in her uncle's castle. A well-mannered young lady must talk very little, walk slowly, and sit quietly in the presence of men, holding her hands on her lap with her eyes modestly turned downward. Lady Anne spends much of her time in a special room off the solar with her female relatives and servants. She keeps busy with her spinning, weaving, sewing, and

A well-educated medieval noblewoman

embroidery, and she has few occasions to enjoy male company (apart from that of Sir Cedric).

Of course, there have been exceptional women. We have already learned about Eleanor of Aquitaine, perhaps the most extraordinary woman of the Middle Ages, but there Were others. For example, the Countess of Buchan successfully defended her husband's castle against Edward I of England. Women can be honorary members of the knightly orders, such as the order of St. John of Jerusalem. In France, the Order of Cordeliers has been established for widows. Among the many poetesses is Marie de France (of Champagne) who has written a collection of poems based on ancient romances entitled the *Lais*. Perhaps you've noticed that all of these women are members of the nobility. This is logical, since only they had the opportunities to exercise any power at all. The courts of love we learned about in Chapter 7 affected only a small elite of wealthy (and rather self-indulgent) ladies.

ENTERTAINMENT

After an early supper at five o'clock consisting of eggs and cheese, Lord Cedric and Lady Anne play a game of chess. The game originated in India in the seventh century, and it has been a favorite pastime of European nobility ever since. Using chess pieces carved in ivory or whalebone in the shapes of knights, castles, bishops, pawns, and, of course, the king and queen, a player tries

to devise the best military strategy to defeat his, or her, opponent. Other popular games are checkers and backgammon.

A dulcimer

Sometimes a minstrel arrives at the castle and everyone gathers in the Great Hall to hear him recite his repertoire of epics and ballads. Minstrels are of humbler birth than the troubadours we have studied, and they expect to be paid for their efforts. Since they travel from place to place, they help to spread the local news. Most minstrels play the lute (an ancient stringed instrument), but some also entertain their audience with music from bagpipes, a dulcimer, a guitar or cymbals. Jongleurs not only sing and play a variety of instruments but they also juggle (hence their name), do acrobatics, and even imitate all kinds of animals. They are always in great demand during the celebrations of the saints' days.

Soon after sunset, the entire household goes to bed so as not to waste tallow candles. (Wax candles are available, but they are reserved for church services.) A watchman walks through the

Chessman represent different medieval figures

castle to make sure the live coals in the fireplaces are covered with ashes (these will be rekindled in the morning). The French words meaning "to cover the fire" are couvrir le feu (remember the couvre feu described in Chapter 6?), and over years of frequent mispronunciation this has evolved into the English word curfew. Today this word means the same as its medieval origin: Lights out!

LIFE AMONG THE SERFS

Before concluding this chapter, something needs to be said about Sir Cedric's counterpart, a serf named John. By learning more about John, we will know about how the vast majority of people were living in England in the thirteenth century.

John awakens at daybreak on a scratchy straw mattress which he shares with his wife, Mary, on the dirt floor of their small hut. He arises and puts on a thick woolen tunic over the shirt and breeches he has slept in. (Although trousers are not fashionable for the nobility, the peasants have been wearing breeches for years.) Then he pulls on long, woolen stockings. The tunic is a deep brown, and he'll wear it for months before it is cleaned. Even if he could afford to do so, John is forbidden by law to wear clothing made from cotton or silk, nor can his attire be dyed in any bright colors. These fabrics and tints are strictly reserved for the nobility, and anyone of a lower class who is brash enough to wear them is heavily fined. Mary puts on her simple green tunic and ties it with a strip of leather. John and Mary both wear shoes fashioned from soft leather.

Breakfast consists of a piece of rye bread. Rye grows in poorer soil than does wheat, and since much of the wheat is paid to Sir Cedric in feudal taxes, his serfs subsist on the rye. They

A serf

call it black wheat, and they make their bread and porridge from it. Actually, they eat little else, apart from cabbage and onions. They cannot afford much salt, and so their meat is very poorly preserved. The rotting meat often makes them very ill.

John and Mary's marriage was arranged by Sir Cedric, and their seven offspring belong to the lord. He is happy to have so many new workers. As is the case with Lady Anne, Mary's main functions are to bear and raise the children and to manage the household. If she complains about John, no matter how badly he treats her, she will be placed on the ducking stool by the village pond. The stool is attached to a wooden framework and can be lowered into the water and then raised again, while the local men laugh at the poor woman's predicament. Fortunately, John and Mary get along quite well.

John will spend his entire day working in the field, taking a break at midday for a small lunch of cabbage soup and bread. At sundown he'll walk slowly back to his hut, have a quick bite to eat with his family, and then fall asleep on the scratchy straw mattress. So ends another hard day.

QUESTIONS

1. What furnishings are in Sir Cedric's bedroom?

2. Describe Lady Anne's daily attire.

3. Who sits above the salt?

4. What is a trencher?

5. What is the buttery?

6. Why are most of the animals slaughtered in the fall?

7. What is the staple food of all classes?

8. How does a hawk differ from a falcon?

9. How does a noblewoman spend most of her time?

10. Why do the peasants eat rye bread?

FURTHER THOUGHTS

1. Medieval dentistry was rather primitive, and by the time a person was thirty he probably had considerable dental problems. This is one reason why even wealthy people who were over thirty preferred stew and soup to the roasts they had enjoyed in their younger days (when their teeth were sounder!).

2. Medieval cooks did not fry their foods in animal fat, because it was much too expensive. The fat was used for soap and candles. A pound of fat cost four times as much as a pound of meat!

3. When Edward III went to France he took thirty falcons and thirty pairs of hunting dogs with him so he could hunt when he wasn't busy fighting the French army! Much of what we know about medieval falconry comes from *The Art Of Falconry* written by Holy Roman Emperor Frederick II.

4. Many games that we consider childrens' games were played by adults in the Middle Ages. A favorite was Blind Man's Bluff. The French had a version of it which they called Colin du Maillet. It was named after a knight called Colin who was blinded in the siege of Liege in 999 yet still fought on.

5. Playing cards were imported to western Europe in the fourteenth century, coming to Italy by way of Egypt. They did not become popular until the invention of the printing press in the fifteenth century, when packs could be produced with identical backs.

6. Medieval cooks did not have access to tomatoes, corn, squash, green peppers, or chocolate. These were all derived from plants that grew only in America.

7. The everyday clothing of the lord and lady were usually dyed a dark blue. The color comes from an herb called woad. It was easily obtained, and so it was the cheapest dye. Even peasants often had dark blue articles of clothing, a welcome change from the usual green, brown, and tan earth tones. A suit of clothes lasted a lifetime, and it was usually listed in the inventory of important possessions upon a person's death.

8. Chairs were fairly rare in medieval times, even among the wealthy classes. A castle or manor would only possess a few. It was considered an honor to be asked to sit on one of them, even though it was probably not very comfortable.

PROJECTS

1. Consult some books in your classroom or Internet about falconry. Study the illustrations. Then draw a picture of a falcon that is ready to hunt.

2. Minstrels sometimes played an instrument called a hurdy-gurdy. Find out what it was. Then draw a picture of one.

3. The people of thirteenth century England liked to gather outside in the spring and dance. One of the favorite songs written at that time was called "Sumer is icumen in." It is still sung today. Find out what the words and music are, practice them with a group of friends, and then entertain your classmates!

4. Have a medieval banquet. This is a class activity. Study several of the books in the classroom, and take notes on what was served at a banquet. Then make a list of what you want to serve at your banquet (chicken can be used to represent swan, pheasant, and peacock, pork can take the place of wild boar, and beef can be called venison—unless the real thing is available). Have your classmates choose what they wish to contribute. In addition to the meat finger foods, you'll need trenchers, uncut loaves of white and brown bread, cheese, and pies. On the day of the banquet, set up tables in the classroom (you will have to decide who sits at the high table). Tapestries (bedspreads) tacked to the walls gives a "castle look." Have everyone come to the banquet dressed in medieval garb. Someone needs to be the jester. These are just a few suggestions. Take it from here, and have fun!

Chicken legs roasted in spices and lemon make great finger food for a banquet

5. The word cockatrice (remember the half bird half pig served at Sir Cedric's dinner?) refers to a legendary creature that was hatched from an egg. Consult some books on mythology and find out what it looked like. Then draw a picture of one.

6. Write a skit about either a day in the life of a noble person or one in the life of a peasant. Make it humorous—remember, these were real people!

Modern actors in medieval dress

The Great Hall of Doune Castle

CHAPTER 10

THE CHURCH AT ITS PEAK

For centuries the Church had been the single unifying force throughout Western Europe. It was better run and organized than any secular (non-religious) government, providing stability and security amid chaos and warfare. The major center of learning, the Church preserved classical scholarship and promoted great works of art, music, and drama. And in a world where everyday life was difficult for most people, the Church offered the promise of salvation in the next world. This explains why the period of the Middle Ages is also known as the Age of Faith.

THE CHURCH AT THE CENTER OF PEOPLE'S LIVES

We've learned that the Latin churches of the West split from the Greek churches of the East in 1054. There were now two Christian churches: the Roman Catholic Church in the West and the Greek Orthodox Church in the East. Let's take a closer look at the Roman Catholic Church in the eleventh century.

Towering above the humble dwellings and shops of every town and village was the church steeple. Nearly everyone attended the church. In fact, the word catholic comes from the Latin catholicus, meaning "universal." Mass was held there every Sunday, and its courtyard was the setting for local trade and community activities. The priest played an important role in the lives of his parishioners, performing baptisms and marriages, conducting funerals, hearing confession, looking after the poor, and, in the larger towns, running the church school. The people had to pay for these services, as well as contributing a tenth of their income each year,

either in money or in goods produced, and this contributed to the great wealth of the Church. Everyone looked forward to the saints' days when work was cancelled and the community gathered to dance, sing, and share specially prepared foods. A saint's day was also called a holy day, from which is derived our modern "holiday".

The nobility gave generously to the church and the monasteries, hoping that by doing so their souls would spend less time in purgatory and make it to heaven. Death occurred all too frequently, and everyone worried about spending eternity in the fiery furnace of hell. For this very reason, no one ever missed Mass except in cases of illness. And yet few people could understand what the priest was talking about as he spouted his Latin (although some sermons were given in the vernacular beginning in the thirteenth century), nor did the ordinary person understand abstract religious concepts like grace. Over the years, artists created altarpieces, stained glass windows, and relief stone statues to tell the stories of the Bible to the people who could neither read nor write.

Even today, the church is the heart of most towns in Europe

SACRED DRAMA AND MUSIC

The Church was the birthplace of medieval drama. Short plays about the birth and life of Jesus (called mysteries) and other biblical subjects (these were called miracles) were written in Latin and presented in the Church at special times, such as Christmas and Easter. They were another excellent device for teaching an illiterate public about the Bible. The roles were played by the priests and their assistants.

In later years, plays were often written in the vernacular (local language) and presented on the church steps or in the town marketplace during special festivals. The people loved to watch reenactments of Noah's Ark and the Great Flood. The most famous of the miracles of the twelfth century was *The Play of Daniel*. In the fifteenth century a new type of drama would evolve from the old miracle. Called the morality play, it was based upon the battle that is constantly waged between the forces of vice and virtue in a person's life.

Music had long been an important part of a church service. The oldest form of church music was the plainsong that was sung in monasteries. This was a simple, monophonic ("single voice") chant set to the words of the psalms (the lyrical poems of Old Testament). A soloist (cantor) or a choir of monks chanted the phrases without the accompaniment of a musical instrument. Sometimes the cantor sang one part and the choir took the other; other times the two halves of the choir alternately took parts. The plainsong had a free, flowing rhythm, and when sung in unison it was melodic and very expressive of the feelings described in the psalms.

Pope Gregory I ordered that the plainsong as it was chanted throughout the many

The church steeple rises above a medieval village

communities of Europe be standardized, and he sent teachers from a school of cantors in Rome to visit hundreds of churches to make sure that everyone performed in a similar fashion. The plainsong as it was codified by Gregory is known as the Gregorian chant. It became the basis for the more complex forms of music written in later centuries, and it remains the official liturgical music of the Roman Catholic Church. An ivory carving on the cover of a tenth century manuscript depicts a dove sitting on Gregory's shoulder, whispering the melodies of a chant in his ear.

Ninth century composers introduced musical variations on themes with complex rhythms, and before long musical instruments were added. Organs were in common use by the tenth century, but they were hardly a medieval invention. They had been used by the Greeks in the third century BC!

A medieval music manuscript

Harmonious voices were first added to the chant in the eleventh century, and soon many chants were being composed that involved two or more melodies that were sung together. This type of music is called polyphonic ("many sounds or voices"). The first soloist began a melody, and then another voice was added, singing a different melody, perhaps even one with a different rhythm. Then a third voice was added, and maybe even a fourth. The music of the fourteenth century was even more complex, and the rhythm was more varied. Guillaume de Machaut wrote the first polyphonic composition for an entire mass during this period.

The earliest music was not written down at all. It was simply passed on from one generation of monks to another. But in the eleventh century inventive composers drew horizontal lines (called staffs) to represent the musical scale. The notes of a piece of music were then drawn onto or between the appropriate lines. The notes also had different shapes to indicate how long the sound should be held (thus providing the rhythm). Much of this breakthrough in the recording of notation was the work of a famous musical theoretician named Guido d'Arezzo.

Although medieval chants were sung by a soloist and/or choir, St. Ambrose of Milan wrote a number of hymns that were designed to be sung by the congregation. And as we learned earlier, Theodulf (one of the scholars summoned to Aachen by Charlemagne) wrote "All Glory, Laud, and Honor"—still a popular hymn in modern churches.

THE CHURCH GROWS IN POLITICAL POWER

As the Church grew and flourished, many of the brightest and ablest minds were drawn to join it. The young boys trained in monastery schools would form an elite corps of highly educated men who dedicated their lives not only to scholarly pursuits but also to the administration of Church or secular (non-Church) governments. Since few people could read and write, the nobles came to depend upon the bishops and abbots to keep written records of local affairs, and it was not unusual for a member of the clergy to become an advisor to a count or duke. But as the power of the Church continued to grow, conflicts with the ruling monarchs of Europe were inevitable.

Much of the wealth of the Church came from the huge amount of property it owned. For example, the Papal States of northern Italy (the Donation of Pepin plus land that was later added) were ruled by the Pope just as any other lord ruled over his feudal territory. The people living there paid him taxes as well as a certain percentage of their produce. In other parts of Europe, large tracts of land were given to bishops and abbots, who held them as fiefs and were vassals to the feudal lords who had donated them. (When a bishop or abbot died, the lord appointed his replacement.) The churchmen, in turn, leased sections of the land to lesser tenants, who paid them taxes and met the other feudal obligations. When the Church was at its peak in the thirteenth century, the income it obtained from its land (it owned one quarter of the land in nearly every shire and county!) combined with the annual payments received from its parishioners exceeded the wealth of all the kings of Europe combined!

During the early years the Pope was advised by a group of bishops called the Curia, whose most important members were the Cardinals. After 1059 a new body, the College of Cardinals, elected each new pope. The Church had its own set of laws (called Canon Law). The people were expected to follow the laws of their secular ruler unless they conflicted with the Church laws, which then took precedence. The highest Church court was presided over by the Pope in Rome. Anyone who disagreed with any aspect of the teachings of the Church or the way that it operated was considered a heretic and was subject to punishment by the courts. The Pope could issue a decree called a papal bull that had tremendous authority. It was called a bull because of the lead seal (bulla in Latin) that was attached to the document.

NEW MONASTIC ORDERS

By the tenth century many of the monasteries had grown lax in their observance of the Benedictine Rule. The monks had farmed the land so successfully that they had a huge surplus of crops nearly every year. The temptation to work less hard and to live more comfortably than their predecessors was hard to resist. As the Benedictine Rule was relaxed, a good many monks became idle, sleeping on soft beds at night and consuming rich foods and fine wine. Benedict would have cringed had he known! Sometimes a lord would appoint as abbot a relative (often a

younger son) whose interests lay in amassing wealth and power, not religion, and the spiritual values of the monastery accordingly suffered even more.

The Abbey of Cluny

There were, however, a number of people who were offended by what they viewed as a corruption of monastic life. They longed for a return to more disciplined behavior. In 910 William, Duke of Aquitaine (not Eleanor's father) founded the Order of Cluny in Burgundy. According to legend, the aging Duke was feeling guilty about a murder he had committed when he was younger. So in hopes of obtaining forgiveness for the act, he summoned the abbot from a neighboring monastery and instructed him to choose a piece of land in Burgundy and to found an abbey there. This became the Abbey of Cluny. The monks of the new order, called Cluniacs, strictly observed the Benedictine Rule. Their leaders were appointed by the Church, not the lords. William drew up a charter stating that

Cluny would have no ties to feudalism but would remain free and independent, subject only to the authority of the Pope.

The Cluniacs were deeply religious, intellectual, and conscientious men. They encouraged the elimination of such Church abuses as simony (the sale of Church offices) and the inconsistent observance of clerical celibacy (non-marriage). At that time, it was not uncommon for priests to marry. The Cluniacs believed that a priest's family should be his congregation, and that a married man would feel torn by his obligations to church and family. Thanks to their efforts, celibacy of all clergymen became the official Church policy in 1100. (The last Pope known to have been married was Adrian II, who was elected in 867.)

It was at Cluny that the celebration of Mass was first dramatized, leading to the development of the mystery and miracle plays. Odilo, the abbot from 994 until 1049, was very interested in improving the physical appearance of the abbey. He supervised numerous renovations and had

Drawing of a Cistercian Monk

beautiful marble columns built around the cloister. Odilo once claimed that he had found the abbey built of wood and left it built of marble (paraphrasing a statement once made by the Emperor Augustus about the city of Rome).

In 1098 Robert, the abbot of Molesme, and a handful of monks left their Benedictine abbey for a secluded area called Citeaux in Burgundy. Known as the Cistercians, they led a strict monastic life reminiscent of the early

years of St. Benedict. Because they wore habits of undyed wool, they were called the White Monks (as we learned in Chapter 2, most Benedictines were called Black Monks).

The Cistercian Monastery of Santa Maria de Poblet, Spain, built in 1150

In 1113 a young Burgundian noble named Bernard (later St. Bernard) was admitted to Citeaux. He was drawn to the austere life style of the Cistercian brothers. He was so determined to avoid personal comfort that he lived in a cell that was so low he could not stand up in it! He spent most of his time studying and praying. St. Bernard wrote that nothing exists that was not made by God. His holiness and forceful personality later made him the spokesman for a monastic reform movement throughout Europe.

By 1151 there were over three hundred new monasteries in Europe and more than 11,000 Cistercian monks and nuns. The Cistercians were united by a constitution (the Charter of Charity) that defined the daily routine of the monks and the government of the abbeys. It bore several similarities to St. Benedict's Rule. Many medieval hymns were written by the Cistercians, some by Bernard himself.

After the death of Bernard, the Cistercians became somewhat less rigid in their philosophy of self-denial. They put their energies into farming the land, bringing many wilderness areas of Europe under cultivation. They drained marshes and established farmland in places that had previously been considered wasteland. Cistercian monks bred animals, especially horses, and they later provided the powerful chargers that could bear the weight of a mounted knight. A Cistercian abbey at Waldsassen in Germany developed a huge fish hatchery, history's first.

In 1131 a band of White Monks sailed across the Channel to England and then walked from the coast northward, where they were drawn to the lonely dales of Yorkshire. On the banks of the River Rie they founded the Rievaulx monastery. This part of England was ideal for raising sheep, and the Cisterians who settled there sold great quantities of wool to obtain what they needed for the monastery. They hired lay brothers (men who wanted to serve god but were not trained to become monks). The lay brothers provided most of the manual labor while the monks kept the books and ran the business. In time, the wool industry made the Cistercians so wealthy that they were able to pay one third of the ransom demanded by Leopold for King Richard.

Even stricter than Bernard's Cistercians were the Carthusians. Their order was founded in 1084 by St. Bruno at the Grande Chartreuse (Great Charterhouse) high in the French Alps. The abbey was said to be built "almost above the clouds and very near to God." It consisted of several stone houses constructed around a central courtyard; all buildings were enclosed by a high wall. Each Carthusian monk lived alone in a separate cell, silently reading and praying.

He prepared his own food (needless to say, it was simple fare). He only went to church for Mass and the night services; the other services he performed alone in his cell. Silence was maintained at all times, since the Carthusians believed that talk interfered with religious devotion.

GREGORY VII DEMANDS TOO MUCH

When a short, thin-voiced Cluniac monk named Hildebrand became Pope in 1073, he made it his mission to end the abuses he had observed within the Church and to free the Church from the control of kings and emperors

A Carthusian Monastery in Granada, Spain

by strengthening his own power. In the Dictatus Papae (Statement of the Pope) of 1075, Gregory VII proclaimed that the Papacy was superior to all other ruling powers, was incapable of error, and could be judged by no one. Henceforth, the Pope was to have the power to depose emperors, to annul decrees (no matter who had issued them), and to release subjects from any oath of allegiance taken to a ruler deemed wicked by the Church. Gregory also issued papal bulls abolishing simony, clerical marriage, and lay investiture (the appointment of clergymen to high Church offices by laymen).

His experiences as a Cluniac had convinced him that only the Church (and, to be more specific, the Pope) should appoint bishops. As we have seen, the kings and emperors were in the habit of appointing Church officials. Under Gregory's new rules, a bishop owed his first allegiance to the Pope (who gave him a ring and staff, the symbols of his office). But at the same time, as a feudal land holder, the bishop also owed allegiance to the king or emperor of whom he was a vassal. This was an awkward situation (where did the bishop's first allegiance lie?), and a conflict was unavoidable.

Henry IV, the Holy Roman Emperor, refused to recognize the Pope as his superior, and he disregarded Gregory's bulls concerning the appointment of bishops. He felt that because Church officials received fiefs from him and performed feudal duties, he ought to be able to select them and install them in office. He then went so far as to appoint a new bishop. When Gregory complained of this action, Henry sent him a letter in which he refused to address him as Pope (he called him a false monk) and demanded that he leave Rome! Gregory responded by excommunicating Henry and releasing his subjects from allegiance to him. Henry was furious! He threatened to depose Gregory, but it soon became clear to him that he would lose the support of his countrymen unless he made peace with the Bishop of Rome.

So Henry set out for Italy to get the Pope to lift the ban of excommunication. On January 21, 1077, he appeared at the gate of the castle at Canossa in the Apennine Mountains, where Gregory was wintering. Now the drama intensified. Gregory refused to see Henry unless he gave up his crown and confessed himself unworthy of the name and honor of emperor. When he reluctantly accepted these rather extreme demands, Henry was admitted to the castle courtyard. There he waited for three days in the bitter cold, barefoot and fasting. On the fourth day Gregory received him. "Holy Father, spare me!" pleaded Henry. Gregory raised him to his feet and absolved him. It appeared to be a victory for the Pope.

Engraving of Henry IV waiting in the snow, barefoot

But the matter was far from settled. The German nobles had used Henry's excommunication as an excuse for electing a new ruler. A civil war followed, during which Gregory tried unsuccessfully to act as a mediator. Once Henry won back his crown, he again ignored the papal decrees concerning the appointment of bishops. Placing himself at the mercy of the Pope had gotten him nowhere, and he would not try that again. Therefore, at the Lenten Synod of 1080 Gregory excommunicated him a second time. Henry countered and, backed by most of the German bishops, declared Gregory deposed and appointed a new pope (Clement III). His army took over Rome and Pope Clement was installed. Henry then besieged the castle of Sant'Angelo where Gregory had fled. Norman lords living in Sicily came to Gregory's aid and set him free (but not before taking time to sack the city of Rome). Gregory died soon afterwards in Salerno. His final years had been unhappy ones, and the appointment issue was still unresolved.

Sant'Angelo, Rome

In 1122 a compromise was reached with the signing of the Concordat of Worms (a German city). According to its terms, a king or emperor could now appoint a bishop, but the Pope had to approve his choice. To symbolize the supposed sharing of the power of appointment, the king (or emperor) gave the new bishop a scepter to signify his ownership of land and his feudal responsibilities; and, as before, the Pope gave him a staff and ring, the symbols of his religious duties. But, as you can see, the papal authority established by Gregory had been greatly weakened.

THE CHURCH IN ENGLAND

The Church in England was more independent of Rome than was the case on the Continent. Its highest ranking official, the Archbishop of Canterbury, often served as the chief advisor of the king. For centuries the Witan and the king had appointed archbishops and bishops as well as summoning church councils. The Norman conquest, however, brought up the question of the power of the Pope in England.

When Gregory demanded that William the Conqueror pay him homage, the king refused. Furthermore, he claimed that no pope would even be recognized in England without his consent, that no papal bull could be issued there without his permission, and that no royal minister could be excommunicated until he (William) had been consulted. Gregory did not pursue the matter further (he knew that William was a very tough competitor), and when the question came up during the reign of Henry I a compromise was reached allowing the Church to appoint a bishop (and give him the ring and staff) but enabling the king to receive his homage for the land he held as his vassal. (This settlement was made before the final compromise at Worms, which gave more power to the monarch.)

Henry II came to the throne in 1154. We learned earlier about his greatest accomplishment—the creation of a system of royal justice now known as the Common Law that guaranteed a trial by jury to all free men. But England also had a system of Church courts, and these were more lenient in the punishments they imposed than were the royal courts (the worst punishment was simply expulsion from the Church). Anyone who could recite six verses from the Bible by heart could claim to be a clergyman and hence be tried in a Church court. Henry believed that this option limited his power (it did!), so he attempted to change the system so that the royal courts would have the final authority. The Church, however, refused to cooperate. (This surprised no one.)

Henry's closest friend and advisor was Thomas Becket, whom he appointed as Chancellor (thereby making him his second-in-command). When the elderly Archbishop of Canterbury died in 1162, Henry chose Becket to succeed him, thinking that by doing so he would have control of the Church in England. However, Becket felt torn between his responsibilities to Henry and to the Pope. The conflict intensified when Henry issued the Constitutions of Clarendon (1164), which required anyone convicted in an ecclesiastical (Church) court to be turned over to a royal court for punishment. Furthermore, they stated that no appeals could be made to the Pope over a royal decision. At first Becket agreed to the new policies of the Constitutions, but when the Pope rejected them, he changed his mind. Henry was furious, and Becket, worried about his personal safety (and rightly so), escaped into exile in France.

After six years the two men were reconciled, and Becket returned to England as Archbishop. But he soon discovered that in his absence Henry's eldest son had been crowned by his rival, the Archbishop of York. (The boy would technically have no power until the death of the king.) This was a violation of Becket's right as Archbishop of Canterbury to preside over coronations. So he obtained from the Pope a

sentence of excommunication against the bishops who had taken part in the ceremony as well as those barons who had sided with the king against him. Henry was so exasperated that he muttered in the presence of four of his knights, "Is there no one who will rid me of this miserable priest?" The knights took him at his word. On December 29, 1170, at the hour of Vespers, they entered the Canterbury Cathedral and killed the Archbishop.

Thomas Becket was canonized (made a saint) in 1173, and the shrine placed in the Cathedral where he died would become a major pilgrimage site. Henry was upset by the death of his former friend (he was angry at him, but he never meant to have him killed). He did penance at Becket's tomb by allowing himself to be publicly whipped by the monks of Canterbury. After Becket's death the Constitutions of Clarendon were largely ignored, and the Church courts continued to function as they had in the past.

Canterbury Cathedral, scene of the murder of Thomas of Becket

In 1198 Innocent III became Pope. Under the control of this intelligent and capable man the Papacy attained the height of its prestige and power. Innocent believed that all secular rulers should be subject to the Pope, "just as the body must be subject to the spirit." This, of course, had been the goal of Gregory VII, but Innocent would meet with greater success. (It was also Innocent who called for the disastrous Fourth Crusade.)

Soon after John succeeded his brother Richard the Lion-hearted as King of England, the question of the appointment of bishops came up again. When the Archbishop of Canterbury died in 1205, John appointed a new candidate, who then went to Rome to receive the Pope's blessing. But Innocent rejected him and appointed someone else as Archbishop, a man named Stephen Langton. When John refused to accept Langton, Innocent placed all of England under an interdict (all church services were banned and no bells could ring). The next year he excommunicated John. John didn't seem to care, but his people were miserable, and many plots were made against his life. Finally, when Innocent threatened to issue a bull releasing all English subjects from allegiance to the king, John submitted. In 1213 he agreed to receive Langton as Archbishop and to surrender England to the Pope, from whom he would receive it back as a fief of the Papacy. Thus, John became Innocent's vassal, a humiliation made even worse by the annual tribute of 1,000 marks that he had to send to Rome. As for Langton, he was an intelligent man and a powerful leader whose presence would have an important effect upon John's government, as we will see in Chapter 13.

THE DESIGN OF CHURCHES AND CATHEDRALS

The word church comes from the Greek kyriakon doma, meaning "the lord's house." At first it referred to the actual place of worship, but it also came to mean the entire religious community. The earliest Christian churches were adaptations of the Roman basilica—a large rectangular structure with a long central aisle which served as a law court and marketplace in ancient times. The interior of such a stone church was dimly lighted by the clerestory, a row of windows just below the wooden roof.

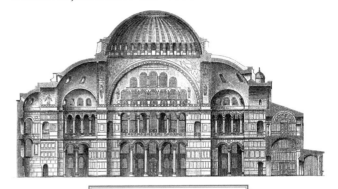

Design of Hagia Sophia

In the sixth century Byzantine Emperor Justinian commissioned the construction of a large church called Hagia Sophia ("Divine Wisdom") which combined the design of the basilica with a huge central dome (one hundred feet in diameter). Viewed from within, the dome appeared to be suspended in the brilliant light that came through the forty windows around its drum. For five years 10,000 men toiled on the project, which cost the equivalent of nearly $150 million! Hagia Sophia was the most important church in the Byzantine Empire for the next thousand years, and it remains one of the world's greatest architectural achievements. (see page 129)

From the sixth to the eleventh centuries, the greatest builders in western Europe were the monastic orders. They used most of the wealth they acquired through donations, feudal fees, and the sale of farm products to construct their abbeys. In the later years, the monks experimented with new designs to give their churches a loftier appearance.

The Carolingian Renaissance marked a resurgence in church construction in Western Europe. Charlemagne, wishing to revive the glories of the imperial past, based the design of his Palace Chapel at Aachen on Justinian's octagonal church dedicated to St. Vitale in Ravenna. In fact, his structure's high, massive columns were brought to Aachen from Rome and Ravenna, and the bronze railings and gratings that decorated its interior were also imported from Italy. The chapel was built in the shape of an octagon with a diameter of fifty feet, topped by a cupola and surrounded by a sixteen-sided gallery of archways. The impressive twin towers that flanked the chapel's entrance were copied throughout Charlemagne's empire and became an integral feature of church design. Part of his chapel has survived to this day.

Charlemagne's octagonal chapel at Aachen

Beginning in the eleventh century, most churches were constructed with very thick walls and rounded arches that were supported by massive piers (pillars). Because these buildings reminded the people of the architecture of ancient Rome, the style became known as Romanesque. Hoping to make the structures more

A Romanesque Church

fire resistant (the old wooden roofs frequently caught fire), the architects designed high vaults (often just a series of arches, known as a barrel vault) in the ceiling to help support a heavy stone roof. But now the walls had to be extremely thick to carry the additional weight, and the windows had to be small in order not to weaken the walls. For further support, the walls were braced on the outside of the church by sturdy (and stubby) stone buttresses. A more complex structure type of vault (called the groin vault) was formed by the intersection at right angles of two barrel vaults; the weight was distributed at the corners and supported by thick stone columns. This produced a large, open space. The Cistercian monks were among the first to experiment with the groin vault.

The interior of the church formed a large cross. The two arms of the cross were called transepts, the short end at the top was called the apse or chancel (it contained the choir and altar), and the long end (the main section of the church) was called the nave. The inner walls were white-

Groin vaults in the cloister of a monastery

washed and painted with colorful scenes taken from Bible stories. The larger churches built in the key cities of the dioceses were called cathedrals. This term comes from the Latin word cathedra which refers to the throne upon which the bishop sat. The Cathedral of Pisa, which is famous for its leaning belltower, was designed by an Italian Romanesque architect.

In the late eleventh century church architects experimented with ways of constructing churches that had higher, thinner walls. The Romanesque buildings were massive and dark, and these men wanted to design buildings that created an ambiance of openness and of closeness with God. But how could they build a wall that was higher without making it thicker to support the increased weight?

The problem was solved in the Ile de France, where architects discovered that by using a pointed arch rather than a rounded one, they could build a much higher ceiling vault. A pointed arch had the extra advantage of pushing downward more than outward (as rounded arches

did), and this somewhat reduced the outward pressure on the walls. They also found that by supporting a vault with a grid of thin diagonal (crossed) arches (ribs) they further lessened the outward pressure of the stone masonry. This new, lighter-looking rib vault was a refinement of the old rounded groin vault. Churches built in this period had a series of rib vaults across the ceiling, which were supported by tall, slender pillars. The outer wall was braced by solid masses of stone called pier (or pillar) buttresses, taller than those seen outside Romanesque churches. The pier buttresses were usually connected to the wall at the points where the ribs of the vaults had the greatest tendency to push outward by slender arched supports called flying buttresses. So the smaller flying buttresses carried the weight of the roof and transferred it to the pier buttresses. Now the walls could be made thinner and the spaces between the pillars could be filled with large stained glass windows.

This type of architecture was called Gothic. Actually, Gothic was a term of derision coined by Italian architects of the sixteenth century who did not admire the style at all. They preferred the more stately design of the ancient Romans to the soaring cathedrals, which they regarded as an inferior product of the Gothic barbarians who had invaded and destroyed classical civilization.

The design of the cross can be seen in the Cathedral of Pisa

Today, however, most people associate Gothic architecture with beauty and elegance.

All lines of a Gothic cathedral pointed up toward heaven: the towering rib vaults of the ceiling, the pointed arches of the doorways and windows, the spire, and the steep roof. It was a graceful structure, spacious and filled with light. The arches above the doorways (portals) were decorated with sculpted figures of saints, angels, and the Apostles, and these, as well as the statues placed in alcoves along the walls, helped to tell the story of the Christian faith. The tops (capitals) of the pillars were intricately sculpted as foliage that often looked like lace. Finely wrought metal work adorned the inner gates that divided the main sections of the church. The

Buttresses supporting a wall of Milan Cathedral

wood of the pulpit and the choir was beautifully carved with scenes from everyday life. Sunlight filtered through the stained glass to illuminate the colorful biblical scenes. Gargoyles, grotesque stone figures of demons and fanciful birds and beasts, were perched along the outer edges of the roof. When it rained, the water spouted out through their mouths (gargoyle means "little throat"). Some of these fanciful creatures, called chimera, were purely decorative and carried no water. They reflect the

A series of vaults in Rheims Cathedral

A chimera

Sculpted portal of Notre Dame

medieval stone cutter's vivid imagination and sense of humor.

A gargoyle

The Gothic style spread from France to Germany, England, and Spain, each nation developing its own version. So many cathedrals and abbeys were built between the eleventh and thirteenth centuries that Europe was once described as being clothed in a white robe of churches. Over five hundred were constructed in France between 1120 and 1270, and more stone was quarried for these churches than had been used in the three Great Pyramids of ancient Egypt!

It took a long time to build a cathedral, and some were never completed. The typical construction crew consisted of teams of stone masons, carpenters, stone cutters, sculptors, metal workers, wood carvers, crafters of stained glass, and many others. The architect (called the master mason) was exempt from taxation and was provided with free housing, fur robes in winter, and a bonus at the end of the year—all this in addition to a high salary and considerable prestige.

In 1140 Abbot Suger of the Benedictine Abbey of St. Denis (just outside Paris) decided to replace the abbey's Romanesque church with a cathedral built in the Gothic style. It is one of the oldest examples of Gothic architecture. The Abbot helped to design glass windows that were so tall that the church was pervaded by the "light of Divine Essence." (The Christian Church had always associated light with truth and divinity.) According to legend, the original abbey was named after a missionary called Denis, who was beheaded by the Romans on Montmartre in 250 and yet walked north carrying his head until he reached a plowed field, where he was then buried. His ashes are the most precious possession of the cathedral, which also contains the remains of nearly all the kings and queens of France who reigned after 768, as well as Pepin II and Charles Martel. Suger's contemporaries were amazed by

Notre Dame Cathedral

the height and dazzling brightness of the interior of the new church, and before long other similar structures were being built throughout France.

In 1163 Pope Alexander III laid the cornerstone for the Cathedral of Notre Dame over the remains of a Roman temple in Paris. The building was not completed until 163 years later. Notre Dame was the first cathedral designed with flying buttresses (St. Denis had only pier buttresses). It is famous for the spectacular stained glass rose windows that dominate the northern and southern ends of the transept.

Stained glass windows in the Cathedral of St Denis

Construction of the Cathedral of Chartres was begun in 1194 and completed in an incredible (for the times) twenty-nine years. It is one of the largest cathedrals in France, its twin-steepled silhouette visible for miles above the flat wheat fields that surround it. Chartres is a masterpiece of finely crafted detail: its 10,000 figures in stone

and glass tell the story of God and man from the creation of the universe. Most of the original stained glass can still be seen in the cathedral today. It was preserved during the two world wars by town authorities, who dismantled over 9,000 square feet of glass and stored it piece by piece until the end of the fighting.

Stained glass in the Cathedral of Chartes

The building of cathedrals brought out the competitive spirit of the architects, and for a while each tried to build the tallest, most majestic structure. This determination to out-do one another is reflected in the increasing height of the vaults in the naves: Notre Dame was 107 feet high; Chartres rose to 118 feet; Bourges was 124 feet; Rheims attained 128 feet; and Amiens towered at 144 feet. (The Cathedral at Rouen has the highest spire, rising a spectacular 495 feet.) In 1272 the architect of the Cathedral at Beauvais designed a vault that was thirteen feet higher than that at Amiens. The chancel was always the first part of a church to be constructed. When the chancel at Beauvais was nearly completed it collapsed. It was rebuilt, this time supported with many more pier buttresses than were originally called for. Soon afterwards work came to a halt on the massive project, due to a lack of funds. The soaring chancel remains, braced by extra supports (even today people seem to worry about another collapse). At the end of the structure that would have led into the nave of the cathedral is the "temporary" partition that was erected in the thirteenth century. The chancel at Beauvais is a majestic reminder of what happens when architectural ambition is pushed beyond what is feasible in engineering (and economics!).

The chancel of the Cathedral of Beauvais

As the Gothic style evolved throughout Europe, less stone was used, as the building became an almost skeletal framework designed to be filled with large stained glass windows. An excellent example of this is the Sainte Chapelle built in Paris in the thirteenth century to house King Louis IX's most priceless possession, the alleged crown of thorns worn by Christ at the time of his crucifixion. Louis had bought the crown for an outrageous price from the Byzantine Emperor. Three quarters of the jewel-like chapel is glass.

How were these magnificent constructions financed? It was no longer the monastic orders that came up with the funds, but the townspeople themselves. They took great pride in having an impressive cathedral in their community, and they were comforted by the belief that their

efforts would win them God's favor. Some money was raised through the sale of indulgences by the bishop. Rouen's south tower, the Butter Tower, was built with money raised by the Church by selling dispensations to permit the eating of butter during Lent! Sometimes the religious relics belonging to a church were sent on tours from town to town; admission was charged for all who wished to view them. And, of course, the local nobility made large contributions (hoping for an easier passage to heaven). Apart from these sources, most of the funds came from the savings of the hard-working peasants and craftsmen, who also contributed their time and labor to the project.

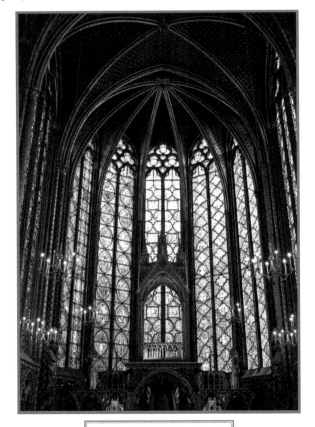

Sainte-Chapelle, Paris

Many of the cathedrals of the Middle Ages have not survived to our times (the wars of the twentieth century destroyed a great deal of our cultural heritage). However, thanks to a master mason named Villhard de Honnecourt, who traveled throughout medieval France, Germany, Switzerland sketching the churches he came upon, we have a detailed record of the design of numerous cathedrals that now lie in ruins.

THE FRIARS

In the thirteenth century the problem of abuses in the Church once again became a major issue. In response to the growing feeling of dissatisfaction with the clergy, two highly motivated and devout men, St. Francis and St. Dominic, founded a new kind of religious order. Known as friars (from the Latin frater meaning "brother"), members of the new orders took a vow to provide spiritual guidance for the common people, especially the poor and the suffering. Although they followed the same rules as the monks we have studied, they lived in the "real world," not the monastery.

Francis Bernadone (1182-1226), the son of a rich merchant, was born in Assisi, Italy. During his early years he lived an extravagant life as the leader of a teenage gang. He was captured while fighting in a war between Assisi and a nearby city. The terrible conditions he observed during the war and while he was imprisoned caused him to reexamine his views about what he valued in life. He concluded that material wealth was meaningless. He decided to give up his possessions and to dwell among the common people, dressed in rags and barefoot, preaching the Gospel and offering aid to those who were suffering. Jesus became his lifetime model. His former companions were so angered by his transformation that they pelted him with mud, and his father, worried that he would give away the entire family fortune, disinherited him. Apparently unfazed by such unkind treatment, Francis left home, singing a French song. He

found great fulfillment working among the poor, even among the lepers (whom everyone else scorned), and he soon had a following of young men who were attracted to his unselfish ways.

In 1210 Francis took twelve of his followers to Rome, where they were recognized by Pope Innocent III (remember him?) as a new order to be called the Franciscan Friars. Since they sold all their personal possessions before becoming friars, the Franciscans depended upon the people they served for food and lodging. They were cheerful men, who believed that God would always help them in their hour of need. In 1212 Francis established the order of the Poor Clares (the women's equivalent of his own order).

The Franciscan order expanded at a phenomenal rate throughout many European countries and even spread into the Holy Land. In 1219 Francis joined the Fifth Crusade and made a futile attempt to convert Sultan al-Kamit while the Crusaders were laying siege to Damietta in Egypt.

In 1224 the Stigmata miraculously appeared on the friar's body. (These were the imprints of the five wounds on the hands, feet, and side of Jesus during the Crucifixion.) When he died two years later he was mourned throughout much of the Christian world. He was canonized in 1228. St. Francis left behind many religious poems, including "The Canticle of Brother Sun," which reflects his love for all living things. A century after his death, a Franciscan friar collected the stories about his order's founder and wrote them down as *The Little Flowers of Saint Francis*.

Dominic (1170-1221) was a Spanish priest who was troubled by the fact that many of his fellow clergymen were nearly illiterate as well as poorly skilled in the art of preaching. Furthermore, he was offended by what he considered heretical teachings within the Church.

Stained glass painting of Saint Francis preaching to the birds

Like Francis, he visited Rome as a young man and met Pope Innocent III, who encouraged him to found an order of friars whose chief aim would be to teach and preach. Every member of the new order, called the Dominicans, was expected to spend many hours of each day in the pursuit of knowledge. Clad in a white habit with a black cloak (so they were known as the Black Friars), they wandered throughout Europe preaching and founding schools. People flocked to hear the sermons of the Dominicans, because they were noted for being witty and entertaining as well as inspirational.

In the thirteenth century Dominican friars traveled into the Holy Land and as far east as China. Being of an intellectual bent, many of them were drawn to the philosophies of such ancient Greeks as Aristotle that had recently been translated into Latin, and Dominicans often joined the faculties of the universities that were springing up (more about these in Chapter 12). The Order of the Dominicans still exists today.

THE BABYLONIAN CAPTIVITY

In the beginning of fourteenth century, King Philip the Fair of France refused to obey Pope Boniface VIIFs order to set free one of his subjects, who was imprisoned for political reasons. In fact, he had Boniface arrested in Anagni, Italy, but the local townspeople immediately set him free. Philip was supported by his nobles in his defiance of the Pope. Boniface died soon afterwards. To prevent any further trouble of this kind, Philip so dominated the election process of the next pope that a Frenchman (Clement V) was chosen, and the seat of the Papacy was transferred from Rome to Avignon, a French city on the Rhone River. This change of the papal residence is known as the Babylonian Captivity of the Church (after the long exile of the ancient Jews in Babylon), and it lasted from 1305 until 1377.

Since he had lost the revenues of the Papal Lands in Italy, Clement needed a new source of income to maintain his court. So he sent orders to all the archbishops and bishops of Europe to levy special taxes on their parishioners and to send him the money. This, of course, caused a great deal of grumbling among the people who were taxed.

The English Church resented any attempt on the part of the French popes to control their affairs, and they totally ignored the papal taxes. King Edward III even passed a law forbidding the Pope to make any appointments in England without his consent and banning any appeals from an English church court to the papal court. (Does this sound familiar?)

The six popes elected during this period were, predictably, all of French origin. They lived in great luxury in a splendid palace, and it was apparent to nearly everyone that their decisions were strongly influenced by the French king. The small village of Avignon soon became a bustling city of eighty thousand, as people of many professions flocked to serve the Pope and his entourage.

The Papal Palace in Avignon

PILGRIMAGES

We learned earlier about the pilgrimages Christians made to the city of Jerusalem, but many other sacred sites were also visited regularly. These were the churches in major cities that possessed such relics of saints as the fingernails of St. Edmund and the skull of St. John. These relics were supposed to have great healing powers, and so they became great tourist attractions. Canterbury had the point of the sword that had been thrust into the brain of Thomas Becket (it

was still lodged in his skull). Bottles of Becket's blood were made available to pilgrims visiting the Canterbury Cathedral. When the scholarly St. Thomas Aquinas died (we'll encounter him in Chapter 12), the monks cut off his head and boiled his body so they could keep the bones as relics! But, as you can imagine, many of the so-called relics were fake. A pig's bone could easily be identified as a part of a saint's skull, and anyone could claim that some splinters of wood came from "the cross" in Jerusalem. Most pilgrims accepted what they were told about a "sacred object" on faith, and the relic merchants made a big profit!

Some people went on a pilgrimage to atone for an immoral life, hoping to receive forgiveness for their behavior. Sick or crippled people went in hopes of being healed. Others simply desired to worship at a holy place. And, of course, some went in search of adventure. (Remember, few people traveled in those early times, so a pilgrimage offered a great opportunity to "see the world.") There were even professional pilgrims: people who went from shrine to shrine, staying at Christian castles or monasteries along the way, and telling their stories to all who would listen. In the twelfth century there was a guidebook that showed the best routes to various shrines and provided information about the purity of local water supplies and good places to spend the night.

A typical pilgrim could be easily identified. He wore a long gray robe and a wide-brimmed hat. He was often barefoot, and he carried an ash wood staff, a script (a small bag slung over his shoulder, containing food and a few necessities), and a hollowed gourd containing water (this hung around his neck). Few women made pilgrimages, because the journey could be dangerous (thieves were abundant). Rich women occasionally traveled to holy sites, accompanied by groups of armed knights.

Statue of a Medieval Pilgrim

Pilgrims visiting a particularly famous site were often given special souvenir emblems to wear. Those who went to Peter's altar in Rome (they were called Romers) were able to view the Holy Vernicle: a cloth on which an imprint of Christ's face appeared after St. Veronica had wiped the sweat from his brow on the way to Calvary. Just seeing this holy relic earned a pilgrim a huge indulgence (remission of punishments for his sins). After visiting the altar, the Romers wore small napkins, symbolic of the one that covered the face of Christ. A few pilgrims visiting Rome also traveled south to Bari on the Italian coast to see the relics of St. Nicholas (the original Santa Claus!).

Pilgrims who went to Jerusalem were called Palmers because of the palm leaf they were given there. Santiago de Compostella in northwestern Spain held the bones of St. James, which had been discovered in the ninth century. Pilgrims visiting there wore scallop shells in honor of a miracle St. James had performed at the nearby seashore. And, as we have seen, visitors to Canterbury were given flasks containing drops of blood of Becket (as well as a small bell). The pilgrims were very proud of the emblems and badges they accumulated, but many medieval writers had great fun ridiculing the odd assortment of trinkets that jingled and clanged as they walked along.

JOHN WYCLIFFE CONFRONTS THE CHURCH

John Wycliffe was an English religious reformer of the fourteenth century. He criticized the parish priests for leading worldly lives and neglecting their duties, the friars for being lazy and ignorant, and the bishops for being so busy looking after their lands that they had no time for their religious duties. By his day the Church had an enormous income from estates that covered a third of England. In 1376 a Parliamentary report indicated that the taxes levied by the Pope in England were five times those collected by the King!

Wycliffe urged the clergy to give up their material possessions and to return to the simple life of earlier times. He believed that every priest had the right to teach and preach whatever and however he chose, and he attacked some of the doctrines of the Church (such as the symbolism of the bread and wine in the Communion service). Wycliffe said that the English king was the appropriate person to reform the church. He denied the authority of the Pope, saying that Christ was the only Head of the Church. The Pope issued five bulls against him, demanding that he be arrested and imprisoned. But the bulls were disregarded.

John Wycliffe

Wycliffe reasoned that if the people could read the Bible for themselves, they would not have to depend upon the clergy at all. So he began a translation of the Scriptures. This, the first English Bible, was completed in 1382. After his death Wycliffe was condemned by the Church Council of Constance, and his body was ordered exhumed and burned.

But Wycliffe's ideas were taken up and spread throughout England by his followers. Known as the Poor Preachers, they went about the country wearing ragged clothes, eating humble fare, and preaching in the open air. Although they were nicknamed the Lollards by their opponents (a lollard is someone who babbles or mumbles), their numbers and influence grew.

Wycliffe's ideas were popularized on the Continent by John Huss, a reformer from Bohemia. They would be an important factor in the Protestant Reformation of the sixteenth century. But for the time being, the Church fought off the repeated charges of abuse and corruption. Huss was excommunicated, condemned as a heretic, and burned at the stake.

THE GREAT SCHISM

In 1377 the French Pope was persuaded to leave Avignon and return to Rome, where he soon died. The College of the Cardinals then elected an Italian Pope (Urban VI). However, the French Cardinals rejected this candidate and appointed a new pope from among their own numbers (Clement VII). Urban then excommunicated Clement as well as the French Cardinals, replacing the fallen cardinals with Italians. So Clement retaliated by excommunicating Urban and the Italian Cardinals! For the next thirty-nine years there were two popes: Urban in Rome and Clement in Avignon. This dual-papacy is known as the Great Schism ("division into two hostile factions"). Each pope claimed supreme power, supported by his own College of Cardinals.

A Church Council met at Constance in 1414 and deposed the two popes, electing a new one (Martin V) who would reside in Rome. Peace was restored, but the Babylonian Captivity and the Great Schism had greatly weakened the authority of the Papacy, and the criticism of the Church continued, unabated.

QUESTIONS

1. What does the word "catholic" mean?

2. What is the Gregorian chant?

3. What is polyphonic music?

4. How did the Church get so rich?

5. Why were new monastic orders formed?

6. What are three important things the Cistercians did?

7. How did Gregory VII define the power of the papacy?

8. What was the Concordat of Worms?

9. What was the main cause of the conflict between Henry II and Thomas Becket?

10. What are three adjectives that describe Innocent HI?

11. What were the special characteristics of a Romanesque church?

12. What is a flying buttress?

13. What is the oldest Gothic cathedral?

14. How were friars different than monks?

15. Where did the popes of the Babylonian Captivity reside?

16. Why did John Wycliffe translate the Bible into English?

FURTHER THOUGHTS

1. Here's how the Gothic stained glass windows were made. First the craftsmen drew the design for the window, indicating with heavy black lines the metal bars that were necessary to hold the glass firmly in place. To make the glass they heated sand, salt, and ashes into a molten mass. They colored it with metallic oxides (copper for red, iron for yellow, manganese for purple, and cobalt for blue). The glass was blown or spun into a crown (plate), and when it cooled it was cut into small pieces. The thin irregular fragments of glass were worked into the grooves of the malleable lead frames. These were strengthened by iron bands. Details, such as a face or the folds of a garment, were painted onto the glass. The art of making stained glass windows was perfected in the twelfth century. The windows represented about half the cost of building a cathedral. For this reason, the windows were often donated by specific groups. Of the 102 windows of the Cathedral of Chartres, forty-four were donated by lords and princes, sixteen by bishops and other clergy, and forty-two by town guilds. Those donated by the guilds include bottom panels that depict their crafts.

Stained glass depicting St. Francis

2. The Inquisition was a church court created to seek out and prosecute heretics, supposedly strengthening the Christian Church. The Papal Inquisition was instituted by Pope Gregory IX in 1231. The court interrogated people suspected of heresy and tried to obtain a

confession, which was necessary for conviction. Physical torture was often used, including such painful procedures as stretching the limbs on a rack or burning the skin with hot coals. If the suspect confessed, he was given minor penances, such as flogging, fasting, or fines. Denial of the charges resulted in terrible punishments: life imprisonment or execution. Since the Church did not allow the shedding of blood, execution meant being burnt at the stake.

3. Many stories of miracles concerning the Virgin Mary were told (and believed) throughout the Middle Ages, particularly after the eleventh century when a cult of the Virgin arose. An interesting example of a miracle concerns a Flemish monk who was painting a picture of heaven and hell on the high portals of his abbey. He portrayed the Devil as a hideous monster, and as he dipped his paintbrush he suddenly spied the Devil himself standing beside him on the scaffold. When the Devil demanded to be painted as a young and handsome man, the monk refused. This so infuriated the Devil that he pushed the hapless painter off the scaffold. But as he fell, a statue of the Virgin in a niche below the portal stretched out her arms and caught him!

4. Three different churches had stood on the site where the Gothic Cathedral of Chartres was built. The original cathedral was built in the fourth century. It was the first church to be dedicated to the Virgin Mary. In 876 the Sancta Carmisia, a long piece of silk believed to have been worn by the Virgin at the birth of Jesus, was presented to the people of Chartres by Charles the Bald (grandson of Charlemagne). From then on pilgrims flocked to the town's Romanesque church (the second cathedral to be built there) to see the sacred relic. The magical powers of the veil were confirmed in 911 when Chartres was attacked by the Vikings. As soon as the local citizens placed the relic on the top of the city

wall, the Norsemen allegedly fled. Their leader was Rollo who, as we know, later converted to Christianity and became the first Duke of Normandy. In 1194 a terrible fire destroyed the church but the veil survived. The parishioners interpreted this as a sign that a new church must be built for the relic. That's when the Gothic Cathedral was constructed. The veil is still on display there.

Chartres Cathedral

5. Pope Celestine V was a hermit monk who became Pope. But he ruled for only a few months and then resigned. He was the only Pope to do so.

6. Many Christian holidays retained a festive touch of paganism during the Middle Ages and even into our own times (the Yule Log, for example). To appease the people in those early times, the Church also tolerated a number of irreverent customs. For example, on certain occasions choirboys changed places with the clergy and led the services. On one feast day, the minor clergy would lead a donkey into the church, drink wine, and munch on sausages before the altar. They wore their vestments inside out, held their Bibles upside down, and punctuated the service with outrageously loud hee-haws, much to the crowd's delight!

7. In the thirteenth century a new style of handwriting (appropriately called Gothic) began to replace the Carolingian miniscule as the standard used by the scribes. It was more elaborate then the older style; the letters were drawn with thick lines and had a relatively stiff, narrow, and angular form.

Gothic letters

PROJECTS

1. Gregorian chants have become very popular in recent times. A CD entitled *chant* was released in early 1994 and rose to the top of the chart for pop music (over two million copies have been sold!). It was recorded by the Benedictine monks of the Spanish monastery of Santo Domingo de Silos. Their monastery was once a resting place for pilgrims en route to Santiago de Compostela. Try to obtain a copy and listen to the beautiful singing.

2. *Everyman* is a well-known medieval play that was once performed by the priests within the church. Find a copy. Read it. Then make a short report to your class. Be sure to explain the meaning of the title.

3. Find out more about St. Bruno, the founder of the Carthusian monks. Think about how his ideas were similar to those of St. Benedict and how they were different. Then write a short play in which St. Benedict and St. Bruno encounter one another in heaven.

4. Watch the DVD *Becket* starring Richard Burton and Peter O 'Toole.

5. Consult a book of modern poetry and find "Murder in the Cathedral" by T.S. Eliot. Read it to yourself several times, slowly. When you understand the images and the mood the poet is trying to convey, read the poem to your class.

6. Read David Macaulay's *Cathedral*. The book is filled with excellent drawings and explanations of the steps involved in building a cathedral.

7. Some scholars have described flying buttresses as examples of architectural crudity. Others maintain that they reflect structural honesty. What do you think? Write a paragraph explaining which definition you agree with, and tell why. Give specific examples to back up your argument.

8. Make a list of the Popes of the Middle Ages. After each name, write one important thing that he did.

9. Matthew Paris was a Benedictine monk who wrote a great deal about daily life in the thirteenth century. Find out more about him and his chronicles.

10. Giotto di Bondone was a Florentine painter who covered most of the inner walls of the Brancacci Chapel (also known as the Arena Chapel) in Padua with life-like frescoes depicting the life of Jesus. His works led to a revolution in painting. Find a website relating to the Brancacci Chapel (or the Arena Chapel) in Padua. Choose one of Giotto's frescoes. Then write a paragraph describing the painting. Tell whether or not the painting appeals to you, and why.

Statue of Giotto in Florence, Italy

PART III
THE SEEDS OF CHANGE

CHAPTER 11

TOWNS AND TRADE

Until the eleventh century the lives of most people centered around a castle or manor whose economy was nearly self-sufficient. But then things began to change. The population increased, and for the first time since the fall of the Roman Empire, births dramatically outnumbered deaths. Strong dynasties in France, England, and Germany put down civil wars and rebellions led by the nobles, bringing peace to their nations. Better farming methods and new technology increased productivity, which meant that fewer farm laborers were required than before. This opened up new possibilities for many peasants to develop special skills and to earn their livings as artisans.

THE RISE OF CRAFTSMEN

In an age when there were no factories or machines to produce everyday items, there was a great need for a wide variety of hand-made crafts. Of course, most families continued to spin their own wool and make their own clothes, but it took an expert to hammer out an iron pitchfork or produce a pair of leather boots. As the number of craftsmen increased, many of them began to add the type of work they did to their first name, such as John the Smith or Henry the Tailor. This also helped to distinguish people who bore the same first name. (Imagine how many Johns or Marys might live in one English community!) Eventually, the article (the) was dropped, leaving a name like John Smith or Henry Tailor (or Taylor). Many modern English last names can be traced back to the profession of a talented medieval ancestor. Potter, Brewer, Wheeler, Fisher, Hunter, Skinner, Weaver, Miller, Glover, and Carpenter are just a few examples.

It takes special skill to make a barrel

There were some crafts that might be unfamiliar to you. For example, did you know that a cooper made barrels by fitting together slats of wood with iron hoops? Barrels were in great demand beginning in the early Middle Ages when it was discovered that wine and beer kept better in wooden containers than in clay pots. And what did a fletcher do? He made arrows from soft wood, using the feathers of forest birds he had slain. A cordwainer made products from leather. The term cordwainer is derived from Cordova, Spain, where the best leather of the times was produced. A currier colored the leather after it was tanned. A loriner made stirrups, bits, and other equipment for horses from steel. A joiner made plows and farm tools. A chandler made candles. A wheelwright made wooden wheels for wagons and carriages from elm, ash, or oak (all hardwoods). Even the spokes of his wheels were made of wood. And John Smith fashioned metal tools, horseshoes, and iron gratings using the heat of his forge.

A blacksmith at work

THE FORMATION OF TOWNS

A surplus of crops and a large number of crafts being produced led to active trade. A potter could easily feed his family and supply his household needs by exchanging his jugs, pots, and cups for the products of other craftsmen as well as the local farmers. But there were certain things that were not locally available. These were brought in by outside merchants, who had to face all sorts of difficulties in order to deliver their products to the manors. Money was rare, roads were poor, there were few bridges, and thieves roamed the highways. Making matters worse, the feudal lords collected heavy tolls from anyone who crossed their estates. But in the twelfth century conditions began to improve. The roads that had been neglected for hundreds of years were repaired and widened so that two carts could pass each other. New bridges were built, and river traffic increased, especially in France.

Merchants could now travel more easily from place to place. Sometimes they congregated at certain locations, such as a major road crossing or along a well-used waterway. These became trading centers, and, when some merchants decided to settle down and work in one place, they evolved into villages, and later towns. The early settlers built wooden houses and surrounded the community with a wooden palisade for protection. Often a trading center grew up near a castle or monastery whose walls provided extra protection in times of war.

Over the years, the population of the towns increased, as the original inhabitants were joined by unemployed professional soldiers, the younger sons of the nobility, and craftsmen from local manors who were looking for a greater market for their products. Serfs also fled from their burdensome feudal obligations. According to the law of the times, if a serf remained in a town for one year he was considered legally free. Since

Fruit like apples could be sold right from the cart

several languages were spoken by the people of medieval Europe, a townsman was referred to in slightly different ways, depending upon where he lived: He was called a burger in Germany, a burgess in England, and a bourgeois in France.

The markets that were set up in the open squares of the towns were bustling places. Once a week the surplus produce of the local manor—eggs, cheese, fruit, livestock, and grain—arrived in carts to be exchanged for such imported goods as cloth, salt, and tar. At first the products were displayed in carts or movable stalls (booths), but these were eventually replaced by permanent ones. They later became small shops. The spirit of competitive trading was held in check, however, by the fact that the Church frowned upon making a profit. It was considered sinful to charge more than the true value of a product. This attitude would influence trading practices for some time, but, in the end, greed would win out.

This sign is marked the shop of a cooper

TOWN CHARTERS

The earliest towns were under the control of the local lord or bishop, to whom they owed feudal services in the form of taxes and agricultural produce. But over the years, the towns struggled to gain independence from these obligations, and beginning in the twelfth century many of them won their freedom by buying charters from their landlords. The charters freed the townspeople from their feudal responsibilities and allowed them to elect their own officials, collect their own taxes, and control their own commerce. Only merchants and craftsmen could hold town offices; knights and clergy were disqualified from them unless they became involved in a local business.

The Crusades benefitted the developing towns, since the kings involved in those holy wars often sold charters in order to obtain money to equip their armies. Richard I raised a great deal of money for the Third Crusade in this way, and he once remarked that he would sell London if he could find a buyer!

Many of the towns in northern Italy withdrew from the feudal system in a different way. They simply ignored the nobles (who were absorbed in other matters) and formed political units called communes, which eventually became independent city-states. Venice, Genoa, and Pisa were run by wealthy merchants. The people of Milan defeated the army of their overlord, Holy Roman Emperor Frederick Barbarossa, in the Battle of Legnano in 1176 and won their independence.

A TYPICAL MEDIEVAL TOWN

By the thirteenth century the wooden palisades surrounding the towns were replaced by stone walls with towers. Townspeople and visitors entered through gates that were shut at sundown and not opened again until the following dawn. The typical house had a framework of wooden beams, probably oak. The walls were filled in with wattle and daub (the latticework of twigs smeared with mud, straw, and cow dung that peasants had been using for centuries to build their huts). The inner walls were covered with plaster.

An outer wall made of wattle and daub

The houses were crowded together on the narrow, twisting streets. Each building had as many as five or six stories, the ground floor often containing a workshop. The upper stories often jutted out over the street, each story projecting out a little further than the one below. The top story might almost meet the one of the house across the street! The family of a successful merchant might occupy an entire house, whereas a weaver's family would have to make do with a single room.

Little thought was given to city planning; dwellings were simply constructed wherever there was room. The sanitary conditions were terrible!

Medieval town buildings in France, with shops on the first floor

Garbage and chamber pots were regularly emptied out windows into the street below. Because of this, it was considered proper for a young man escorting his girlfriend to walk on the outside of the walkway (away from the building) in order to shield her from whatever might be thrown down from the stories above! Even today a well-mannered gentleman walks beside a lady on the street side of the sidewalk. The narrow medieval streets were mostly dirt (although some had cobblestones), so they were very muddy when it rained. There were no drains, and the channel of water that ran down the center of a street became a smelly open sewer. Pigs and rats roamed about, feasting upon what had been dumped. In a later chapter, we will learn how the unhealthy conditions of the towns contributed to the spread of terrible plagues.

This medieval town in Spain is still inhabited

In the center of a town was a market square surrounded by community buildings, including the town hall and the church. The town council dealt with taxes, road repairs, and other local issues. There were also local courts to try civil cases. Some of the punishments were harsh. A person found guilty of murder was hanged (the executions drew huge crowds), and theft was punishable by the loss of an arm or a hand. For a minor crime the culprit was whipped or placed in the stocks (a wooden frame with holes in which his hands and feet were locked) where he was ridiculed by every passer-by and often pelted with rotten food.

The average town had about 5,000 inhabitants, mostly tradesmen. Each evening a curfew bell was rung. (Do you remember the derivation of the word curfew?) No one was allowed on the streets when it stopped ringing until the gates were opened the next morning.

THE GUILDS

The merchants living in the towns formed organizations (called guilds) to protect their businesses from non-resident traders. The guilds regulated the prices of products and standardized weights and measures. It became unlawful for a stranger to come into the town to sell goods, except under the regulations of the guild. He had to pay the guild a toll, and he was forbidden to buy goods and sell them at a higher price than that determined by the guild, or to buy products on the way to market to corner the supply. Most people in those early times believed that anyone who made a profit by buying and selling things must be cheating someone. And we know how the Church felt about this!

Craft guilds were later formed by groups of artisans who did the same type of work. There were guilds of spinners, weavers, tailors, furriers, brewers, silversmiths, goldsmiths, bakers, and so forth. Some guilds were made up entirely of women, such as spinners, embroiderers, and seamstresses. Members of a particular craft guild usually lived and worked in the same area of town. No one was allowed to engage in a craft unless he was a member of a guild.

During the early years of the craft guilds, the members met in one-story buildings called guildhalls. Each guild had a distinctive banner, bearing the design of a thimble, loaf of bread, or some other object that symbolized its craft. In later years, the more important guilds built beautiful Gothic buildings to house their offices. One of the most elaborate is the Hall of the Clothmakers' Guild which is still standing in Ypres, Belgium.

The old guild hall in Burssels, Belgium

The guild regulated the work hours and decided the fair price of goods. It determined the standards of quality, which were very high.

Inspectors (called searchers) were always on the prowl among the local workshops to keep the craftsmen on their toes. The penalties for bad or slovenly workmanship were harsh. If the number of threads in a weaver's cloth were too few, his looms were destroyed. If a baker sold loaves of bread that were inferior either in weight or quality, he would be dragged on a sledge through the streets of the town with the unacceptable loaf hung around his neck. If a vintner sold poor quality wine, he would be forced to drink a cup of it, the remainder being ceremoniously poured over his head. Other substandard goods were confiscated, destroyed, or given to the poor. A product that was deemed of high quality, on the other hand, was stamped with a hallmark (the guildhall seal of approval). The beautiful iron grillwork, stained glass, and other outstanding examples of medieval craftsmanship that have survived to our times attest to the high standards of quality required by the guilds.

Each guild chose its own officers and looked out for its members, who paid annual dues. (In fact, the word guild comes from the German word geld which means "gold" and hence money.) A guild would bail a member out of jail or pay for his daughter's dowry. If someone was ill or out of work, the guild looked after him and even provided food and clothing. When a member died, the guild prayed for his soul, paid his debts, financed his funeral, and supported his widow. Guild members were expected to conduct themselves properly, and anyone who displayed poor behavior was expelled from the organization. This was a terrible punishment since it barred him from practicing his craft in that town.

No craftsman was allowed to work on Saturday afternoons, Sundays, or other holy days. Every guild had a patron saint and kept a light burning before his altar in the local church. The saint of the needlemakers' guild was St. Sebastian, who was killed by a very sharp arrow, and the perfumers' guild chose St. Mary Magdalen, who had once poured oil on Jesus' feet. (Can you see the connections?) On their chosen saint's day, the members of the guild marched in a procession to the church for the service and then went to their guildhall for a festival of plays, music, and good eating.

How did a craftsman join a guild? It was a long process. First he had to serve an apprenticeship of from two to ten years, depending on the type of craft (the apprenticeship of a goldsmith took the longest). During this time the young man worked under the direction of a master in his trade. In return for his labors, the master provided him with clothing, food, and lodging.

It took great skill and training to make a golden chalice like this

When the apprenticeship was over, the young man was examined by members of the guild, and if he had done his work well, he would become a journeyman. He would most likely continue to work under a master, but now he received a daily wage. The word journeyman comes from the French word journee meaning "day" (his rate of pay). He also had the option of traveling about from town to town, perfecting his craft under the guidance of numerous masters.

When a journeyman thought he had learned all he could (usually after another seven years), he would be examined by the officers of his guild: Under their careful scrutiny, he would produce something—a pair of shoes, a piece of cloth, or whatever his craft happened to be. This was called his masterpiece, and if it was approved by the guild officers, he became a master. After receiving instructions concerning his duties to the guild, the new master put his hand on the Bible and solemnly pledged to meet all his professional obligations. Then, after paying a substantial fee, he could establish his own workshop. (Those who could not afford the fee remained journeymen until they could. Some never became masters for this reason.)

The craft guilds thrived for several centuries, but when vast trading networks expanded throughout Europe, Asia, and Africa, many of the guild practices and procedures became out of date. And when the guilds gave in to the pressure to embrace competition and sanctioned profit-making, a new class of wealthy merchants came into being, many of whom lived more splendidly than the nobility. Slowly, the old principles upon which the organizations had been founded disappeared. Before long the guilds were forgotten.

THE FAIRS

We learned earlier about the luxury products from the East that were introduced into western culture as a result of the Crusades. Knights returning home from the Holy Land brought pack animals laden with silk, velvet, damask cloth, perfumes, spices, tapestries, and exotic fruits. The European nobility soon developed new tastes in food, fashions, and castle furnishings, and enterprising merchants were quick to take advantage of the rapidly expanding market.

Some of the larger towns began to hold fairs once or twice a year which were attended by merchants coming from many distant regions. These fairs were sponsored by the local lords, who collected taxes on the products sold (this was an early form of sales tax). The trading usually began on a saint's day (the word fair comes from the Latin feria, meaning "festival") and it lasted for several days.

The most famous fairs were held in Champagne, a region in northeastern France where the trade routes from northern Europe crossed those from Italy. Eventually permanent fairgrounds were established, and six fairs, each lasting for two months, were held, making Champagne a permanent year-round market for the Continent. Each fair had a schedule according to which specific products were sold at the same time. The first ten days were devoted to the sale of cloth (cotton, linen, silk, damask, and so forth), then the focus turned to animal hides, then to something else. Finally, after the long series of single-item markets concluded there was a sale of all those materials which were sold by

A medieval fair was much like a modern open-air market

weight (sugar, salt, dyes, grains, spices, fruits, and wines).

Of course, most fairs were not as large as those held in Champagne. But each one was a festive occasion marked by general merrymaking and much anticipated performances by jugglers, acrobats, puppets, and specially trained animals. People from different regions mingled together and shared bits of news and stories about their communities, a real treat in the days before television, radio, and even newspapers.

At first the people bartered (exchanged one good for another), but later silver coins (called deniers) were introduced. Italian money changers set up booths and estimated the value of the currency in one region in relation to that in another. They made their estimates while sitting upon a special bench (in French it's called a banc), and this is the derivation of our word "bank". By the thirteenth century all the bankers were using Arabic numerals, thanks to their contacts with the eastern merchants; the use of zero enabled them to indicate units, tens, hundreds, and thousands, a system that was much simpler than the clumsy Roman numerals of the past.

VENICE BECOMES A CENTER OF TRADE

Constantinople had been the richest trading city in the Christian world until it was sacked in 1204 by the Crusading knights (with the aid and support of the merchants of Venice). As we learned in Chapter 8, the long, drawn-out assault of the Fourth Crusade so weakened the Byzantine economy that Venice was able to replace Constantinople as the trading giant of the western world. But before going further, let's look more closely at the events that led up to Venice's commercial monopoly.

The city was founded in the fifth century by Roman families fleeing from the Germanic barbarians (the Lombards). It was built on many islands in the lagoons that lie at the head of the Adriatic Sea. According to an old legend, when St. Mark landed on one of the islands an angel appeared and told him that one day his body would rest near the spot where he was standing. This prediction would come true in the ninth century, when his body was exhumed and

brought to Venice for reburial. On that occasion he became the city's patron saint.

The settlers of Venice were fishermen and traders from the very beginning, since their land was not suitable for farming. They built ships and sailed to ports along the Adriatic coast, exchanging their local crafts for wheat and other necessities. Over the years, Venetian merchants ventured farther and farther from home, obtaining products from one distant port and trading them with merchants in another. In this way, they eventually gained control of the commerce of the Adriatic Sea. The Venetian navy helped to drive the Muslims from the eastern Mediterranean so that Italian ships could sail safely to Asia.

Venice was also well located for land travel: Just to the north was the Brenner Pass, a major crossing point through the Alps for those traveling between Italy and Germany. Venetian merchants led pack trains along this overland route to the northern towns and fairs, returning home with their animals heavily laden with furs, leather, and wool. These products would then be loaded onto Venetian ships bound for Constantinople, where they would be traded for luxury items like silk and spices. The next step, of course, was to transport the eastern products back to the markets of northern Europe. At every stage of this process, some Venetian merchants were making a tidy profit. Unlike the guilds we have just learned about, the Italian traders ad no qualms about acquiring wealth through their business transactions. By the tenth century Venice had become very rich by exploiting its location as a mid-way point between Constantinople and western Europe.

In 697 the Venetian government was consolidated under a leader known as the Doge (Duke), who was advised by a Senate. By the eleventh century, however, even though the

One of the many islands of modern Venice

Republic was officially ruled by the Doge, it was really controlled by the Council of Ten (ten wealthy merchants). This shows how important trade was to Venetian society. Every year, beginning around this time, the Doge flung a gold ring from a huge state galley (the Bucentaur) into the sea, saying, "We wed thee, sea, in token of our perpetual domination."

The Palace of the Doge, Venice

The Crusades were perhaps the most crucial factor in establishing Venice's economic power in Europe. During the Third Crusade Venetian merchants gladly sailed huge numbers of knights to the Holy Land (for a good price) and then brought back cargoes from the East. Other independent Italian cities, such as Genoa, Milan, and Pisa were also involved in the maritime trade, but from the beginning Venice clearly dominated. During the Fourth Crusade, it was the wily, old (and blind!) Doge Enrico Dandolo who imposed the terms of the settlement with Constantinople that gave Venice commercial control of the Adriatic, Aegean, and Black Seas as well as ownership of a large number of rich ports and islands (formerly belonging to the Byzantine Emperor). Venice maintained a huge trading empire until the late fifteenth century, when a Portuguese explorer named Vasco de Gama discovered an ocean route from Europe to India and the East. When this happened, the Mediterranean trade route was all but abandoned.

But that story belongs to another era—the Age of Discovery (the Renaissance).

THE WOOL TRADE

One of the most important products traded during the Middle Ages was wool. Much of this came from sheep raised in England (remember the Cistercian monks?) and Flanders, a low, marshy region in northwest Europe (part of modern Belgium and northern France). The Flemish developed a profitable weaving industry, and since English wool was considered the best in Europe (and superior to Flemish wool), they established a partnership with England. Raw English wool would be shipped across the Channel to Flanders, where it was woven in cloth. Much of this was then shipped back to England to be sold there, but some of it was also sent to the fairs in Champagne. In later years, the English would start their own weaving industry.

Flemish towns like Bruges, Liege, and Ghent soon became important ports for cargo ships sailing between Scandinavia and the

Raw wool ready for spinning

Mediterranean Sea. Twice a year Venetian fleets sailed through the strait of Gibraltar and then north to Flanders and England, where they exchanged products from the Mediterranean and the East for woolen cloth. Later on, enterprising Italian craftsmen began a cloth industry of their own and started to compete with the northern cities in the dying and weaving of wool as well as the production of velvet, damask, and even silk. (A Florentine guild of weavers adopted as part of its coat of arms an eagle clutching a corded bale of wool in its talons.)

THE HANSEATTC LEAGUE

The Hanseatic League (known as Hansa) was a trading confederacy formed during the late twelfth century by the northern German trading towns near the Baltic and North Sea coasts (such as Hamburg and Bremen) for protection against acts of theft and piracy. It had its own fleet, which successfully wiped out most of the pirates on the northern seas. The League captains also prepared numerous charts which proved extremely useful to later navigators. At its height in the fourteenth and fifteenth centuries, Hansa had eighty member cities stretching from Novgorod (Russia) in the east to Bruges in the west. The League now controlled most of the trade in northern Europe just as Venice did in the south.

Hansa set high standards for the products of its member cities. Every year an assembly of representatives met to determine new policies and settle disputes. Any city that failed to abide by League policies lost its trading privileges, a punishment that could destroy its entire economy. Special offices called Kontors were built in the cities. They had facilities for Hansa merchants to sleep, eat, and trade.

Hansa became so powerful that it claimed equality with the kings of Europe. But in the later Middle Ages, England and the Netherlands grew sufficiently strong to challenge the League and effectively compete with its merchants. As a result, the organization lost considerable power. It remained in existence in Germany, however, until the nineteenth century.

QUESTIONS

1. Why did the medieval craftsmen take last names?

2. What group of people created the first towns?

3. What rights did town charters provide?

4. Why did a gentleman always walk on the street side of the sidewalk when escorting a lady?

5. What did the guild searchers do?

6. Who was a journeyman?

7. Where were the biggest fairs in Europe?

8. Who was a Doge?

9. How did the Crusades contribute to Venice's power?

10. Why was the Hanseatic League formed?

FURTHER THOUGHTS

1. During the Middle Ages, tolls were often collected by placing a pike (pole) in the road. Once the traveler paid a sum, the pike was turned aside to allow him to pass by. This is the origin of our modern word turnpike.

2. A number of English words and expressions can be traced back to the medieval wool industry. For example, the wool could be dyed at any stage (as raw wool, as yarn, or even as cloth), but if the process took place in the raw stage, it was called "dyed in the wool." What does this expression mean today? A spinster was a woman who supported herself by spinning. Who are the spinsters in modern society? Once the wool was woven, it was taken to a fuller, who soaked the fabric in a trough of water and fuller's earth to shrink it and give it body. The fuller and his assistants actually trampled on the cloth in their bare feet (and for this reason a fuller was also called a walker). Then, after the cloth had been soaked, it was hung to dry on a large wooden frame called a tenter. It was fastened by tenterhooks that were placed along parallel bars which could be adjusted in order to stretch the cloth to the right length and width. Do you know what it means today to be kept "on tenterhooks?"

3. The Catholic Church disapproved of towns. They considered them hotbeds of vice and sin, where tradesmen and merchants exhibited terrible traits, such as selfishness, greed and materialism. But couldn't the merchants say the same thing about the clergy?

4. In the fifteenth century there were many more sheep than people in England—the average flock contained between 20,000 and 30,000 animals!

5. Leather was an important material in medieval times. This is how a hide was tanned. After the hair and epidermis were scraped away from the skin, the hide was softened by rubbing it with cold poultry or pigeon dung (or warm dog dung). Next it was soaked in a mildly acidic liquid produced by fermenting bran in order to wash off the traces of lime left by the dung. Then the hide was submerged in a trough containing water and ingredients such as oak bark and acacia pods which added tannin. The next step was to remove the hide from the trough and lay it flat to dry on a pile of other hides, each one separated by a layer of crushed bark. Finally, the leather was ready to be made into shoes, bridles, or whatever.

Modern replica of medieval leather shoes

6. The average citizen of Venice had little say in the government. In fact, at the height of the city's commercial power, half of the members of its citizen assembly (the Grand Council) came from twenty-seven wealthy families!

PROJECTS

1. In 1275 a Venetian named Marco Polo reached Peking and opened a trade route between Europe and China. His written accounts of his experiences helped to educate western Europeans about the Far East. Find out more about Marco Polo and write a report.

2. As we have learned, many of the last names of people living in medieval England were derived from the craft a person was involved in. But sometimes a man's last name was based upon that of his father: for example, Dickson was the son of Dick, Harrison was the son of Harry, and so forth. A wealthy baron would add Fitz before his father's name (Fitzgerald). But let's get back to the names derived from crafts. Think of the names of people you know or have heard about that might have originally been connected with a person's trade. Many have been mentioned in this chapter, but there are lots more. If you need help, consult the lists in your telephone directory! Select a name, write it in large letters on a piece of blank paper, and then draw a picture of a person working at this craft (for example, write the word smith and then draw a person making an iron horseshoe). Or make a collage of pictures that seem to illustrate names derived from specific professions.

3. *Dick Whittington* is a classic children's story about a poor boy who, with the aid of his pet cat, became the Mayor of London. Whittington was a real person. The son of a knight, he became a prosperous merchant and was elected mayor three times between 1397 and 1420. Find a copy of the book in your school library and read it.

4. Think about how the craft guilds felt about making a profit. Then consider today's competitive economy. In general, which society

made the highest quality products, medieval or modern? If you chose medieval, how do you think the modern work ethic could be improved to produce better work? Write a short essay in response to these questions. If you chose modern, write an essay explaining how you came to this conclusion.

5. The growth of towns signaled the end to the feudal system. Write a paragraph explaining why this statement is true. Use specific examples to support your ideas.

6. A craftsman always hung a sign outside his shop with a painted picture of his tools or his product. For example, a sign might display a pair of scissors, a needle and thread, a spindle, a bellows, a grape vine, or a wooden chest. Do you know why the craftsmen couldn't simply write the names of their trades on the signs? Think about what some of the signs might have looked like in a twelfth or thirteenth century town. Then draw three examples. Now think about modern products. Pretend that most people have forgotten how to read. What sorts of symbols would appear on signs hanging outside modern shops? Draw three.

7. Why do you think a well-known greeting card company selected Hallmark as its name? Can you think of any other commonly used words or expressions that are derived from the medieval guilds? Name two, and use them in sentences.

8. *Adam of the Road* by Elizabeth Jane Gray (a Puffin book) is an absorbing story about the adventures of an eleven-year-old boy in the countryside of thirteenth century England. Read it, and write a short report.

CHAPTER 12

ADVANCES IN LEARNING

During most of the medieval period, a boy's education had little to do with reading and writing. He trained for knighthood in the castle of a nobleman, or he learned a trade by serving as an apprentice to a master craftsmen. Of course, the majority of the young boys who were growing up in medieval Europe simply learned how to farm the land, while most girls focused their attention on the basics of running a household. From the time of St. Benedict, only those boys destined for a career in the Church had the opportunity to learn to decipher and then reproduce a written text in the schools set up in the monasteries. There were some exceptions, such as the palace schools established by Charlemagne and Alfred to train young people for government positions. And a few fortunate girls of the noble classes were tutored in languages and literature at home. But until the eleventh century the vast majority of literate men (and women) continued to be the clergy.

THE CATHEDRAL SCHOOLS

One of the most profound effects of the Crusades was the mental reawakening it produced in medieval society. As a result of the many eastern ideas transmitted to Europe, more and more people, nobility as well as townspeople, became interested in learning to read and extending the scope of their knowledge. Cathedral schools, originally established to teach the clergy, were opened up to laymen (non-clergy). As new towns sprung up, so did new cathedral schools. Among the most famous were those in Paris, Chartres, and Rouen (France).

The curriculum taught was basically the same in every school. Since Latin was the universal language of the Church and therefore of scholarship, the first years of schooling were

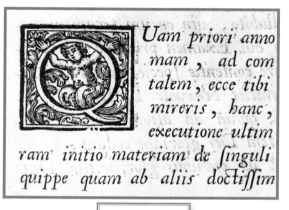

A Latin text

devoted to courses in the grammar of that ancient tongue. (This is the origin of the term grammar school.) The students worked hard, putting in nine hours of study a day, six and a half days a week. Imagine spending all that time reading, writing, and speaking Latin! Books were valuable and scarce, and often only the teacher had one. The students had to copy down and memorize what he read aloud. No explanations of the text were given. The next day the teacher would ask questions about what he had read. If a student could not answer in the exact words presented in the lesson of the previous day, he was beaten across the shoulders with a stick! Students were also punished for speaking their native languages. When Latin was finally mastered, the class could move on to subjects like arithmetic, geometry, and astronomy. (Remember the seven liberal arts of Alcuin's curriculum?)

Medieval buildings of Pembroke College, Cambridge University

THE UNIVERSITIES

In the twelfth century groups of teachers often assembled in some of the larger towns. Anyone could set himself up as a teacher (called a master); all he had to do was attract students, who paid him a fee for his services. As the numbers of scholars increased, guilds of students and masters were formed. Such a guild called itself a universitas, a Latin term meaning "an association of people." (Today, of course, a university is simply a place of higher learning.) The universities (as we will refer to them) enabled students from many regions to study under a group of teachers, each of whom specialized in a particular area. They could study the traditional seven liberal arts, as well as advanced subjects— law (canon and civil), medicine, and theology.

All university classes were taught in Latin. As the master read passages from a book on a particular subject (the French word for reading is lecture), the students took notes on wax tablets. A lecture could last an entire morning. A disputation was a discussion or debate between two or more masters about the material that had been read. Today, a lecture given by a university professor is a talk followed by questions. A university was run by a church official called the Chancellor. Gradually sets of rules were established. For example, classes on particular subjects were to be taught at specific times. Masters continued to be paid by collecting fees from their students.

After studying the liberal arts for five years a candidate could present himself for an examination. If he passed, he became a baccalaureus ("bachelor of arts"), a title which entitled him to be an assistant teacher. After more years of study, he took another exam, and then wrote a thesis which he had to defend before a group of his teachers. If he passed, he received a degree of Master of Arts and was crowned with

The buildings of Merton College, Oxford University date back to the thirteenth century

a master's cap. This qualified him to teach the seven liberal arts. At this point he was admitted to a guild of teachers at a ceremony called commencement (marking his "beginning" as a full-fledged teacher). In England he was given a special cane with a flattened disc on one end to smack the palms of disobedient students! Should he wish to become a master of a specific discipline, he needed to study a few more years and take another examination. If he passed, he would become a Doctor of Letters. He could now teach at the most advanced levels.

By the thirteenth century there were twenty-two universities in France, Italy, Spain, and England. The more well-known were in Salerno (this was the first one), Paris, Bologna, Naples, Montpellier, Oxford, and Cambridge. In Paris the masters organized themselves into groups according to what they taught. These groups were known as the faculties of theology, law, medicine, and liberal arts. The masters were a proud group of men. They taught while sitting upon a kind of throne, and they wore long gowns and gloves. At Oxford and Cambridge lectures were given in the morning, and a fine was imposed if a student missed daily Mass, gambled, practiced with a sword, brought a knife to the dinner table, or made any unnecessary noise during class.

The University of Bologna in northern

Even today Oxford professors wear academic gowns

Italy became famous for its instruction in law and medicine. The guilds of students were very powerful there. They hired the masters whom they considered the most qualified, decided upon which courses should be taught, and fined those instructors who missed a class, left out material they were supposed to include, or dodged a difficult question.

At first there were no campuses. The students in Paris gathered in the cathedral cloisters, those in Italy met in town squares or rented rooms, while in Cambridge classes were held in sheds. The students lived in boarding houses. In Paris these centered around a region that came to be known as the Latin Quarter (for obvious reasons!). By the late thirteenth century, however, residential colleges had been established with dormitories where students and masters lived together, and buildings had been constructed solely for teaching purposes.

THE SCHOLARS BEGIN TO THINK FOR THEMSELVES

With a few exceptions, early medieval scholars were not encouraged to think for themselves. They were expected to accept the writings of the Church Fathers (such as St. Augustine and Pope Gregory the Great) whose authority was considered absolute. The Church frowned upon any questioning of the traditional interpretation of a work, since everything had to fit in with its teachings.

Gerbert of Aurillac was one of the exceptions. He was a French monk of the tenth century who visited Spain and learned about the ancient works that formed the basis of Muslim scholarship. (We learned about him in an earlier chapter.) He decided that it was not sufficient to simply study the words of the Church Fathers, and so upon his

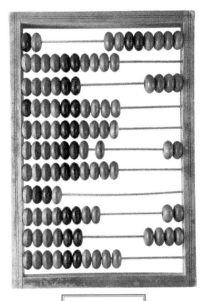

An abacus

return to France he set about making copies of original Roman classical writings. Gerbert taught at a cathedral school at Rheims until he was elected Pope (he would be called Sylvester II). One of the most learned men of his time, he added what he had learned in Spain to the school's mathematics curriculum: He introduced the Arabic numerals and revived the use of the abacus (a frame with rods on which beads are moved, the rods representing digits, tens, and hundreds). He had learned from his reading of the ancients that the earth was round and orbited the sun, and he shared this revolutionary knowledge with his students. Gerbert also included the writings of such Roman authors as Virgil, Horace, Terence, and Juvenal in his curriculum.

Adelard of Bath was born in 1090. He traveled to Greece, Asia Minor, and Africa, where he learned Arabic. He later translated many of the ancient writings from Arabic into Latin, and in the process he developed an interest in the scientific thought of the early writers. This led him to appreciate reasoning over the blind acceptance of Church authority. He once referred to the Church as a halter that keeps a beast from going anywhere on its own. Adelard translated Euclid's *Elements*, and his own work, *Natural Questions*, contained all he'd learned about Greek and Arabic science.

PETER ABELARD

Many scholars who gathered quotations on various topics from the writings of the Church Fathers were amazed to discover that the authorities often contradicted one another. So the scholars had to use their own common sense and reasoning powers to determine which statements were valid. This logical analysis of theological works is known as scholasticism. It represented an attempt to bring together two disparate factors: faith and reason.

One of the first scholars to challenge the authority of the Church Fathers was Peter Abelard (1079-1142). He was the eldest son of a noble of Brittany, but he gave up his inheritance because, he said, he preferred to fight with his brains rather than with his hands. After studying in Paris, he became a popular teacher there. Students were drawn to him because he always gave clear reasons to justify his statements. (Among his pupils was Thomas Becket.)

Although scholars were forbidden to marry, Abelard fell in love with one of his students (Heloise) and they were wed. They had a child, whom they named Astrolabe (do you know what an astrolabe is?). But Heloise's uncle (Canon Fulbert of Notre Dame) was a powerful Church leader, and he had the marriage annulled. Publicly disgraced, Abelard became a Benedictine monk, and Heloise spent the rest of her years as a prioress and teacher in a convent near Troyes. The series of love letters that the two exchanged remains one of the most beautiful pieces of romantic literature.

But it is Abelard's scholarship that concerns us here. He, too, was opposed to a blind reverence for the authority of the Church Fathers. In his book, *Sic Et Non* (Yes and No) he presented 158 general statements (theses) such as, "nothing happens by chance" or "sin is pleasing to God,"and he followed each one with a series of quotations related to them, coming from such sources as the writings of Church Fathers, Church council statements, and papal decrees. As you may have guessed, the quotations frequently contradicted one another. Abelard never said who was right, leaving it to the reader to consider the different points of view and then decide for himself. His motto was: "By doubting we are led to questioning, and by questioning we arrive at the truth."

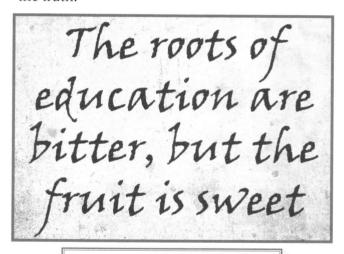

A famous quotation from Aristotle

Of course, the Church was not pleased with Abelard's writings, which it condemned as heresy. He spent his last years at the monastery at Cluny. After he died, the abbot of Cluny wrote Heloise a moving letter, praising Abelard's spirituality and assuring her that her soul would one day be united with his. They were later buried in a common grave.

After the scholar's death, Peter Lombard wrote *A Book of Sentences* that used the same method as

Abelard but, instead of raising doubts, he tried to explain the apparent contradictions raised among the various Church Fathers. This work was accepted by the Church, and it became the textbook used by medieval students of theology for centuries.

A statue of Aristotle

THE REASONING OF ARISTOTLE

In the thirteenth century the questioning of Church teachings intensified, as vast quantities of Greek and Arabic writings in Latin translation became available to European scholars. The works of the Greek scientist and philosopher Aristotle particularly angered the Church leaders, since his systematic approach to obtaining knowledge seemed hostile to their reliance on faith. (Aristotle had once formulated a detailed theory to rationally explain the existence of the universe.)

In 1210 the Church passed a decree that forbade any student at the University of Paris to read a book or even a commentary of a book by Aristotle. The punishment for anyone caught doing so was excommunication! But after a great deal of protest on the part of the scholars, the Pope agreed to a compromise. The works could be read, but students were cautioned to disregard what the Church considered the "useless" parts (which must have been a major part of the writing!).

ST. THOMAS AQUINAS

The most famous scholastic thinker was St. Thomas Aquinas. He was an Italian nobleman educated at Monte Cassino and the University of Naples. He became a Dominican Friar in 1244 and later taught philosophy and theology in Paris, Rome, and Bologna.

St. Thomas met the challenge posed by the classical and Arab writers to the Christian faith by creating a philosophical synthesis (blending) of reason and belief. Unlike many theologians, he welcomed the Latin translations of Aristotle's writings. His greatest work, *Summa Theologica*, was a summary of all the theology and philosophy of his time and an attempt to reconcile Aristotle's scientific ideas with Church doctrine. St. Thomas followed the method of Abelard, asking questions and presenting various opinions in response to them. Then, using logical reasoning, he set forth his own conclusions. He took up each point of the Christian doctrine, examined it, and tried to show that it could be arrived at by logic as well as by faith. He saw no conflict between reason and faith but considered them both part of a single truth. Reason was necessary to help man understand this world, he said, while faith helped him to understand life after death.

St. Thomas even employed Aristotelian logic to justify faith. For example, referring to the Greek philosopher's principle that every effect has a cause and every cause a prior cause, all the way back to a first cause, St. Thomas argued that the existence of God could be proven by tracing all creation back to a divine first cause.

Some clerics were offended by what St. Thomas wrote, believing that he was compromising the authority of the Church. The Bishop of Paris referred to some of his ideas as heresy and threatened to excommunicate anyone who supported them. The Archbishop of Canterbury did the same thing. The Dominicans, however, warmly praised the scholar's teachings (remember, he was a member of their order), and his works were later accepted and even promoted by the Church. *Summa Theologica* is now the basis of teaching in most Roman Catholic schools.

ROGER BACON

Scholasticism trained medieval scholars to make careful distinctions between ideas and to arrange the ideas in an orderly way. This careful approach was effectively applied to areas beyond philosophy and theology. Robert Grosseteste was a master at Oxford who studied the writings of Aristotle and other early scientists and concluded that mathematics provided a means of understanding the universe. Grosseteste taught his students to follow the scientific method, which is based upon observation and experimentation.

Roger Bacon (1214-1292) was a Franciscan Friar who also taught at Oxford. He was a follower of Grosseteste. Bacon complained that scholars

were paying too much attention to the ancient writings and were willing to believe things just because other people said they were so. He added that if he had his way he would burn all the books of Aristotle! True knowledge came, he said, not from arguing but from observing nature and testing one's suspicions of why things happened by experiments.

He certainly followed his own advice. He set up a laboratory and allegedly invented a steam engine. He built an observatory to study the stars and planets. Sometimes his experiments didn't work out the way he had planned. When he tried to mix saltpeter, charcoal, and sulphur, the materials exploded. (Bacon was the first European to write down the formula for this very significant explosive: gunpowder.) Superstitious townspeople were frightened by the noise, and became convinced that Bacon was practicing some sort of black magic. The Franciscan Order became so alarmed that they forbade him to teach his new methods of scientific inquiry. Going even further, they accused him of questioning some of the teachings of the Church related to the creation and makeup of the universe. When Pope Clement IV heard of Bacon's activities, however,

Early design of spectacles

he was so impressed by the friar's intellect that he encouraged him to continue with his work.

But when Clement died, Bacon lost the support of the Church and he was imprisoned. He sadly described himself at the time as "unheard, forgotten, and buried." He died two years after he was released.

Bacon was perhaps the first modern scientific thinker, and he will never be forgotten. Many of his predictions were amazingly accurate. For example, he said that one day ships would move without sails or rowers, carriages would be drawn without horses, and man would fly. He was a pioneer in the development of the microscope, and his idea of using a segment of glass to improve vision led to the invention of spectacles. (A Venetian glassmaker developed an optical lens in the late thirteenth century, and by the fifteenth century spectacles were in common use among those who could afford them.) Of course, not all of Bacon's ideas were valid. For example, he dabbled in alchemy, hoping to find a way to make gold out of ground up minerals. But even alchemists stumbled across a great deal of useful knowledge about various substances, and this would be invaluable to later scientists.

LITERATURE

Much has already been mentioned about medieval literature, so let's review what we've learned about the subject. First, there's the language itself. The spoken Latin of the Roman Empire gradually blended with the languages of the people living in various regions (and later nations) of Western Europe until the modern Romance (from the Roman) languages of Italian, Spanish, Portuguese, French, and Romanian evolved. The language of the people (as opposed to the Latin of the Church) is referred to as vernacular. In the old frontier provinces along the Rhine and Danube as well as in Britain, where the Roman influence was less marked, the Celtic languages (Irish, Welsh, and Breton) and the Germanic languages (Swedish, Danish, Norwegian, German, Dutch, and English) developed.

Most of the books produced during the Middle Ages were, of course, written in Latin and religious in nature: They included the lives of saints, sermons, the writings of the Church fathers, and the like. But, as we have learned, there were also historical chronicles and (in the later years) books about science and philosophy.

Poetry first appeared in France in the epics and ballads of the troubadours, trouveres, and other bards of the eleventh and twelfth centuries, although the origins of these works could be traced back to the heroic verses of *Beowulf*. But certain works like *The Song of Roland* and *The Cid* were written in the vernacular of the region in which they were produced. They marked an important step in the development of a popular literature that was no longer shackled by the

Arthurian Tales of Sir Lancelot and Queen Guinevere were very popular

rather burdensome language of the Church. When the epic and the lyric poem merged, a new form, the romance, was born; minstrels now sang about the chivalry of the knights of King Arthur's Round Table and expressed the sensibilities of courtly love. Toward the end of the medieval period much of the poetry had become so sentimental (and downright sappy) that the satire expressed in the last section of *The Romance of the Rose* was viewed by many as a welcome change.

All of these literary forms—the epic, ballad, lyric, and romance—were written for and enjoyed by the nobility. But what about the other people? The citizens of the rapidly growing towns had their own brand of literary entertainment. They loved to read and hear stories, called fabliaux (fables), that poked fun at various members of their society—priests, merchants, craftsmen, and even the nobility. The fabliaux were bawdy and vulgar; in fact, even by modern standards, many of them are considered too crude to be enjoyable. The townspeople also enjoyed animal fables that seem reminiscent of our tales about Brer Rabbit (told by Uncle Remus). Since most of these dealt with a fox called Renard, they are known as The *Romance of Renard*. The main characters were a lion (Noble), a bear (Bernard), and wolf (Isengrin), a cock (Chanticleer), and, of course, the fox

(Reynard). It was the fox that always outwitted the other animals, and, all too often, wickedness and cunning triumphed over simple-mindedness or innocence. Needless to say, the fabliaux were written in the vernacular.

Statue in Florence of Dante

Dante Alighieri (1265-1321) was an Italian poet whose masterpiece, *The Divine Comedy*, helped to establish his Tuscan dialect as the literary language of Italy (it evolved into modern Italian). The poem is an account of the poet's spiritual journey from life on earth to the eternal bliss of Heaven. Guided by the classical Roman poet Virgil, Dante travels through the nine circles of the damned in the Inferno (Hell) and the mountainous wasteland of Purgatory. When he finally arrives in Paradise (Heaven), he has come to understand God's divine plan of justice. He is joined there by the spirit of his beloved Beatrice (the symbol of pure love). Throughout the poem, which is actually an allegory of medieval moral, religious, and scientific views, Dante expresses the aspirations and anxieties of his times. He also uses the poem to criticize and vent his anger at certain important figures— past and present—by placing them in different levels of Hell.

Characters in *Canterbury Tales*

In the fourteenth century Geoffrey Chaucer wrote The Canterbury Tales, a collection of stories told by pilgrims as they made their way to the shrine of Thomas Becket. Chaucer was greatly influenced by Dante's works, and, like the Italian poet, he wrote in the vernacular (English) rather than the Latin of the Church scholars. In the opening pages of his work, each of twenty-nine pilgrims is described as the group gathers at the Tabard Inn in Southwark (outside London). The host of the inn makes this proposition: Each pilgrim is to tell two tales on the way to Canterbury and two on the return journey, and whoever tells the best tale will have supper when the group returns to the inn at the expense of the rest. Chaucer's descriptions of the pilgrims, who come from many classes of society, give us a good picture of fourteenth-century life in England. Chaucer clearly admires the devout and sincere priest, but he revels in belittling the friar and the monk, who have obviously strayed some

distance from St. Benedict's Rule. He also takes delight in describing the Pardoner (a hypocrite), a drummer who sells fake relics to unsuspecting pilgrims, and the Prioress (head of a nunnery) who is a terrible snob. The tales are a blend of reverence and bawdiness, and they make good reading even today. Chaucer had completed only twenty-four of them when he died. The work ends with a curious Retraction in which Chaucer asks forgiveness for most of his writings. Why do you think he did that?

QUESTIONS

1. How were the cathedral schools different from monastery schools?

2. What is the original meaning of the word "universitas?"

3. Name four medieval universities.

4. How did the Latin Quarter in Paris get its name?

5. Name four good things Gerbert of Aurillac did for medieval education.

6. What is *Sic et Non* about?

7. Why didn't the Church like Aristotle?

8. How did St. Thomas try to reconcile Church teachings with logic?

9. What were three of Roger Bacon's inventions?

10. How did Dante make fun of certain people he disliked in his *Divine Comedy*?

11. Describe Chaucer's *Canterbury Tales.*

FURTHER THOUGHTS

1. The facade of the Cathedral of Chartres was adorned with sculpted figures symbolizing the Seven Liberal Arts: Grammar (an old woman), Dialectic (who holds the serpent of

wisdom), Rhetoric (who carries tablets of poetry), Arithmetic (counting on his fingers), Geometry (holding compasses), Astronomy (holding an astrolabe), and Music (striking bells with a hammer).

2. The oldest university building still standing is at Merton College, Oxford. Merton had the first university library in the 1370's. As we know, books were scarce during medieval times, and in the university libraries each book was chained to a desk. The student had to stand while he read. A special librarian was on hand to see that no one brought either a pen or a knife into the library, and readers were refused admittance if they appeared in wet clothing. Upon entering the room, the student had to take an oath that he would not in any way mutilate a book.

3. Books were so expensive that few people possessed any of them. In the later Middle Ages, kings began collecting books and foundations were laid which became the great libraries of Europe. The fifteenth century popes, Nicholas V and Sixtus IV, began a collection of books that is now the library of the Vatican. Somewhat later, King Francis I of France built up a library that became part of the Bibliotheque Nationale in Paris.

4. Chaucer's name means "Shoemaker." It is derived from chaussure, the French word for "shoe."

PROJECTS

1. Believe it or not, alchemy was a forerunner of chemistry. It was based on Aristotle's theory of Four Elements, namely that matter is composed of earth, water, fire and air, and that all material bodies had four properties: hot, moist, cold, and dry. Alchemists' experiments showed that when cold, wet water was heated it became hot, wet air, and they wondered if all matter could be changed in a similar way. So they searched and searched for the key that would enable them to do this. Could they find through their experiments an elixir that could make old men young? Could they turn dirt into gold or silver? Even Roger Bacon dabbled in alchemy. Find out more about the medieval alchemists and write a report. Explain why you think magic and superstition played such an important role in the Middle Ages, even among scholars.

2. The concept of the university began in ancient Greece. Find out about Plato's Academy and Aristotle's Lyceum. Then write a short report comparing the Greek concept of higher learning with the medieval university.

3. Many books have been written about the love between Abelard and Heloise. Find one and read it. Then make an oral report to your class.

4. One of the greatest poets of the late Middle Ages was an Italian poet named Petrarch. Find out more about him. Then read five of his poems, and share them with your class.

5. Read five of *The Canterbury Tales*. Then write a short descriptive paragraph about each tale, explaining what aspect of medieval culture Chaucer is describing or satirizing.

6. Several of William Shakespeare's plays take place in medieval times. *Romeo and Juliet* is a wonderful story of youthful love that is stifled by the prejudice and stupidity of rival Italian families. Read the play (modern versions are available). Then write an essay comparing the rivalry between the Montagues and the Capulets to a similar type of conflict in modern times.

7. Boethius was a Roman scholar of the sixth century who began a Latin translation of the works of Aristotle. Find out what prevented him from completing his task.

Romeo and Juliet

CHAPTER 13

THE GROWING POWER OF THE COMMON MAN

During and immediately after the Crusades, the major rulers of Europe tried to strengthen their hold on their kingdoms. The feudal system was slowly dying, and the growing towns needed a strong central government to protect their interests and enable them to thrive. In some cases, the monarch managed to subdue the power-hungry nobility and run the kingdom according to his own whims (this happened in France). But in others, a confrontation with the nobility resulted in a diminishing of the monarch's power (this happened in England). The Holy Roman Emperors resolved their differences in yet another way.

So let's take a closer look at the political situation in the three major nations of the thirteenth century to see how their rulers dealt with challenges to their authority and where the ordinary people fit into the national scheme. Afterwards, we'll examine two major events that profoundly altered medieval society: the Black Death and the Peasants' Revolt.

ENGLAND

When John succeeded his brother Richard, the power of the English monarchy entered a downward spiral from which it would never totally recover. We already learned in Chapter 10 how John quarreled with the Pope. He also imposed huge taxes on his subjects to support his ill-fated military campaign in France. When his father, Henry II died in 1189, England owned as much land in France as it did in Britain. But John was a poor leader, and he managed to lose everything in France except a portion of

Aquitaine. (Imagine how greatly Henry would have mourned this loss!)

Do you remember how Stephen Langton had become Archbishop of Canterbury? When the English barons decided they could endure John's oppressive rule no longer, Langton called them together and told them about a charter that Henry I had once drawn up. In it he promised to rule according to the old Anglo-Saxon customs. Why not ask the same of John? The barons thought this was an excellent idea, so they sent John a list of what they considered their rights and demanded that he honor them.

Lincoln Castle, England holds one of the four surviving copies of the Magna Carta

The king refused to even consider making any concessions, but when the clergy joined the nobles in protest, he finally agreed to meet with them at Runnymede, a meadow beside the Thames River (twenty miles outside London).

On June 15, 1215, John reluctantly affixed the royal seal to the Magna Carta ("Great Charter"), which the nobles had prepared for him. This document significantly lessened the king's power and increased that of the nobles. It included sixty-three provisions. Many of these seem unimportant in our times, but two of them would have a lasting influence on the development of the English system of justice. The first one made it the official policy that no one could be thrown into prison without just cause (previously this happened all the time), and the accused had the right to a trial by jury. The second one guaranteed that no new taxes could be raised without the the consent of the King's Council. Furthermore, the king now had to obey the laws just like everyone else. Although the charter was intended by the barons to protect their own interests (they had little concern for the rights of the common people), it became an important milestone in the evolution of human rights.

A word cloud based on the Magna Carta

The Magna Carta was written in Latin on a parchment scroll. Many copies were made and sent to churches throughout England to be read to the people. It was reported that when John returned to his castle he was so furious about what he had been forced to sign that he gnashed his teeth like a madman, threw himself upon the floor, and gnawed the rushes strewn there!

John's son Henry III was also a weak monarch; he was always in need of money to

Ruins of Odiham Castle, where King John was staying when he rode to Runnymede to sign the Magna Carta

fight the Welsh and the French or to give to the Pope. So he disregarded the Magna Carta and taxed the people without the consent of the Council. In 1264 Simon de Montfort, the Earl of Leicester and Henry's brother-in-law, led a resistance movement. Henry was defeated at the Battle of Lewes and taken prisoner. For a while de Montfort ran the government single-handedly, but in 1265 he called for a new meeting of the Council, which was made up of barons and churchmen. Believing that his government would only survive if the common people were represented as well as the wealthy, he expanded the Council to include two knights from each shire and two burgesses (citizens) from each town. Thus was formed the English Parliament (from the Latin ad parlamentum, meaning "to discuss"), with its two major divisions, the House of Lords (nobles and clergy) and the House of Commons (ordinary people). When de Montfort was killed in the same year, Henry climbed back on the throne.

Henry's son, Edward I, was an excellent king. In 1295 he called a meeting of Parliament and announced that all matters concerning the people should be settled by those who could speak for them. He thereby established the principle of representative government, in which all those

Houses of Parliament in London

who obey the laws have a voice in the making of them. The Parliament of 1295 is known as the Model Parliament because it set the standard for later assemblies. It voted that no tax could be imposed without the consent of its members. This meant that the king was henceforth dependent upon the people for any funds he required. By the fifteenth century Parliament would control the finances of England, and both Houses would have a share in making and passing the laws of the nation. Parliament usually met in the hall in the royal residence at Westminster. Today, the modern Houses of Parliament stand on the site of the old Westminster palace.

FRANCE

In 1180 Philip II (called Philip Augustus) became King of France at the age of fifteen. As you will recall, Philip joined Richard I in the Third Crusade, and afterwards the two fought over territory in France. Not long after John inherited the English throne, Philip captured Richard's favorite French castle, Chateau Gaillard, and Normandy was lost to England. Ten years later Philip had won back nearly all the English territory in France from John.

Philip arranged for the beautification of Paris. He had the streets paved, ordered a twenty-eight-foot wall to be erected around the city, and built the Louvre as a fortress to guard the Seine. It was during his reign that Notre Dame Cathedral was begun. Philip supported the French cathedral schools, and he promoted trade by bringing merchants to Paris from all parts of northern France.

The Louvre along the Seine River in Paris

Philip created a new system of government offices to maintain order, administer justice, and collect taxes in the French provinces. He appointed commoners (baillis) who were trained in law to these positions and paid them fixed salaries. Now the top government officials were no longer the nobles but untitled civil servants who depended upon the king for their livings. So while the English barons were obtaining more liberty and power from King John, the power of the French nobility was being seriously eroded. In fact, Philip emerged as the strongest monarch in Europe. He was given the title Augustus by his fawning courtiers, who compared him to the legendary Roman Emperor of ancient times. Perhaps they hoped this would cause him to give them more power. It didn't.

Louis IX, grandson of Philip II, ruled from 1226 until 1270. Because of his piety and pacifism when dealing with his fellow Christians, he became known as St. Louis. (He was canonized in 1297, the only monarch to be so honored.) And yet, he was extremely intolerant of non-Christians, and this is what motivated him to lead two Crusades. On the home front, Louis

Statue of St. Louis

was concerned about the struggling lower classes of Frenchmen, and he forbade his barons to tax the people living on their land too heavily. He abolished trial by combat, and attempted to end fighting among his nobles by imposing a forty-day "cooling off period." He established a royal mint (until then the barons had been making their own coins), and he set up a royal court to which anyone could bring disputes. This would later evolve into the Parlement de Paris, France's

The Sorbonne, University of Paris

supreme court. During Louis' reign the university in Paris became a major intellectual center.

It was Louis' grandson, Philip IV (the Fair), who established the papacy at Avignon in 1305, thus creating the Babylonian Captivity we read about earlier. In the conflicts with the Pope (Boniface) that led up to this action, Philip had assembled a group of his countrymen known as the Estates General made up of nobles, clergy, and townspeople (each category was known as an estate). This assembly, which supported the king against the Pope, marked the beginning of a national government in France that included commoners as well as the traditional ruling classes. However, the Estates General would never have the power or authority of England's Parliament. Philip had no male heir, and when he died in 1328, the Captetian Dynasty came to an end.

THE HOLY ROMAN EMPIRE

Holy Roman Emperor Frederick I (Barbarossa) tried to guarantee the loyalty of his nobles by placing them in high positions in his government, but his attempts to control them actually worked against him. The nobles merely accumulated more wealth from their offices while maintaining their independence from the monarch. It was under Frederick's rule that the northern Italian city-states banded together (with the support of the Pope) and won their independence from the Empire. As we learned, the red-bearded emperor died on the Third Crusade at the age of seventy.

Frederick II became Emperor in 1212. He was born and raised in Palermo, Sicily (at the time it was still part of the Empire), and when he came to the throne he basically ignored Germany and concentrated his attention on the affairs of the

Vintage flag of the Holy Roman Empire

island he knew so well. He was a brilliant man and the best educated monarch of his time. Frederick was an amateur scientist, with a particular interest in animals and birds (especially falcons). He wrote a book about birds, and his sketches are remarkably accurate. He kept a menagerie of creatures, which often traveled with him. The Sultan of Egypt once sent Frederick a giraffe (the first in medieval Europe).

We learned in Chapter 8 how Frederick was excommunicated by Pope Honorius III in 1227 because he delayed in setting out on his Crusade, and how he ultimately won back Jerusalem by sheer diplomacy. (He was the only Crusader who managed to do that!) When Frederick later returned to Sicily, he established an Eastern style court at his castle and devoted much of his time to scholarly pursuits. He founded a university in Palermo, and he supported artists and scholars who came there to study. However, his preoccupation with Sicily led to the further disintegration of the central government in Germany and even greater power among the nobles. As for the common man, he had no say at all in the decisions of his government.

THE BLACK DEATH

In 1348 a terrible plague swept over Europe that would cause the deaths of many thousands of people. It all began when twelve Italian cargo ships crewed by dying men arrived in Messina (Italy) from trading ports in the Black Sea. After taking one look at the pathetic, swollen bodies of the mariners, the Italian officials immediately ordered the ships out of the harbor. But it was too late. Black rats carrying the infected fleas that caused the illness had already hopped off the ships, and before long the disease began to spread throughout Italy.

The plague originated in China in 1334 and had slowly moved westward until it reached Europe. It was called the Bubonic Plague because an infected person developed large swellings (buboes) the size of eggs in the lymph glands under the armpits or in the groin. This condition was accompanied by a sore throat and a high fever. Slowly patches of skin darkened as hemorrhages occurred just beneath the surface. This is why the Europeans also referred to the disease as the Black Death.

The illness was extremely contagious. It was first spread by the fleas that abandoned the bodies of dead rats and, seeking other sources of food, attached themselves to nearby humans. As they fed upon the blood, they infected their new hosts. The disease was also spread from one person to another by sneezing and coughing.

Once infected, a victim suffered in agony, often delirious and vomiting blood, but the end came quickly (within three days). Only a lucky few survived. The two other forms of the disease (pneumonic and septicemic) were as deadly as the bubonic type.

Once the plague appeared in a town there was little escape. Remember those filthy, rat-infested streets? They provided the perfect environment for the bacteria to spread. All normal routines and activities came to an abrupt halt as the townspeople vainly tried to save themselves by sniffing herbal concoctions or chanting magical spells. People often died alone, since everyone was afraid of the contagion. Most priests forgot their religious duties and isolated themselves from their parishioners. Many nuns in Paris, however, risked their lives to help the afflicted, only to die at their patients' sides. The Franciscans lost 125,000 brothers in this way. At a Carthusian monastery in Montreux, one monk (Gherardo) cared for his brothers, burying them one by one until he and his faithful dog were the only ones still alive. Gherardo survived to tell his story. (So did the dog.)

Sometimes the only clue that a person had died was the awful stench of rotting flesh.

Criminals were released from prison to drag carts through the streets and collect the dead bodies that had been placed outside the doors of the houses. They transported their gruesome cargo outside the city gates, where they threw the bodies into deep trenches and covered them with shovelfuls of dirt.

Giovanni Boccaccio was an Italian nobleman whose book, *The Decameron*, concerns a group of ten wealthy ladies and gentlemen who rode out the storm of the plague at a country manor, passing the time by telling each other somewhat racy stories. Boccaccio also describes in his book how the people of Florence dealt with the Black Death. Many of them apparently adopted a fatalistic attitude: Their solution was to eat, drink, and be merry until death took them away. Others tried to isolate themselves, afraid to help even family members who were dying. Many of the animals that freely roamed the streets also contracted and helped to spread the disease.

Much of medieval medicine was based upon guesswork and superstition. Although schools had been established in Italy to teach the scientific principles derived from classical and Arabic medicine, there were relatively few qualified physicians available to treat the vast numbers of dying Europeans. And even those educated men were influenced by astrology and magic. For example, they believed that there were lucky and unlucky days for bloodletting (in itself a primitive procedure), and a doctor always asked his patient what star he had been born under (certain remedies were associated with certain planets). And just imagine: The moon had to be in a favorable position before most medical procedures would be performed at all.

Since the people didn't understand about germs or the relationship between filth and disease, they ignored the unsanitary conditions of their towns and tried the "cures" they had heard about from their neighbors. Among these were the following: 1) Drink vinegar; 2) avoid moist food; and 3) boil wax, milk, and frankincense, add oil, and then put the mixture on the skin. Other magic potions combined herbs with urine, dung, or powdered earthworms. They didn't work.

The Grim Reaper, symbol of death

Some doctors thought the plague was caused by bad air. Since the influence of the atmosphere around a person seemed to make him sick, they referred to the sickness as influenza (the origin of the word flu). They instructed their patients to burn incense or to wear bags of spices around their necks and to sniff them every few minutes. Church bells were rung frequently to help stir up the bad air. Some people carried around bunches of flowers or fragrant herbs and spices simply to lessen the stench of the dead bodies.

But let's not forget that this was the Age of Faith. Many believed that the plague was God's punishment for their sins, and they knelt in prayer, begging forgiveness. Some made pilgrimages. The flagellants were a group of people who marched in processions from town to town, dressed in rags with their backs bare.

They carried whips made of knotted strings with jagged pieces of iron attached at the ends. When they arrived at a town they formed circles and beat each other's backs with the weighted whips. All the while they sang hymns. They flagellants were convinced that the only way to win God's forgiveness was through physical suffering.

Some town councils in Italy responded to the disaster in a more practical manner. They removed the filth from the streets and ordered the clothes of plague victims to be burned. They even established quarantine: a forty-day period of isolation for all persons wishing to leave an infected city or to enter an uncontaminated one. (Quarantina means "forty days" in Italian.) In Flanders laws were also established to promote cleanliness of food and water. Amazingly, certain regions, such as the Kingdom of Bohemia, escaped the plague entirely without resorting to any of these measures. No one knows why.

This terrible calamity finally died down in around 1350 after claiming over a third of Europe's population. The plague reappeared in 1360 (killing twenty-two percent of its victims), in 1369 (killing thirteen percent), and in 1375 (killing twelve percent). Of those who died in the later plagues, the majority were children, probably because their bodies had no resistance to the disease.

HOW THE PLAGUE CHANGED THE ECONOMY

Before the outbreak of the Black Death, Europe's agricultural economy was still dependent upon the feudal system. After the devastation of the plague, however, there were tremendous shortages of goods and labor, and the serfs, realizing how much they were needed, began making certain demands. In 1358 peasants in northern France banded together in a revolt against their subservience known as the Jacquerie (after Jacques Bonhomme, the nobility's scornful name for a typical peasant). They plundered the homes of the nobles, but they had no proper arms (pitchforks and scythes were no match for swords!). The rebellion was easily quelled within a month. Serfdom would not be abolished in France until 1789. Similar revolts broke out in Germany, Hungary, and Denmark, with similar results.

Things were different in England, however, where the landowners waived some of the old feudal rules, allowing serfs to move from place to place and even offering them wages. But the serfs were not satisfied and demanded still higher wages, deserting those lords who refused to pay them what they wanted and hiring themselves on with others who would.

To create some sort of order, Parliament passed laws to keep wages at the rate originally set. Those workers who continued to demand higher wages were to be branded on the forehead with a hot iron. However, the feudal lords so desperately needed field laborers that the serfs often got what they wanted, despite the new laws.

The government had other problems to deal with as well. England was at war with France (we'll learn about this war in the next chapter), and so new taxes were proposed to help finance it. In 1377 a poll tax (poll means "head") of four pence was placed on every person rich or poor. Formerly, taxes had been placed only on land or possessions. The new tax was a terrible hardship for the peasants, since four pence was more than a day's wages.

Discontent about wages and taxes could be felt everywhere, but no solutions were found. For twenty years a priest named John Ball traveled throughout England trying to stir up opposition to the inequality between rich and poor. Ball, a follower of John Wycliffe, hated authority, and he strongly criticized the wealth and idleness of many Church leaders. When he was prohibited from preaching in the churches, he began speaking in villages marketplaces, in fields, at street corners, and wherever he could attract listeners. He proposed that all the land should be owned communally, a serf having the same amount as a noble. And he predicted that things would never get better until there were no more lords to exploit the workers.

Meanwhile, there were more poll taxes, in 1379 and again in 1380. Many peasants in southeastern England, unable or unwilling to pay the taxes, attacked the tax collectors and then escaped into the woods. When new officials were sent out to round up the tax-evaders, the peasants armed themselves with pitchforks and threw the officials into the local ponds. In Essex, some officials were killed, and their heads were stuck on long poles and paraded throughout the villages. Crowds gathered to protest what they considered the unfair demands of the government, and they marched to the homes of those who would not join their forces, smashing down buildings and setting them afire. The nobles quickly fled to London or other parts of the country. Thus began the Peasants' Revolt.

THE PEASANTS' REVOLT

In 1381, nearly 60,000 peasants, tradesmen, priests, and outlaws marched to London. They were led by a former soldier named Wat (Walter) Tyler. When they arrived at the city, sympathetic craftsmen opened the gates. Chaos quickly erupted, as the crowd surged forward. One group of peasants freed the prisoners from jails, including the recently arrested John Ball. Another

group attacked and burned the palace of John of Gaunt, one of the king's uncles. They gleefully broke up the gold and silver bowls and plates with their axes and then threw them into the Thames River.

Engraving of Richard II

The king at the time was Richard II, a fourteen-year-old boy who ruled under the regency of his uncles. When there was no sign of things settling down, Richard agreed to meet with Tyler just outside of London. There Tyler set forth the peasants' demands: the abolition of feudal services, a new rate of rent amounting to four pence an acre, and the deaths of all "traitors" to the people. Richard agreed to the first two requests but said that only a court could decide who was a traitor. Tyler then demanded written charters of freedom that the peasants could take back and present to their lords. Richard also agreed to this, but while the charters were being prepared, a group of rebels burst into the Tower of London, where they found the Archbishop of Canterbury and the ministers responsible for the dreaded poll taxes. All were beheaded, and the Archbishop's mitre was nailed to his skull.

Engraving of Wat Tyler attacking a tax minister

one of the peasants shouted, "Let's slay them all!" But Richard had the presence of mind to save the day. As the rebel archers raised their bows, he rode among them, shouting, "Will you shoot your king? Let me be your captain." The peasants had no personal quarrel with the young monarch, so they put down their weapons and agreed to go home.

Richard consented to everything Tyler had asked, but he didn't keep his word. Any peasants who remained in London were arrested. The rebel leaders were captured and put to death in grisly ways. Some were drawn and quartered, while others died on the gallows, their bodies left to rot beside the roads as a reminder of how dangerous it was to question the king's (or Parliament's) authority. Among those executed was John Ball. Every city resident had to swear his loyalty to the king on a Bible. Soon afterwards the royal army marched throughout the English countryside, putting down any remaining resistance. The charters, of course, turned out to be worthless.

The revolt had failed, but the cause was not lost. Slowly the peasants would gain more independence. The poll tax was never again levied in medieval times, and within ten years all attempts by Parliament to keep down wages were abandoned. Besides, as the towns grew and flourished, more and more laborers were able to leave the fields and seek employment there. The feudal system was slowly vanishing. By the end of the fifteenth century there would be no serfs in England.

Nonetheless, the charters were handed out, and once they received them most peasants returned home. However, the leaders remained in London, for all the issues had not yet been addressed. Another meeting was arranged between Tyler and Richard, this time at Smithfield, just outside the city walls. Tyler now requested that the lords' lands be reduced and the lands of the Church be divided among the people. Richard agreed. Then, because it was rather hot, he offered Tyler a cup of water. Tyler allegedly rinsed his mouth with the water and then spat it out on the ground (there are many differing accounts of what actually happened). One of the king's courtiers was so dismayed by what he interpreted as an affront to Richard that he drew his sword and struck Tyler dead. For a moment, there was a terrible silence. Suddenly,

QUESTIONS

1. Who was Stephen Langton, and why was he important?

2. What were the three most important provisions of the Magna Carta?

3. What did Simon de Montfort contribute to English government?

4. What did Philip Augustus win from John?

5. Was Louis IX tolerant of other religions?

6. List three adjectives that aptly describe Frederick II.

7. How was the Black Death spread?

8. Name three ways that Europeans tried to protect themselves from the plague.

9. Did any good things result from the plague? If so, what?

10. What were Wat Tyler's demands?

FURTHER THOUGHTS

1. Of the numerous copies that were made of the Magna Carta in 1215, four have survived. Two can be viewed in the British Museum in London.

2. During the early medieval period surgery was not closely associated with medicine. Operations were often performed by barbers! In fact, the red and white stripes on the traditional barber's pole represent the blood spilled and the bandages used during surgery. Experiments were made to discover a sleeping potion for use during surgery. Here's one that worked quite well. A mixture was made of hemlock, opium, mulberry juice, ivy and lettuce. This was then dried on a sponge. Before an operation, the sponge was moistened and then inhaled by the patient, who slowly drifted off to sleep. (It was the opium that did the trick!) The patient was later aroused by fennel juice applied to his nostrils.

Robin Hood takes aim

3. Monasteries were the best place to be if you were ill. They had the first hospitals (built to treat ailing brothers). In the thirteenth century Pope Innocent built the Hospital of the Holy Spirit in Rome to treat the general population of the city. Other medieval hospitals, including St. Bartholomew's in London and the Hotel de Dieu in Paris, are still functioning.

4. The tales of Robin Hood were first set down at the time of the Peasants' Revolt. Robert Hoode was an outlaw in York in about 1225, but he was not a noble, nor was he a benefactor of the poor. Nonetheless, many scholars believe that he is the origin of the legend. The story as we know it (with such characters as Friar Tuck and the Sheriff of Nottingham) was not written down until the sixteenth century.

5. When the judges in a medieval English court sat on their bench, a space was kept clear before them by a waist-level bar. The attorney for an accused person stood at the bar to plead his case, and for this reason he was known as a barrister. Similarly, in modern times lawyers (barristers) must belong to a bar association in order to practice their profession.

6. Medieval doctors had some strange ideas about how the human body worked. They believed that the stomach was a cauldron in which food was cooked; if it was filled too full, it would boil over and the food would remain uncooked. The liver, they said, supplied heat for the body's furnace. The body's humors (phlegm, blood, bile, and water) had to be kept in perfect balance relative to heat and moisture. If the balance was thrown off, it could be adjusted by bloodletting (cutting a vein and letting a certain amount of blood flow out).

7. Medieval housewives believed that certain herbs and plants had specific healing powers: Wormwood cured a fever and headache, marigold and fennel aided weak eyes, lavender induced sleep, horehound cured a cough, lad's love kept moths away, thyme provided a person with courage, and sage offered him a long life (if it was eaten in May!).

8. Richard II met an unhappy end. In fact, every English king named Richard died violently. Richard I died in battle from a crossbow wound, Richard II was forced to abdicate the throne (in 1399) and was probably murdered in prison, and Richard III was killed in battle in 1485. No British monarch since then has had the name. Can you see why?

Ruins of Chinon Castle in France

PROJECTS

1. Make a timeline indicating the reigns of the major rulers of England, France, and the Holy Roman Empire during the Middle Ages. Beside each name, write one important thing that he did.

2. When Henry II died in 1189 at his castle in Chinon, France, his heart had been broken by the news that even his youngest son (his favorite) John had plotted against him, just as his other three sons had done in the past. Not long before his death, he had ordered that a decoration be painted in his chamber at Winchester Castle showing an eagle being attacked by its fledglings (representing himself and his disloyal offspring). Find out more about Henry II and his four ungrateful sons: Henry, Geoffrey, Richard, and John. *Lion in Winter* is an excellent movie available on video cassette about this subject. Then write a short family history. Include anything you learn about Eleanor of Aquitaine, the boys' mother.

A medieval town in Tuscany

3.   King John has been portrayed as a bad king by many writers. He was selfish and arrogant, and he is rumored to have murdered his rival for the throne (his young nephew Arthur of Brittany). He appears especially villainous in *The Tales of Robin Hood* and several plays of Shakespeare. But he had his good points, too. For example, he was the first English monarch to order that written records be kept of government decisions. Read three sources about this controversial ruler. (Be sure to find out why he was called John Lackland both at the beginning of his life and toward the end.) Then write a biographical portrait of King John. Be sure to include his good points as well as his bad ones!

4.   Frederick II was a brilliant and eccentric man. In fact, he was called Stupor Mundi ("Wonder of the World") for his wide-ranging abilities. Find out more about his scientific experiments and writings, his poetry, and his philosophy of life. Then write a report.

5.   Find out more about medieval medicine. Compare it with the medicine of ancient Greece (check out the discoveries made by Greeks living and working in Alexandria, Egypt). Write a report.

6.   Until the Black Death, the most feared disease in Europe was leprosy. Learn more about this disease and how patients were treated in medieval times. Write a short report.

7. Medieval executions were grisly. Find out what it meant to be drawn and quartered. What was the gallows? Write a short report about how condemned prisoners met untimely ends.

8. *The Door in the Wall* by Marguerite de Angeli is a poignant story about a crippled boy living in fourteenth century England. Read it, and then make an oral report to your class.

Lavender was considered a sleeping aid

CHAPTER 14

THE HUNDRED YEARS' WAR

In the early fourteenth century the English still held a small part of southwestern France, which produced large quantities of excellent wine. Each year hundreds of crates of the wine (which the English called claret) were shipped from Bordeaux to London. The cargo vessels returned home heavily laden with woolen cloth. It was a profitable business, and when the English merchants heard that the French might try to take over the region, they urged the king, Edward III, to fight to protect their rights.

OTHER PROBLEMS

The English had a number of other reasons to be angry with France at this time. Ship captains frequently complained that their vessels were attacked by French pirates as they crossed the English Channel that divides Britain and France. Then there was the matter of Scotland. Edward had been trying for some time to bring Wales and Scotland under his control (it seemed reasonable to him that all of Britain should be united under one monarch), but the French consistently aided the Scots in their armed resistance to the English troops. And when it was rumored that the French might try to conquer Flanders, another of England's most important trading partners, the Flemish appealed to Edward for aid.

In 1328 Charles IV, the last of the Capetian kings, died leaving no son to succeed him, so the French crown was passed on to his cousin Philip of Valois (the King's nearest descendant in the male line.) Edward contested Philip's coronation and even went so far as to name himself as the rightful heir to the French throne, basing his claim on the fact that his mother Isabella was Charles' sister. But the French Estates General dismissed Edward's claim on the grounds that the old Frankish laws forbade a woman to inherit or to transmit inheritance of the French throne.

Edward must have realized that he stood little chance of actually becoming the King of France, but he continued to insist that he was the rightful heir. His actions were largely motivated at this point by an alliance he had made with the Flemish merchants. (Claiming the French crown provided a convenient excuse for going to war to defend English as well as Flemish commercial interests.) Edward had three lilies (fleurs de lys), the traditional symbol of the French king, incorporated into his royal coat of arms along with the English lions, and he took the French motto Dieu et mon Droit ("God and my Right") as his own. This, of course, made the French furious!

Those lilies and the French motto are still on the English coat of arms

A TERRIBLE WAR

In 1337 a long serial conflict began between France and England that is known as the Hundred Years' War. There were three major periods of intense fighting with long stretches of peace in between, and, despite its name, the conflict covered somewhat more than one hundred years. All the land battles took place on French soil, and during the peaceful interludes, much of the French countryside was pillaged by bored professional soldiers. Most scholars view the Hundred Years War as a continuation of the rivalry between England and France that began when William the Conqueror defeated King Harold at the Battle of Hastings. England had held property in France ever since, and, as we have seen, this was a major source of conflict between the two powers.

We know a lot about the war because of the four-volume *Chronicles of France*, England, Scotland, and Spain, written by French historian and poet, Jean Froissart. He traveled widely in Europe and enjoyed the patronage of Edward's wife, Queen Philippa, as well as that of numerous noblemen. Froissart's works cover European political affairs during the years 1325-1400 and focus upon the Hundred Years War. For the earlier sections (up until 1356) Froissart borrowed from the notes of writer Jean le Bel, but he based the rest of his descriptions on eye-witness accounts of the major events. Although not always accurate and often biased, Froissart's books still provide a great deal of useful information about the war.

CRECY

In 1340 Edward's forces crossed the Channel on a fleet of two hundred ships. Although the French fleet was much larger, it was still at anchor when the English vessels sailed into view. Edward immediately attacked, giving the French little opportunity to defend themselves. By defeating the French navy at Sluys, the English won control of the Channel. Now they could invade the mainland.

By 1346 Edward had raised enough money (largely by imposing a huge tax on wool) to hire and equip an army to attack France, so he crossed the Channel and landed in Normandy. The French army was much larger than one that Edward could maintain so far from home. In fact, the French soldiers outnumbered the English two to one, and any men who were killed could easily be replaced, since the French population was very large (nearly four times that of England). But, as we will soon see, their smaller numbers did not prevent the English from succeeding on the battlefield. Edward was accompanied by his sixteen-year-old eldest son, known as the Black Prince (so called because of the black armor he wore).

From the coast the army moved southeast, looting the villages it passed through. It approached Paris, where Philip was waiting with his troops, then suddenly turned and headed north towards Flanders. The French forces immediately set out in hot pursuit, catching up with Edward near the village of Crecy.

The English army consisted mainly of professional soldiers who fought on foot. Many of them were armed with the longbow. During the lengthy wars against the Welsh and Scots, the English had been introduced to this new weapon, and they had learned how to arrange their troops to make the best use of it. A longbow was made of a straight stave of wood the height of the man who used it, and it shot a steel-pointed yard-long arrow that carried with deadly accuracy for over five hundred feet. The arrow could easily penetrate the armor of a knight or horse. The bow was cheap, easy to maintain, and unlikely to malfunction. A bowman could shoot six arrows a minute, and at close range an army of highly skilled archers could create an arrow storm by firing up to twelve a minute. The fast-moving missiles would literally fill the sky and then fall like hail upon the enemy soldiers.

Archer with a longbow and arrows

The French army, on the other hand, had a unit of Genoese archers who were masters of the crossbow. This powerful bow of tough whalebone or hardwood had a string made from a thick cord of twisted linen that was drawn back with handles and pulleys. The bow fired iron-tipped ten-inch bolts which fitted into a groove and were released by a trigger. Because the bolts spun in the air like rifle bullets, feathers were often attached to them to keep them steady. The bolt from a crossbow could penetrate armor at two hundred yards, a longer range than that of the longbow. However, a crossbow took a long time to reload, and it could fire no more than two bolts a minute. The bowman had to rewind the string by placing his foot in a stirrup at the bottom of the bow. (In later years a crossbow could be loaded with a mechanical device called the windlass.)

A crossbow

The French army was mostly knights, backed up by a relatively small group of crossbowmen. Just before the battle took place at Crecy there was a brief rainstorm. The English archers wisely removed their bowstrings during the shower, keeping them dry. But removing the strings of a crossbow was a more complicated and time-consuming process, so most of the French weapons were left as they were to be drenched by the rain. As a result, the strings were stretched and the bows couldn't fire as effectively as they usually did.

Edward had previously chosen a position on the edge of a small plateau rising above some marshy land. The wings of his army were protected by deep woods. He formed most of his regular troops into two units, each one flanked by archers. Philip ordered a division of crossbow men to march forward and engage the English in battle. But they were hampered by the setting sun, which shone directly in their eyes, as well as the steep incline which made it difficult to shoot their crossbows. (And don't forget those wet strings!) At the signal, the English bowmen shot a storm of arrows that forced the French bowmen to retreat. When the French knights charged through their retreating crossbowmen, the English archers brought down both men

Windsor Castle

and horses. Edward also had a secret weapon: five-foot iron "thunder tubes" that were loaded with gunpowder and fired balls of stone and iron. So now the sky was filled with arrows and missiles the size of golf balls, and men and horses screamed in agony. Although the French gamely charged again and again, they could not penetrate the English line. By dusk, they had retreated from the battlefield. Over 1500 French knights were killed. The Black Prince had fought so bravely (he commanded one of the units) that he was knighted on the field of battle. (We learned about this in Chapter 7.)

From Crecy Edward marched to the port of Calais and set a siege. After eleven months, the starving citizens of that city finally surrendered on August 3, 1347. Calais would become an important trading port for English merchants. When he returned home, Edward was welcomed as a great hero. Tournaments and festivals were held in his honor throughout England.

POITIERS

The year after the surrender of Calais the Black Death broke out in France, and it soon spread to England. Nonetheless, the English continued their raids in France. Many of these were led by the Black Prince. In 1356 he and about 7,000 men were surrounded by a much larger French army at Poitiers (on the border of Aquitaine). Once again, the longbow (and the cannon) gave the English the advantage, and after three days of hard fighting the French surrendered.

During this battle the French king (Jean II) was captured, and the Black Prince proudly carried him off to London. The French monarch was ransomed for 500,000 English pounds (about $1 million). King Jean did not suffer during his imprisonment, however. According to Froissart, he was provided with a large household staff at the castle of Windsor, where he passed the time entertaining the English royalty and nobility at lavish banquets and hunting with them in the local forests!

In 1360 a peace treaty was signed at Bretigny. According to its terms, Edward gave up his claim to the French crown; in return he kept Calais and the land around it as well as the southwestern provinces of Gascony and Guienne (in Aquitaine). King Jean's ransom was paid, and this huge sum temporarily relieved the burden on the English taxpayers.

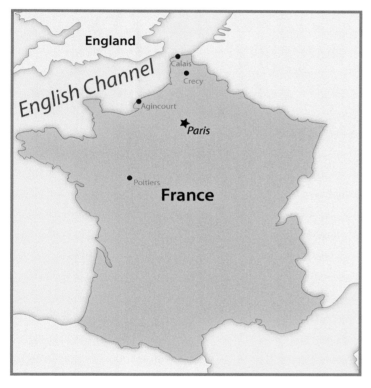

Although the treaty ended the English raids for the time being, the situation in France was far from peaceful. As was mentioned earlier, large numbers of mercenary soldiers (who fought for both French and English armies) found themselves with too much time of their hands, so they occupied themselves by plundering the French countryside. Bertrand du Guesclin, who was placed in charge of the French army, tried to restore peace. He ordered the strengthening of the fortifications of castles and towns to make it

more difficult for the raiders to obtain supplies. Meanwhile, by attacking small groups of English troops that were separated from the main army, the French military leaders were able to recover most of the land they had lost. When Edward died in 1377, England held only a few coastal towns, including Calais and Bordeaux. The Black Prince had died the year before, and his son, who was crowned King Richard II, was just a boy. We learned about him in our study of the Peasants' Revolt.

AGINCOURT

At the opening of the fifteenth century the French government was in disarray. The reigning French king, Charles VI (Charles the Mad), often had to be locked up because of his fits of insanity, and the nobles, particularly the Duke of Burgundy (his uncle) and the Duke of Orleans (his brother), were fighting for control of the kingdom. It was the perfect time for the English to stage another assault.

In 1415 Henry V of England, an ambitious and clever leader (fondly referred to as young Harry by his people), renewed the claim of the English kings to the crown of France. He crossed the Channel in the late summer with about 8,000 men and, like Edward, landed in Normandy. He besieged and captured the port city of Harfleur, but during the fighting many of his troops became ill with dysentery. Two thousand of them died. So with his remaining men Henry marched north to Calais, hoping to return home from there to gather replacement soldiers.

Along the way he was surprised by a huge French army of nearly 20,000 men that barred his path, forcing him to defend himself. The fighting took place at Agincourt, a village not far from the scene of his great-grandfather's triumph at Crecy.

The English soldiers were tired and hungry as well as water-logged from a heavy rain. The last thing they wanted to do was fight. But when Henry heard one of them complain that their numbers were too few to survive against the French, he replied that he would not have a single man more. "If God will give us the victory," he said, "it will be plain that we owe it to His grace. If not, the fewer we are, the less loss for England." (Henry's statement was recorded in Froissart's writings.) The courage of the young king in the face of such tremendous odds inspired his soldiers to "give it all they had."

Henry thoughtfully chose the terrain where he would make his stand. Then he lined up his men in a narrow gap between two dense woodlands just behind a marshy area. (Does this strategy sound familiar?) Six-foot wooden stakes were stuck in the soil with their sharp points directed toward the enemy. The French army continued to depend upon the knights to break through its opponent's lines. But only a few knights could pass through the gap between the two woods at one time, and as they charged the arrows of the English bowmen filled the sky and drove them back. When the French foot soldiers marched forward, many of them became bogged down in the mud, sinking in up to their thighs. At this point, the English foot soldiers dashed forward and defeated the struggling enemy troops in hand-to-hand combat. Hie French losses were tremendous: 7,000 were slain. The English lost only a few hundred men.

Within five years, Henry had conquered northern France, and the treaty he signed at Troyes in 1420 allowed him to keep the lands he had won. Charles the Mad even offered Henry the hand of his daughter Catherine in marriage and agreed to recognize him as his heir. This was a most unusual agreement, since Charles had a son

(also named Charles). The French people were not happy with the prospect of an English king grabbing the throne from the young man they considered the rightful heir, but the Duke of Burgundy, who had been Henry's ally all along, couldn't have been more pleased.

As it turned out, Henry died in August 1422, and Charles passed away the following October. The infant son of Henry and Catherine (Henry VI) was proclaimed the new King of France and England. His royal uncle, the Duke of Bedford, assumed control of his interests in France. He laid siege to Orleans, the gateway city to central and southern France, where resistance to the English was particularly strong. The French, meanwhile, determined that no Englishman would ever rule them, and they looked to Charles (known as the Dauphin, French for "Prince") as their lawful king.

JOAN OF ARC

Joan of Arc (Jeanne d'Arc) was a peasant girl born at Domremy in Champagne three years before the battle of Agincourt. From the soldiers who passed through her village she learned of the desolation the English occupation had caused in the French countryside. Joan was deeply religious, and at the age of thirteen she claimed to have heard the voices of three saints (St. Michael, St. Catherine, and St. Margaret). The voices told her she had been chosen to help the Dauphin recover his land and his crown from the English.

Joan was seventeen when the Duke of Bedford began the siege of Orleans. She managed to persuade the captain of a nearby fortress (Vaucouleurs) to take her to see the Dauphin at his headquarters in Chinon. Then she convinced Charles that she could liberate Orleans if he would provide her with an army. We must remember that in those times magic and miracles were readily accepted by most people. So, mounted on a white horse, clad in a man's suit of armor, and carrying an old sword once belonging to Charles Martel, Joan led the French troops to Orleans. Her white standard was embroidered with two angels, each holding a fleur de lis. The soldiers were so inspired by her courage and confidence that they succeeded in driving the English from the city on May 3, 1429. Joan was hailed as the "Maid of Orleans." The liberation of the city marked the beginning of the end of the Hundred Years' War, because from then on the English hold on France grew steadily weaker.

From Orleans the French army, led by Joan, fought its way through regions controlled by the Burgundians until they reached the city of Rheims. On July 17, 1429, Joan stood near the Dauphin as he was crowned Charles VII in the cathedral (where French kings were traditionally crowned). Content that she had fulfilled her mission, she asked permission to return home. But Charles ignored her pleas and forced her to take the field again. Not long after, she was captured while defending Compeigne against the Duke of Burgundy. Her captor delivered her to the Duke, and he sold her to the English.

Joan was imprisoned in the Norman town of Rouen for a year. Although she had restored the French crown, Charles never made any effort to save her. The English were concerned about the tremendous influence Joan had over the French people, so they decided to expose her as an imposter. She was tried in an ecclesiastical (church) court, presided over by the Bishop of Beauvais. Every effort was made to trick her into saying that her voices came not from the saints but from the devil. Even the masters of theology at the University of Paris were consulted. Joan defended herself heroically, but at one moment of weakness (understandably caused by five months of constant harassment) she admitted that she had been mistaken. When she later regained her courage and reconfirmed her belief that the voices were genuine her critics would not listen. It was too late.

Joan was condemned as a witch and burned at the stake in the marketplace of Rouen on May 19, 1431. She was only nineteen. Before she died

Statue of Joan of Arc in Orleans

she asked for a cross, and one of the English soldiers standing nearby made one for her with two bits of wood. As the flames licked at her feet, she uttered the word "Jesus" over and over again. Another soldier turned away and whispered to his neighbor, "We are lost; we have burned a saint." And he was right. Two years later her case was reopened and she was declared innocent of the charges. In 1920 she was canonized.

Despite her untimely death, Joan's courage served as a model for the French soldiers, and they rallied behind Charles with a new determination to drive out the English. Joan had united them as no king had been able to do. The fighting went on for another twenty years, as one by one Charles reclaimed castles, cities and provinces. By 1453 the English held only Calais (they would continue to do so until 1558) and the Channel Islands.

England had gained little by the long years of fighting, and when it was all over the monarchy was greatly weakened. It would not be strong again until the late fifteenth century. In Joan's country, however, a new spirit of patriotism strengthened the national government, and virtually all of France now belonged to the French.

QUESTIONS

1. On what grounds could Edward III claim the French throne?

2. Who was Jean Froissart?

3. Why was the longbow a superior weapon to the crossbow?

4. What important person was captured by the Black Prince at Poitiers?

5. What did the mercenaries do when they weren't fighting?

6. In what ways did the Battle of Agincourt resemble that of Crecy?

7. Who was the Dauphin?

8. Who was the Maid of Orleans?

9. Where was Charles crowned?

10. Why was Charles able to drive out the English?

FURTHER THOUGHTS

1. Edward I fought hard to subdue Wales. When he finally defeated the Welsh in 1281 he built strong castles along the coast of northern Wales to keep the people under control. Hoping to pacify the patriotic Welshmen (who hated the English), he promised them they would have a ruler who spoke no English at all (the Welsh spoke Gaelic). Whom did he have in mind? His son, who, being a baby at the time, spoke no language at all! Ever since, the heir to the English throne has been given the title of Prince of Wales.

2. The English archers had to be very strong. Pulling the string of the longbow was the equivalent of lifting 100 pounds. This requires two times the effort needed to shoot with a modern sports bow. The skeletons of medieval archers that have been found have twisted spines, a condition that developed from years of exerting a tremendous sidewise pull.

3. Although cannons were used by the English and later the French (Charles had several), gunpowder was not used as a major weapon for another two hundred years. By then, soldiers would depend upon guns, not swords and arrows. Gunpowder had been invented in China around 800. It reached Europe in about 1240, and by the next century Italian engineers in Florence were making their thunder tubes. As we know, the first known recipe for the explosive mixture was written down by Roger Bacon (in

secret code): seven parts of saltpeter to five of charcoal and sulphur. The word cannon comes from the Latin carina meaning "tube." Although the early cannons often backfired and were inaccurate, they would permanently change the way battles were conducted.

4. French was the language of the court in England until the time of Edward III. It was during his reign that English became the official language of the court and of Parliament.

5. English poet Geoffrey Chaucer was a page in the royal household when he was captured near Rheims during the Hundred Years War (in 1359). His ransom was paid by Edward III, who later appointed him an esquire (an honorary title for a commoner).

6. By the end of the fourteenth century warfare had changed radically as knights were replaced by disciplined foot soldiers marching shoulder to shoulder. The new breed of soldier carried twenty-foot long pikes, which easily broke a cavalry charge and impaled the horsemen. A battle fought in Courtrai, Flanders early in the century (1302) indicated what was to come when 7,400 Flemish footsoldiers defeated 50,000 French troops, most of whom were mounted. Besides being "piked," thousands of knights were trapped on marshy ground and, weighed down by their heavy armor, drowned.

PROJECTS

1. Find a copy of Froissart's *Chronicles*. Read some passages, and then share them with your class.

2. Find out more about the Black Prince. Write a report.

3. Robert the Bruce (1274-1329) fought hard to win Scotland's independence. When Edward I of England tried to make Scotland part of his empire, Robert seized the Scottish throne and began to reconquer the lands that had been taken. The Battle of Bannockburn was a decisive one for him. Scotland became independent in 1328, with Robert its king. Find out more about this ambitious man and write a short report.

Flag of Scotland, bearing the cross of St. Andrew

4. Kenneth Brannagh stars as Henry V in an excellent movie by that name (*Henry V*) based on Shakespeare's play about the Battle of Agincourt. See the movie (it's available on video cassette) and then write a report explaining why Henry was such a popular king.

5. Many books are available on the life of Joan of Arc. Find one in your school library, read it, and write a short report.

Medieval town in Brittany

EPILOGUE

The Black Death and the Hundred Years' War jointly killed off nearly half the population of western Europe. In so many ways the fourteenth century was marked by destruction, suffering, and despair. And when the people desperately needed something to believe in, support for the Church was at a low ebb. Weakened by the Babylonian Captivity and the Great Schism, the Pope now confronted a steady barrage of complaints about the abuses and corruption of the clergy. The old ideal of Christian unity throughout the civilized world was rapidly fading; Church lands were neglected, tithes were not collected, and monasteries were abandoned.

Where could the people turn for hope? What could they believe in? Joan of Arc and her miraculous campaign offered an answer. "La France pour les frangais" ("France for the French"), she had proclaimed as she led her soldiers into battle. Even after her death, her vision inspired her countrymen to drive the English from their soil, once and for all. Before long, this new spirit of patriotism spread to the other nations of Europe.

The old feudal system, which had once held society together so efficiently, completely disappeared as strong central governments provided the stability necessary for new industries to flourish. Castles had outlived their usefulness (the use of cannons in siege warfare had been the final blow), and many of them crumbled in ruins. The economy was no longer based on land but on currency, and the commercial activities of the bustling towns and cities provided the monarchs with large tax revenues. And as the wealthy merchants extended their power by serving as advisors to the king, the role of the nobility gradually diminished. Gone were the days when the lords and their knights controlled the lives of the majority of the population. Furthermore, the high cost of mercenaries and new weapon technology meant that only kings could afford to engage in warfare.

Europe was now divided into nations, many of which have survived until modern times. And what lay ahead for them? The Holy Roman Empire was led by a new dynasty (the Habsburgs) that would rule until the nineteenth century. However, their power was dependent upon the group of powerful princes who elected them (fortunately, with one exception, they always voted for Habsburgs). In the second half of the fifteenth century Martin Luther would be born in Saxony and grow up to lead a reform movement that would radically change the Christian Church. In Italy, powerful families took over the governments of many of the city-states. Their patronage of the arts would spearhead a great intellectual and creative revival known as the Italian Renaissance. In France, the Valois dynasty strengthened its royal authority and even launched a military campaign into Italy. In England, the Tudors would eventually emerge as victors of the long Wars of the Roses. They were destined to usher in significant changes in religion and literature (particularly drama) while making their nation one of the most formidable powers in Europe. Meanwhile, Ferdinand of Aragon married Isabella of Castile and brought unity to most of Spain.

One of the most important inventions of the fifteenth century was the printing press. The technology for making paper had arrived earlier in Europe from China, and parchment was gradually replaced by the cheaper, more durable material. In the late 1430's Johann Gutenberg, a German goldsmith, experimented with movable type, and by 1456 his new printing press had copied an entire book. It was, of course, the Bible (known ever since as the Gutenberg Bible). Of the three hundred copies he printed, forty have survived to our times, and they are among the most valuable books in the world. The printing press made it possible for tremendous amounts of material to be made available to large segments of the European population, and literacy skyrocketed.

Remember those Latin translations of the works of the ancient Greek philosophers that had led to scholasticism? By the end of the medieval period they had become the basic texts of scholars, inspiring a new enthusiasm for the power of reason and an excitement about the great feats man could achieve by using his mind. This led to a movement known as Humanism. Rather than accept everything as it was and hope for something better in the next life, educated men now wanted to know more about the universe and sought to make the most of the

"here and now." The Age of Faith was rapidly being replaced by the Age of Discovery.

In 1453 Turkish Sultan Mohammed II attacked Constantinople and dramatically brought to a close the thousand-year era of Byzantine civilization. Emperor Constantine XI died in the fighting, and his capital city was renamed Istanbul. The magnificent Santa Sophia church was transformed into a mosque, and many of the city's greatest scholars fled to Italy. The Turks blocked the eastern end of the Mediterranean, forcing European traders to look for other routes to Asia. The Middle Ages were over, and a new age was dawning.

INDEX